D0975419

The New Deal at Work

The
New
Deal
at Work

MANAGING THE MARKET-DRIVEN WORKFORCE

Peter Cappelli

HARVARD BUSINESS SCHOOL PRESS
BOSTON, MASSACHUSETTS

03 02 01 00 99   5 4 3 2 1

LIBRARY OF CONGRESS CATALOGING-IN-PUBLICATION DATA

Cappelli, Peter.
    The new deal at work : managing the market-driven workforce / Peter Cappelli.
    p. cm.
    Includes bibliographical references and index.
    ISBN 0-87584-668-8 (alk. paper)
    1. Industrial management. 2. Organizational change. 3. Corporate reorganizations.
    4. Downsizing of organizations. I. Title.
    HD31. C3433 1999
    658.3—dc21   98-42221
                                                                CIP

The paper used in this publication meets the requirements of the American National Standard for Permanence of Paper for Printed Library Materials Z39.49-1984

Contents

Preface

THE IDEA for this book began with a research project sponsored by the National Policy Association (NPA) in Washington, D.C. Jim Auerbach, senior vice-president of the NPA, asked me to pull together a report summarizing what we knew about changes in the workplace, particularly regarding new systems for organizing "high performance work." In the book that resulted from that project, *Change at Work*,[1] my colleagues and I identified a pattern in the changes that had occurred in the workplace since the early 1980s. Much of the cost of restructuring U. S. businesses had been pushed onto employees in the form of developments such as downsizing and related changes that reduced the security and predictability of employment relationships. There was, however, some disagreement among us about the extent to which the old arrangements—where careers were built largely inside a single organization and organized around internal rules—were giving way. It was unclear what would take their place, and therefore we stopped short of trying to describe systematically what the new arrangements looked like.

A number of books have been written about other changes in the employment relationship. Among the most prominent are: *The End of Work*,[2] warning of a long-term decline in jobs; *Job Shift*,[3] arguing that tasks are broadening inside organizations in ways that make traditional job descriptions less applicable; *The Boundaryless Career*,[4] a collection of essays around the theme of how greater mobility across employers will change careers; *We Are All Self-Employed*,[5] offering advice about how employees should adjust to a world with sharply reduced job security; and *White-Collar Blues*,[6] describing how the work culture and values of managers changed as a result of corporate restructuring.

Almost all of these studies were written from the perspective of the employees and focused on the problems of adjusting to the tremendous changes driven by corporate restructuring. At least some of those problems were temporary in that they were caused by, or at least exacerbated by, slack labor markets. It became clear that jobs were not disappearing once the labor market tightened, and not all jobs are temporary even if the idea of a lifetime with the same employer is in decline. Whether—and how—the employment relationship has changed in ways that transcend downsizing remained to be examined, as did how such changes would affect management practices.

The theme of *The New Deal* is to describe the new employment relationship that has emerged from more than a decade of corporate restructuring and to consider how it is changing the practice of employee management. The centerpiece of the story is the rise of the labor market, perhaps the most important development in the world in the past generation. Just as the barriers between nations have been redrawn through global trade and regulated industries reshaped by deregulation, so too are the internal management practices of employers being redrafted by the growing power and influence of the labor market. In part, some of the pressures on employers that led to *The New Deal* have been driven by responses to more volatile product markets, especially the difficulty in financing long-term investments in employees associated with life-time careers. But arguably the most important pressures have been generated by new management practices that have essentially brought the market inside the firm. Techniques such as benchmarking, backed up by the ability to outsource high-cost operations, make even the most insulated aspects of an internal bureaucracy feel the pressure of the market. In most cases, the threat of going to the outside market is enough to change the relationship. As economists might describe this development, the threat of going to the market has made the employment relationship contestable in the same way that the threat of competition in product markets regulates the behavior of producers.

The change in the employment relationship can be described as the substitution of market solutions for the internal, administrative rules associated with corporate employment policies. The compensation for a particular job is increasingly shaped by the market wage for that job outside the firm, and not by how it fits into the hierarchy of an internal compensation system. The older, internalized employment practices, with their long-term commitments and assumptions, buffered the employment relationship from market pressures, but they are giving way to a negotiated relationship where the power shifts back and forth from employer to employee based on conditions in the labor market. Even when the relationship remains long-term, the fact that it is now governed by the market and not by internal administrative principles makes it fundamentally different. (Much of the skeptical thinking about changes in employment, particularly by economists, is wrong in assuming that employees must actually move more frequently across employers before the relationship can change.)

Unlike slack labor markets associated with recessions, restructuring waves, or fads in management practices, the rise of the market in employment relationships is such a fundamental and long-term development that it is likely to generate profound changes. This new, market-mediated relationship appeared to work like a charm for employers when the labor market was slack because they were in the driver's seat. But it is proving to be something of a nightmare for employers when the market tightens. The internalized practices associated with long-term employment relationships have always been designed in large part to help retain employees, develop their skills, and ensure certain levels of commitment to the employer necessary for jobs that cannot be closely managed. Once these arrangements have been swept aside and the labor market becomes a factor—most notably when it tightens—employers must find alternative ways to solve these problems and their efforts to do so are described in detail within.

An issue worth more attention than I am able to give it in this book is the public's interest in these developments. What does it mean, for example, when employees must take on more responsibility for their own training and for managing their own careers, or when they assume more of the business risks and uncertainty previously associated with shareholders? Surely this will increase the inequality between the "haves," who have the resources to provide for their own skills and career management, and the "have nots," who do not. And what about the entry of young workers into the labor market where traditional, entry-level jobs that provide training in basic, work-based skills no longer exist? Where will these workers get such skills? Can traditional education providers fill this gap? How will managers in particular adjust to a world where the type of commitments between employer and employee that shaped their identities in the past give way to relationships based on bargaining power? Will managers become, as Charles Heckscher suggests,[7] like professionals, simply seeking out the best career opportunities possible, or is there something about the nature of managerial work, the firm, and the project-specific nature of the tasks, that will prevent that? These are fundamental issues that I hope others will continue to explore.

Most authors, I suspect, would describe writing as more cathartic than fun. Even though the process of finding out where a particular argument will lead is certainly interesting, just the prospect of getting started, let alone sustaining an entire book, is overwhelming enough to send most projects back into the box and under the bed. Thanks to my editors at Harvard Business School Press, first Marjorie Williams and then Nikki Sabin, for gently but persistently nudging me along to finishing the manuscript. Several generations of research assistants, especially Clint Chadwick and Teni Mardarossian, helped me track down examples of changes in the workplace. Sue Torelli at the Center for Human Resources was a great help with published materials. The employers who participate in the Wharton School's Center for Human Resources programs were a terrific source of real-time information about changes in the workplace, as were Jim Walker and his colleagues at the Walker Group. Where I do not cite a published source for the information used in the text, it comes from interviews with participants, often from these groups, whom I identify except in those few instances where they requested to remain anonymous. Kathryn Pearcy continues to spare me from the consequences of my otherwise unedited prose and from the fact that I appear unable to place references and tables together with text.

My family, I hope, was blissfully unaware of the process of writing this book, the result of a conscious policy of keeping a firm boundary between work and family life, although I appreciate their understanding in navigating the ever-increasing piles of paper that filled the house as the project moved along. Sir Henry Phelps-Brown, one of my earliest mentors, died as I began this project. I like to think that I have followed his example by asking big questions about issues that matter.

An Overview of the New Employment Relationship

MOST OBSERVERS of the corporate world believe that the traditional relationship between employer and employee is gone, but there is little understanding of why it ended and even less about what is replacing that relationship. What ended the traditional employment relationship is a variety of new management practices, driven by a changing environment, that essentially brings the market—both the market for a company's products and the labor market for its employees—directly inside the firm. And once inside, the market's logic quickly becomes dominant, pushing out of its way the behavioral principles of reciprocity and long-term commitment, the internal promotion and development practices, and the concerns about equity that underlie the more traditional employment contract. The policies and practices that buffered the relationship with employees from outside pressures are gone. The end of employee loyalty to an organization, replaced by greater attachment to careers, is but one manifestation of this change.

Most attempts by companies to draw up a new contract represent wishful thinking. Their managers seek simply to lower the expectations of employees by limiting the employer's obligations on job security and career development—the dreaded "employability" doctrine that pushes responsibility for careers onto employees—while assuming that most other aspects of the relationship, including high levels of employee performance, will continue. In fact, virtually every aspect of employment changes now that the market governs this relationship. From the difficulty that employers have in recouping training investments to the substitutes that must be found for employee motivation and commitment, the new relationship changes dramatically how firms must manage their employees.

If the new employment relationship is not defined unilaterally by employer attempts to dictate a new deal, then what is it? It is tempting to think of the new relationship as something like free agency, where legal contracts can be used to govern all aspects of the relationship, much as they do for professional sports players or temporary workers. For most positions, especially those in management, contracts struck in the market cannot define an employment relationship. At least some of the skills are unique to the employer and developed on-the-job, the tasks are interdependent with others or with systems in the organization, and performance is difficult to monitor accurately, all of which make contracts imperfect at best. Nor are managers professionals. Their work is governed by standards inside the organization, not professional codes, and their success is inextricably linked to that of their employer. The most important rewards for managers are still associated with promotion inside a company hierarchy.

The contradiction inherent in the new relationship comes from the fact that the nature of the work that most managers perform does not lend itself to market-based relationships and contracts. It is much more suited to open-ended relationships in which the obligations can be adjusted, performance can be observed, and rewards allocated accordingly as situations change. Some level of mutual commitment and trust to facilitate changing needs is inevitable, as is the need to develop some unique skills inside the organization and to retain them indefinitely. At the same time, the pressures from markets and the need to change organizations mean that truly open-ended, long-term employment relationships are largely dead. The pressures on firms to shed obsolete skills (compounded by the uncertainty of knowing which ones will be obsolete) and the problem of skill "poaching" by other employers make it difficult to maintain commitment and trust, develop skills internally, and retain important skills. The defining problem of the new relationship, therefore, is how to graft the model of the market onto occupations for which it is poorly suited.

If the traditional, lifetime employment relationship was like a marriage, then the new employment relationship is like a lifetime of divorces and remarriages, a series of close relationships governed by the expectation going in that they need to be made to work and yet will inevitably not last.

Suppose that both sides entered a relationship with the same expectation that it could be temporary. There are many successful relationships involving mutual commitments that we know going in will not last. What is different about the new employment relationship is that while both parties know that the relationship is unlikely to last forever, neither knows exactly when it will end, while either side can end it unilaterally when it so desires.

So the new employment relationship is an uneasy dance between an open-ended relationship and the pull of the market, with the parties constantly renegotiating their commitments. Pressures from the labor market are now the important forces shaping the nature of the relationship.

As is the case with any change, the new situation in which the labor market dominates employee behavior is creating a new set of winners and losers. For most of the past two decades, it was easy to keep score: Employers won and employees lost. This is because slack labor markets allowed employers to push most of the costs of restructuring onto employees. The advice for employees was simple: Try to develop other job options, just in case, and prepare psychologically to get whacked. For employers, the management of employees was such a simple matter that observers seriously questioned whether the human resource function was even necessary.

As labor markets begin to tighten, however, the situation becomes more complex. When bargaining power becomes a bit more equal, the problem of negotiating this open-ended relationship in the context of a market becomes very tricky indeed. Even though employers may not have all the power, the job of shaping the employment relationship in response to these negotiations and making it work falls to them because they control the mechanisms through which the relationship can adapt—how jobs are designed, compensation structured, training delivered, and so forth. Which employers will come out on the winning side of this new relationship depends on how well they can adapt, whether they can find ways to manage employee commitment, develop the skills they need, and retain needed workers in the context of a much more open and powerful labor market.

WHAT CAUSED THE CHANGE?

In fact, what we think of as the "traditional" employment relationship is really a very recent phenomenon. At the turn of the century, most industrial employees either worked for contractors within a company's facilities or turned over so quickly that they were essentially "temps," very much like what we see happening now. Companies that kept accurate records of costs found that contractors working inside their facilities were very efficient. Contractor costs were often well below those incurred by direct employees—as many companies who are outsourcing today have discovered.

What ended the contracting system, bringing the workforce into long-term relationships inside the firm, was the need to coordinate more complex organizations and to ensure that the skills were there to make that happen. The skill of human resource planning, forced on industry by wartime controls, first in World War I, eventually led to what we now see as the traditional employment relationship. Companies had to safeguard the supply of labor for their vast, integrated operations.

Especially in the managerial ranks, long-term relationships and systems of internal development, including promotion, served three key purposes. First, they facilitated investments in training, which were recouped by the employer over time as the employee's performance improved. Particularly in large corporations, a crucial skill was understanding the organization's systems and procedures, a skill that could be developed only by means of long-term service to the corporation. Second, the security that employees found in these relationships helped produce loyalty and commitment. In large, complex organizations, loyalty was especially important because it was difficult to measure any individual's performance. Third, the possibility of moving up the ladder provided powerful motivation at relatively little cost, since few employees could ever make it to the top.

These long-term relationships were not without their downsides, however. Even in their heyday, they were rightly criticized in books such as *The Organization Man* for creating something like an industrial feudalism, where employees essentially could not leave (corporate managers could not move to similar jobs elsewhere because other corporations would not hire them) and where inbreeding stifled new thinking.

The developments that eroded the benefits of these long-term relationships became noticeable in the 1980s. They include the following:

- More competitive product markets that not only created pressure to cut costs but, more important, reduced time to market and pursued differentiated market niches. These changes made long-term, fixed investments—in people as well as in capital—problematic because they became obsolete much more quickly.

- Information technology that could take over the functions of coordinating and monitoring, tasks traditionally performed by middle management. With these technologies in place, outside suppliers could easily be monitored and integrated into an operation. No corporate staff was necessary to manage them. As a result, a huge range of functions could now be outsourced. For those employees who remained within the company, the threat of being outsourced was always present.

- New arrangements that have made it possible for the financial community to advance the interests of shareholders far ahead of other traditional stakeholders within publicly held companies. Pressures to increase shareholder value put the squeeze on costs, especially fixed costs.

- New management techniques—profit centers, outside benchmarking, core competencies—that brought the discipline of markets inside the firm and exposed every aspect of the business and every employee to market pressures.

EFFECTS OF THE CHANGE

These developments make it very difficult for firms to retain long-term relationships with employees and much easier to rely on the market to meet their needs. One way to think of the change is that the planning horizon for firms is now much shorter than can be accommodated by an individual's career. The behavior of employees has changed as a result, as has the way in which they are managed, altering fundamentally the relationship between employer and employee. And that process is far from over. Indeed, some of these developments now appear to be a permanent part of the business landscape. The downsizing trend, for example, not only has continued nonstop since its beginnings around 1982, largely independent of the business cycle, but appears to have increased in recent years, especially for managers. The goal of downsizing is no longer simply to get down to a more efficient size. It is to rearrange the competencies of the organization. Companies continue to hire while they are downsizing because they are shedding workers with obsolete skills while taking in new ones with skills in demand.

While the challenges facing employees under these new arrangements are clear, very little attention has been given to the substantial problems that they pose for employers. For example, turnover, especially of key employees, is almost always a crucial issue for employers, and it becomes much more difficult to manage in this new environment. Research on employee turnover finds that most people who quit generally do so to take jobs elsewhere. The more employees are focused on the labor market and the more information they have on other jobs, the more likely they are to leave. New workplace contracts that push workers to focus on their "employability" direct their attention outside the firm.

Voluntary turnover has been less of a problem for the corporate world because virtually all corporations have been downsizing at the same time, creating a big surplus of talent on the market and also restricting those who quit voluntarily. But in tight labor markets, such as information systems, companies are already bemoaning the lack of loyalty such employees show and the difficulty of retaining them as they hop from one opportunity to a better one. And as labor markets tighten further, turnover even of traditionally loyal employees can be expected to skyrocket as they pull away to jobs elsewhere. Employers lose their investments in employees when they leave, so the ability to recoup those investments declines as the expectation that workers will remain with the firm erodes. Investments in training for new workers—that is, investments in teaching them how to do their jobs—are declining. In some cases, this reduction in training creates a vicious circle in which more and more outside hiring is done to fill skill shortages that never go away. This phenomenon has not only bid up wages but has further reduced corporate interest in developing any of its own talent. Managers fear—rightly—that they will lose their investments in new employees to a higher bidder who can pay more for a trained worker. As employee development declines, the shortage of skilled labor can worsen.

Likewise, virtually all organizations need their employees to make investments in company-specific capabilities, but this becomes more difficult to accomplish as employees begin to understand that those investments may not pay off for them. Will an employee be willing to take an undesirable assignment that is crucial to the company if the promised payoff of a plum job at headquarters two years later may be wiped out by a downsizing or restructuring? Again, recent evidence suggests that employees today don't want to take this kind of risk.

The traditional reliance on mentoring that companies used to develop employees has eroded as both turnover and restructurings have led to frequent changes in supervisors and reporting arrangements. Because employees can no longer expect to get help from a supervisor on all technical issues, some organizations have created specialized "centers of excellence" where employees can take such problems. For career advice, managerial employees increasingly have to look for help outside the organization. The exploding field of management coaches, or mentors, for hire exists because managerial employees want development so desperately that they are willing to buy it in the market.

Compensation is widely accepted as being the most important mechanism for managing and motivating employees, especially in the United States. These changes in the employment relationship turn most existing compensation principles on their head. Traditional compensation policies, based on job evaluation, were designed to promote internal equity between employees in different jobs. Those concerns have gone out the window. Instead, wages are set based on prevailing levels in the labor market; if not, people holding skills that are in demand walk for better offers, and it becomes impossible to bring in skills from the outside. But complaints about equity skyrocket, typically as junior people with "hot" skills end up making much more than their senior colleagues. The widespread use of contractors, consultants, and temps, each with different pay rates, sets up another group of invidious comparisons.

In fields such as information systems, where the demands are constantly changing, the wage structure within the firm may have little apparent order: older skills may suddenly have virtually no market value, since new programming skills do not build on old ones. Young programmers find their wages may be highest when they first enter the labor market because their skills are on the cutting edge. From that point on, their value and market compensation erodes, and they may well find themselves unemployable unless they update their skills regularly.

There are also consequences for the macroeconomy and associated financial markets now that the outside labor market has become so dominant. With employees much more likely to move to other employers and employers having to raise wages to keep them, wage inflation is likely to escalate more rapidly when labor markets tighten. Conversely, the greater focus on the labor market means that companies are no longer as interested in maintaining wages when the economy is slack, thus contributing to deflation. These developments should make wages and, in turn, inflation much more sensitive to the overall level of demand in the economy.

Beyond simply securing a skilled workforce lies the much more complicated challenge of ensuring its performance, a task that focuses on issues like motivation and commitment. This task is made more difficult by the new employment relationship because work-related attitudes are now driven much more by outside circumstances that are beyond the control of the employer. Companies that work hard to maintain good morale find that the results of their climate surveys rise and fall with outside events, such as the state of the labor market. Some of the most interesting research on employee commitment finds that it is driven by the employee's labor market options: the more employees search and the more job options they find, the lower is their commitment to their current employer. On the other hand, downturns in the economy and in opportunities elsewhere raise employees' satisfaction with and commitment to their current job.

The possibility of promotion has long been the most important incentive for individuals to act in the interests of their employer. Flat organizations and reduced job security have lowered the probability of promotion dramatically and so have reduced its power as an incentive. Securing cooperation within the organization becomes much more of an issue as employees come to see their interests as more and more distinct from—rather than linked to—the overall success of the corporation. Competition between individual employees to build their resumes for the outside market means greater competition for choice assignments and more fights to secure credit and avoid blame when projects are finished. These situations are particularly intense in professional organizations such as law firms or investment banks, where employees on the same level must work together on discrete projects.

MANAGING THE CHANGE

A range of options are available to employers for addressing the problems associated with this highly market-regulated workforce. Some companies, for example, are attempting to rebuild their long-term employment relationships with investments in employees and commitments to job security, going back to the old model. Whether these efforts will succeed is another matter. So far things do not look promising. Even if these companies are stable enough to make long-term relationships effective, poaching from competitors may be enough to do them in. One of the key lessons for companies is that they may no longer be able to define their own, unique employment relationships. Markets have a way of breaking them down, not only by pulling out key employees but by shaping the attitudes and behavior of those who remain.

Similar efforts to buck the trend toward free agency in employment involve explicit contracts that tie employees to the firm or make them repay investments the firm has made in them should they leave. One way that more and more companies are dealing with the conflict between the need to invest in training on the one hand and to manage higher turnover and poaching on the other is through explicit training contracts that require employees to stay for some minimum period after receiving their training or to pay back some portion of training expenses. The courts have recently affirmed the enforceability of these contracts, and companies like Texas Instruments, EDS, and Nissan all use them.

The other general approach is to forget about trying to reverse the trend and instead try to adjust management practices to the requirements of a more arm's-length employment relationship. Some of the adjustments that companies have made to function with these new relationships include the following:

- *Adjust the nature of the tasks.* Adopting the assumption that skilled workers will be leaving changes fundamentally what companies decide to do themselves. When choosing how much to customize an information system, for example, companies need to factor in where the skills will come from to run such systems. When turnover among employees is greater, it is better to pick an off-the-shelf system because the skills needed to operate it will be readily available in the outside market. The risks of operating legacy systems skyrocket in such an environment, and if companies have them at all, they are best off turning the whole system over to an outsourcer who will operate and staff that legacy system.

- *Own the project.* New employees in particular are concerned about building their resumes with accomplishments that increase their marketability. Rather than fighting that interest, smart companies carve work up into distinct projects over which an individual or team has ownership.

The potential to add a valuable achievement to a resume provides an incentive to work hard.

As companies outsource more and enter into more joint ventures, specific work projects increasingly span more than one organization. We might expect to see a rebirth of the kind of employment arrangements prevalent in the aircraft industry in the 1950s, where workers would follow the project, changing "employers" in the process, as it moved from subcontractor to contractor—the avionics engineers went with the project to the cockpit assembler and then on to the airframe manufacturer that put the plane together.

Compensation needs to reflect the more contingent nature of the employment relationship. The probability of promotions can no longer serve as the long-term incentive. In its place are compensation strategies that provide clear incentives by specifying in detail exactly what outcomes will be rewarded in what way. These practices will eventually change the norms of fairness and pay as they shatter the old pay schedules based on internal equity: there will be large differences in compensation across workers in the same jobs, high-flying subordinates will earn more than their supervisors, and seniority will have little to do with pay. Human resource programs that attempt to unite a company with a single set of practices or pay scales across all employees are disappearing.

Part of the effort needed to make rewards more contingent on performance is to monitor individual performance more carefully. Reductions in supervision associated with teamwork and reengineering have reduced the traditional forms of monitoring. In their place are peer review and 360-degree appraisals that tap new sources of information on performance or internal accounting systems that count performance components (such as orders processed per hour) or break down financial results at lower levels. All of these methods better track the performance of individual employees.

- **Substitutes for commitment.** Even with redesigned work and compensation systems, most organizations still cannot function without some employee commitment. Some organizations, such as GTE and Banker's Trust, have pulled back from arm's-length relationships with employees toward a position where *some* mutual obligations, including employee commitment, are expected. More common are efforts to direct employee commitment toward something within the company now that commitment to the organization as a whole is gone. The interpersonal dynamics of teamwork, for example, help create a sense of identification with and commitment to other members of the team, and company practices often work to reinforce this effect. Eliminating relief workers in production means that when a team member is absent, the rest of the team has to make up the work, creating peer pressure for good attendance. For many jobs, commitment to the corporation as a whole is largely irrelevant as long as the employees feel commitment to their team or project.

- *Employee selection.* As more and more jobs are filled from the outside, employee selection becomes increasingly important. But most companies are wildly unsophisticated about selection techniques. Most have no systematic selection practices, and virtually none bother to assess the results of their decisions.

    Companies like AT&T have begun to worry about their dependence on the outside labor market for critical skills. AT&T's Talent Network represents an effort to organize like-minded employers into a network for swapping workers with key skills. They believe it is cheaper to share information and workers within this network than on the open market. It has many of the efficiencies of the old internal labor markets of giant corporations without having to be giant. Something similar is underway in San Francisco's hotel industry with a government-sponsored program to transform the high turnover, casual nature of many hotel jobs into something more like a craft with credentials and certifications that allow workers to move within that industry more easily.

- *Different skills are rewarded.* In the past, the key to a successful corporate career was to understand a company's systems and procedures. This is because the big rewards came with promotions to headquarters, where the key competency was coordinating the company's disparate operations. Now, at corporations like IBM, these are the competencies that are selected for outplacement, as they are less and less necessary. Instead, because workers no longer reside in large departmental hierarchies, functional skills matter more for individuals. New assignments afford no time to learn them. Further, a whole set of new competencies begin to matter, such as the ability to manage contractors—negotiating arrangements and performance specifications, creating incentives for performance, monitoring compliance, and drawing up contracts.

For employees who are increasingly in the market and in competition for work, interpersonal skills have become enormously important. Contractors and contingent workers have always known that, other things being equal, employers will choose to deal with the person who is easiest to deal with. Even inside organizations, there is competition for business: should we give this plum job to that partner or this one, to our in-house people or the outside consultants? As workers spend more time seeking and securing jobs, the interpersonal skills associated with job hunting become more important. And being "nice"—accommodating and easy to get along with—is now an attribute with an even bigger payoff.

The fact that employees are spending less time with a given employer but more time in the same occupation creates a real dilemma for employees who need to develop their skills. Investments in occupational job skills will have a greater payoff for employees because they will use them longer, but the employer is less likely to provide them because the organization will not benefit. The mechanism through which employees are addressing this dilemma is the market. Increasingly, they are turning to educational institutions and other outside vendors to get the skills and training that employers used to provide. One quarter of all the students in community colleges in the United States already have bachelor degrees, and most of those degree holders are already employed. They are returning to school not to take basic college courses but to learn things like how to run a TQM (total quality management) program or how to build teamwork skills.

Particularly in areas where skills become dated quickly, as in information systems, employees who are not working with cutting-edge systems see the value of their skills in the market steadily decline. The best way to keep skills current is to work with new systems. To attract and retain talented workers, companies therefore find that they must keep their systems near the state of the art. Staffing out-of-date legacy systems, for example, requires either hiring workers whose skills are also dated or promising workers that such assignments will be combined with work in other, more current systems.

IMPLICATIONS FOR THE FUTURE

The history of employment relationships in the United States makes clear that what we think of as the "traditional" model of long-term attachments, internal development, and mutual obligations likely existed for little more than a generation. The current move toward a more market-mediated employment relationship is in some ways a return to earlier arrangements. It is a particularly powerful transition in that markets represent especially elemental and resilient mechanisms for managing relationships.

The transition from one set of arrangements to another is rarely smooth, and new problems are often generated in the process. The problems managers face in trying to address basic human resource issues are the focus of this book. How organizations will function in the absence of employee commitment, with workers who have a more individualistic, short-term orientation, is a far-reaching question that raises serious concerns for employees and society as well.

One consequence of these new arrangements seems to be a number of internal contradictions. Organizations are demanding more from employees but offering them less. Bureaucratic control systems are replaced by systems with reduced supervision that require more commitment from employees at a time when employers are reducing their commitments to employees. More skills are required, including more knowledge and skills specific to an organization, when the employer's ability to fund those investments is decreasing.

Another fundamental concern is the issue of fairness. A great many of the practices in the more traditional employment relationship were designed to accommodate the equity concerns of employees. Compensation practices, for example, tried to reflect the view that seniority and responsibility should be rewarded and that employees performing tasks of comparable value should be treated similarly. Markets, in contrast, are not good at equity. Market-based employment relationships reward skills that are in demand and in short supply, but only as long as that situation lasts. The results they generate may be fundamentally at odds with the perceptions of employees and the broader society about what is fair.

How skills are valued and developed is also central to the problems raised by these new arrangements. Many of the skills that are valuable in society are developed at the workplace through investments made by organizations in their employees. When the ability of the employer to fund those investments declines, especially when the overall demand for skills begins to rise, then the search for alternatives becomes imperative. Some employers will continue to invest in firm-specific skills and training when they can be reasonably certain that their employees will not leave. Other employers will become net exporters of skill, relying on the productive work of trainees who then move on to other organizations. Firms that can find ways to combine work and learning, making it possible to support training, will have a competitive advantage in attracting employees.

The prominent solution at the moment is to push the problem of skill development off onto employees and, in turn, onto the market. The surplus of skilled workers that was associated with downsizing efforts may at least delay the development of a market for training, and there may be certain work processes or technologies where training cannot be efficiently provided other than at work. But efforts are already under way to develop these new arrangements. Employer-generated skill standards, for example, are in effect credentials for skills and are currently being drafted by industry associations.

Individual workers now bear not only more of the responsibility for acquiring skills and managing their careers but also much more of the risk and uncertainty of doing business. Where individuals will get both the skills and the information to manage careers themselves is another source of concern. They have been turning to postsecondary education for help. Community colleges have been particularly responsive, with new coursework offering some job skills, especially for non-management work. Help in career management is not readily available yet. What kind of entrepreneurs will enter this market and what their products will look like remains to be seen.

These changes have important consequences for society as a whole. For example, employees with good skills, superior information about opportunities, and an overall high level of marketability may find that their job prospects are enhanced under the new market-oriented system; those who lack skills and information and are less marketable may find their prospects deteriorating. Together, these changes may further the trend toward increasing inequality in labor market outcomes that is already underway.

Much of contemporary American society has been built on stable employment relationships characterized by predictable career advancement and steady growth in wages. Long-term individual investments such as home ownership and college educations for children, community ties and the stability they bring, and quality of life outside of work have all been enhanced by reducing risk and uncertainty on the job. There is already at least anecdotal evidence that younger employees are more worried about accumulating a "nest egg" for financial security and may be willing to take more risk to get it. How these characteristics may change with the new employment relationship is an open question.

Both a high level of information and a series of contracts to enforce training agreements are needed to make the new employment arrangements function effectively. Meaningful credentials are needed as a signal to employers about skills and as a goal for employees. Potential employees need to be able to judge the quality of a training experience, just as employers need to judge the quality of a potential employee. Internalized systems of employment offered employers detailed and accurate information about the abilities of their employees that will be difficult to duplicate with the outside labor market. One consequence, then, is that there may be more "slippage" with these new arrangements—employees with the necessary abilities and talent who are passed over because they lack the necessary credentials.

Increased importance of the labor market means more transactions and, in turn, more contracts to enforce them. With more hiring and presumably more dismissals, the labor law governing such actions will certainly get a workout that will make clear how out of step its 1930s New Deal roots are with the contemporary scene. Both employers and employees will need strong incentives not to cheat in these transactions (reneging on training contracts, for instance).

Markets demand infrastructure to make them operate honestly and efficiently. As the labor market becomes more important, the need for information about jobs and workers, guidelines and enforcement of contracts, and other aspects of infrastructure will rise. Some industries have developed mechanisms for providing aspects of this infrastructure. But at present, the government is the only player in a position to deliver the credential systems, remedial training programs, protection for the displaced, and other arrangements on a national scale that could make the new system operate effectively.

OUTLINE OF THE BOOK

Chapter 1 introduces the basic contours of the "new deal" at work and discusses ways employers have tried to rewrite their psychological contract with workers. The central problem areas that the new deal creates for managers—commitment, attrition, and skill development—are explored in detail. Chapter 2 steps back and investigates the historical roots of the modern employment relationship, looking to a time when things looked remarkably like the current situation. The surprising lesson is that what we think of as the "traditional," long-term employment relationship is a relatively recent phenomenon that arose in response to a particular economic situation and the challenges it posed to companies. The pressures that began to erode that situation are outlined in Chapter 3. While many of them can be traced to economy-wide issues, the most important ones lie in innovations in the way businesses are managed. Exactly how these pressures have affected the employment relationship and employees in particular is addressed in Chapter 4, which presents the hard evidence that documents the various dimensions of the changed relationship in the workplace.

The next two chapters examine efforts to make market-based employment relationships work. Chapter 5 looks at occupations and industries that have long had such relationships and outlines the often unique adaptations that have been required to address these problems. Chapter 6 describes adaptations that contemporary employers have made to address the problems of commitment, retention, and skill development. In Chapter 7, a series of broader issues associated with the new employment relationships is explored, considering the implications for the individual and for society of an employment relationship in which employees face many more decisions and risks.

CHAPTER 1

The New Deal at Work

THE OLD employment system of secure, lifetime jobs with predictable advancement and stable pay is dead. What killed it were changes in the way firms operate that brought markets inside the organization. In the process, labor markets were also brought inside the firm, and the pressures they create are systematically undermining the complex system of human resource practices that made long-term careers the staple of corporate life.

While employers have quite clearly broken the old deal and its long-term commitments, they do not control the new deal, which is fundamentally an agreement negotiated between employer and employee. It is an open-ended relationship that is continually being redrafted. Which side gains and loses depends on bargaining power, which in turn stems from the state of the labor market.

The end of the old system created a crisis for the employees who were in it. The administrative arrangements that had buffered employees from the market came to an end and, with that, job security. But what about employers? How does it change the way they operate? What we see as the traditional model of employment, in which employees were developed inside the firm and managed according to principles internal to the company, was designed to solve many problems for employers. And as that traditional model erodes, those problems resurface, this time against the backdrop of new constraints in the form of the labor market.

The new deal at work, where the employment relationship is now an open-ended negotiation based on market power, creates fundamental challenges for management. Addressing them begins with an understanding of the nature of the relationship between employers and employees in the workplace and how it serves the interests of employers.

THE PSYCHOLOGICAL CONTRACT

One aspect of employment that sets it apart from other economic transactions is the virtual impossibility of managing employees through explicit contracts. Most jobs are complex enough, especially inside organizations, that it is impossible to specify in advance all of the duties and performance levels that are required, and the cooperation of employees is needed to fill in the blanks. For example, one of the most effective techniques of industrial action that unionized employees use to punish management is the "work to rule," in which employees carry out their tasks precisely according to written employer instructions or union contracts, doing only what those contracts indicate. When they withdraw their cooperation and do only what they are told, the unique problems that occur daily in a workplace but cannot be specified in advance are left unaddressed, and the time-saving techniques that workers have developed themselves are put aside. The performance of the workplace comes to a halt.

Observers of society have long recognized the limits of coercion as the basis for compliance and the advantages of having individuals comply voluntarily with rules or expectations. In the workplace, what causes employees to cooperate with management in pursuit of the organization's goals? The answer turns on the nature of the deal, or contract, between employers and employees, an understanding about mutual obligations and responsibilities that is both explicit and implicit.

Individuals pursue the interests of their employer in part because they believe they will eventually be rewarded for doing so. The key element in this model is how long the period of reckoning is. The more immediate it is, the more time and effort are spent haggling over the terms. One of the problems that plagued the British economy through much of this century was the daily negotiating and recontracting involved in exchanging effort for reward. Every change in the workplace that affected the pace or nature of the tasks performed led to time-consuming negotiations between shop stewards and supervisors for additional compensation, negotiations that had to be completed before the work could progress because the parties did not trust each other.

When the period of reckoning increases, the nature of the exchange requires trust and the related concept of commitment. In the absence of an explicit contract, employees have to trust that their efforts will be rewarded in the longer term. That trust requires first that they believe there is a longer term, that the relationship will continue, and second that the employer has policies in place that will ensure the employee is properly compensated in the long run. In most corporations, these policies include income security in the form of stable careers and lucrative pensions. But the most important has been promotions. There is a long literature documenting both in theory and in practice how promotions are used to reward good performance. From the employer's point of view, promotions provide a very efficient means for rewarding and motivating superior performance. The reckoning period can be a long one, with the promotion typically given in return for many years of good performance. There's no need to specify exact performance targets, and because there are no targets, there's no need to constantly monitor performance. Promotions work well for employers. The employer relies on competition between candidates to drive performance levels higher and to push the employees to do whatever it takes to meet the employer's needs. For the employee, promotions are a very desirable prize in that they typically represent sizeable increases in compensation, increases that several studies have found more than compensate for the additional job demands.[1]

What persuades workers that, years down the road, they will get the reward of promotion for good performance is that they have seen it happen before. At this point, the relationship goes beyond a simple economic contract to a process that psychologists refer to as *modeling*. The accomplished workers who receive big rewards serve as role models for the employees they supervise. Those employees subconsciously model the behaviors and job performance that their supervisors exhibit.

With modeling, the explanation as to why employees comply with the interests of the organization moves from the calculus of self-interest to more behaviorally based explanations. These focus on the concept of commitment, how employees come to see their own interests as being similar to those of the organization. The concept of reciprocity is central to understanding how employment relationships foster employee commitment. Reciprocity refers to the sense of obligation that one feels to repay gifts, a value that has been identified as underlying every culture on the planet.[2]

A clever laboratory experiment illustrates the power of reciprocity. In the control group, a student is assigned to a room and given some menial task to perform. Another student is sent into the room to work on the same task. The new student then strikes up a conversation and mentions that she is selling lottery tickets to benefit a college organization. In a typical case, the first student agrees to buy some tickets, although generally a small number. In the experimental group, when the new student enters the room, she comes in with two bottles of soda—both opened—and says, "I got one of these for myself and thought you might like one as well." A gift. This time, when the pitch to buy lottery tickets comes, the first student buys four times as many as the student in the control setting.[3]

Imagine how new employees experienced that reciprocity norm under the traditional corporate model. Right after leaving college, where they paid large amounts of tuition, they enter a training program that seems a lot like college and may go on for more than a year. Unlike college, they don't have to pay anything. In fact, they are being paid a salary even though they don't have to do anything for the organization, and they would not know how to do it even if they had to. Surely this experience must feel like a gift to the new employees, and it creates a sense of obligation to reciprocate. They reciprocate with commitment to serve the goals of the employer.

Studies that follow employees in such circumstances over time have found that new entrants believe that they owe their employer a great deal and that the company owes them relatively little. As time goes on, their view of the relationship changes. The longer they are with the company, the more they believe the company owes them.[4] Perhaps this reflects their own investments in the organization. The longer they stay and the more they have contributed, the more they believe the company owes them in return. Most companies do act like they owe long-service employees more by giving them special benefits that are at least implicitly linked to seniority. Studies find that, as long as they continue to meet acceptable performance levels, employees tend to get more rights and privileges in organizations the longer they stay.[5]

Psychologist Denise Rousseau has described in detail how these assumptions about obligations come to create psychological contracts.[6]

Contracts are voluntary agreements based on promises about the future behavior of the parties. What differentiates psychological contracts from legal contracts is that they are based on an individual's *perception* of the appropriate obligations and generally are not tied to any formal or written documents. Long-standing practices create expectations among workers that are incorporated into their psychological contracts. For example, the fact that large companies in particular generally gave workers job security created a sense that companies were obligated to do so. A survey of employees in the mid-1980s documented this perception in finding that a majority believed employers could not fire workers without just cause, that is, unless the individual workers were in some way poor performers. In fact, employers had the legal right to dismiss workers virtually at will.[7]

The psychological contract that accompanied the lifetime corporate employment model represented an exchange of job security and predictable advancement for loyalty and good performance. And employees complied voluntarily with the goals of the company not only because they saw it as being in their long-term interests but also because of a perceived obligation to the organization. That contract was important, especially for managerial jobs, because so much of the work done in large corporations involved discretion, making it virtually impossible to set explicit performance requirements in advance. Employers had to find some way to secure the cooperation of employees because explicit contracts and compulsion would not work. Managers were committed to the organization not only because they thought they would be rewarded for their loyalty but also because they could not leave. Freedom to move to other companies, especially for middle managers, was generally quite limited. The lifetime employment model helped produce desirable behaviors and attitudes on the part of employees, such as low turnover, the development of organization-specific skills, and commitment. Long-term job tenure complemented the company's need for a predictable set of skills and for the development of the relationships and knowledge needed to coordinate its increasingly complex organization.

It is worth pointing out that the deal for blue-collar workers was never quite like the one for managerial employees. In unionized settings, the deal was a hard-fought contract, a legal document, around which both sides were constantly seeking an advantage. The deal required employers to provide much more job security than employees would have on their own, and it certainly helped encourage long-term relationships with employees. But it did not develop what we generally think of as commitment on the part of the workforce in the same way as did the deal for white-collar workers. That is, blue-collar workers did not necessarily identify with the goals of the organization. In many workplaces, the goals of the employees as represented by their union were explicitly in conflict with those of the company. As a result, any violation of this relationship meant something quite different for these workers from what it meant for the management workforce.[8]

As we will see in Chapter 3, the advantages of the old relationship essentially evaporated when the competitive environment changed. Long-term investments and obligations became burdens as it became difficult to predict what skills would be needed in the future. Loyalty became dependence on employers who could no longer deliver on their side of the deal.

THE NEW DEAL

A great many employers have attempted to articulate a new relationship, a new contract with their employees. What this new deal really means, however, may not bear much resemblance to the carefully crafted language coming from human resource departments. And its effect on employers is likely to be just as profound as it is on employees—and much less appreciated.

The changes in the employment relationship that have occurred since the early 1980s that represent a break from the old deal include reductions in employment security, declines in internal development, and increases in the risks that employees must bear. They represent the backdrop against which employers are attempting to rewrite their deal with the workforce. Most employers understand the profound way in which they have unilaterally broken the old deal: two-thirds report that they have ended policies of job security, as indicated in Figure 1-1.[9]

Just as employers did not broker the old deal out of altruism, they did not break it out of spite. Harsh economic realities made it necessary. But within companies, human resource departments in particular began to worry about the long-term consequences of this broken contract. In particular, they were shocked by the collapse of employee morale. Many HR executives believed that its collapse would cost their organizations in terms of employee performance. (Whether or not they were right in this belief is another matter, as noted later in this chapter.) Figure 1-2 suggests the extent to which those companies which eventually re-drafted the deals with their employees perceived various problems with their workforce, strongly suggesting that these morale and trust issues were the motivating force.

These HR executives found a receptive ear among the cadre of senior executives who had ordered the downsizings and restructurings that broke the old deal. Dennis Sullivan, vice president of organizational development at GTE, noted that one of the motivating factors behind the old deal was to make senior management feel good about the way it was treating their workers: "I think a lot of corporate executives during that period really had a need to feel loved by their employees."[10] They were being made to feel pretty guilty about breaking the old deal by their communities and the press. "Corporate killers" was a commonly used epigram for these executives. Their concern about the negative effects of morale and their own guilt led them to articulate new deals for their workers.

Employers are generally extremely reluctant to put anything in writing about employment, even abandoning established employee handbooks, as they were counseled by their lawyers that written state-

Figure 1-1. The Changing Employment Compact

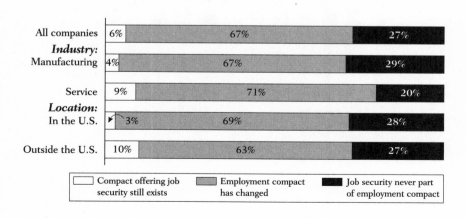

Source: HR Executive Review: Implementing the New Employment Compact (New York: Conference Board, 1997), 5.
Reprinted with permission.

Figure 1-2. *What Employees Expect from Companies*

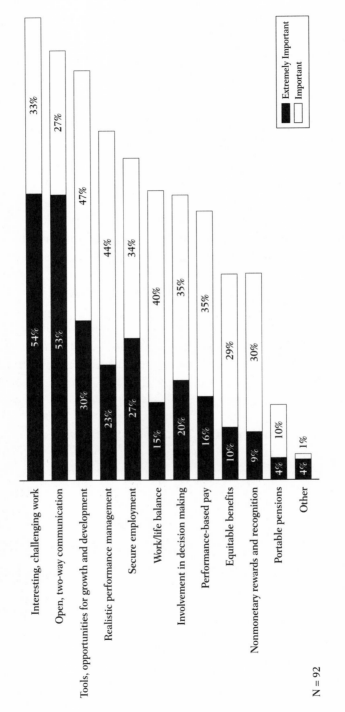

N = 92

Note: Data reflects managers' perceptions based on internal employee attitude surveys and/or other feedback from employees.
Source: HR Executive Review: Implementing the New Employment Compact (New York: Conference Board, 1997), 12.

ments can tie their hands and create legal liabilities. Given this, the fact that almost half of U.S. employers in 1996–1997 produced written material outlining new deals for their employees is astonishing; it suggests how important the employers believed this effort to be. The vast majority, 84 percent, reported that their policies and actions conveyed the essence of a new contract to the workforce.[11]

What does the new deal say? Many of the first attempts to outline it were driven simply by the interest on the part of top management to limit employee expectations, to make certain that they understood that the old deal was dead. Here is a typical example of such a presentation:

> *You have to accept responsibility for your own personal excellence, be accountable for your commitments, and understand that the customer is the most important factor in our business life. We cannot guarantee you job security any more than we can guarantee our success in the marketplace. Job security is earned by market success. Each of us must keep the company alive, vibrant, competitive, and growing. You can expect us to trust you, and you need to have trust in management. You can expect us to respect you and create a positive work environment.*[12]

What is particularly notable in this description of the new deal is that it demands a lot from employees but offers little in return. And what it does offer employees is platitudinous and vague: trust and respect. In its initial restructuring in the mid-1980s, General Electric issued similar statements to its employees that were designed to break the old deal:

> *On Job Security:* "The only job security is a successful business."
> *On Loyalty:* "If loyalty means that this company will ignore poor performance, then loyalty is off the table."
> *On Values:* "Performance without values will not be rewarded. Values without performance earn a second chance."[13]

The General Electric statement goes further in managing expectations by making it clear that loyalty per se is not that valuable in the new deal, but it also differs from the preceding statement in that it is clear about what the company expects from employees: behavior consistent with company values is the key outcome.

Apple Computer "Apple Deal," a written contract between the company and every full-time employee initiated in the 1980s, reflects an approach to employee relationships that is common in Silicon Valley and predates most of the other new deals. While equally blunt in

limiting employee expectations of the company's obligations, it offers
more from the company in return:

> Here's the deal Apple will give you; here's what we want from you. We're
> going to give you a really neat trip while you're here. We're going to teach
> you stuff you couldn't learn anywhere else. In return . . . we expect you to
> work like hell, buy the vision as long as you're here. . . . We're not interested
> in employing you for a lifetime, but that's not the way we are thinking about
> this. It's a good opportunity for both of us that is probably finite.[14]

AT&T has experienced one of the most dramatic changes in its employee relationships and has introduced a series of new policies to help
define the new deal. AT&T executives described the old deal as one in
which "the employee provided a fair day's work and a tremendous sense
of loyalty, commitment, and dependability. For its part, AT&T rewarded
most employees with a fair day's pay, a secure future, and an opportunity
to rise through the ranks. Managers and professionals were virtually
assured of lifetime employment."[15] With the breakup of the Bell System
and the competition of deregulation, an AT&T executive noted, "the
company moved to encourage entrepreneurship, individual responsibility, and accountability. Rewards were more closely tied to performance
and, most dramatically, surplus employees were let go. Thus, AT&T's
psychological contract died in the 1980s."[16] When security ended, loyalty and commitment became casualties as well.

AT&T's effort to draft a new deal began with pressure from unions.
Mary Anne Walk, the company's vice president for labor relations,
observed that "Both sides agreed that we needed to prepare our employees for the future—either with AT&T or another company."[17] Several
new programs contribute to the new deal:

- The Alliance for Employee Growth and Development is a company-
  funded subsidiary operated jointly by the company and its unions. Its
  goal is to identify trends in workplace demands and skill needs, pass
  the information on to employees, and provide them with help in
  making themselves marketable both within AT&T and to outside employers.
- Resource Link (for managers) and Skills Match Center (for union employees) are programs that place surplus employees in an internal pool
  that the company draws on for temporary assignments. While the initial
  interest in these programs grew out of a desire to reduce the churning
  of the workforce—firing and then hiring from the outside market—

40 percent of the participants in the Resource Link program have joined voluntarily, not as a result of being declared redundant. They do so to broaden their skills. Half of these volunteers are in information systems and technical positions where skills deteriorate quickly and the need to update them is more intense. Particularly for these workers, the internal temping programs may also create some stability by offering a buffer against changes in the business.[18]

- Workplace of the Future is a series of representative councils with union representatives intended to allow for participation in more business decisions affecting employees.

- Changes in management compensation link it to employee satisfaction levels, helping to create a sense of accountability among top managers to the concerns of lower-level employees.

As with most companies, GTE's effort to redraft its relationship with employees began with evidence of sharp declines in morale following corporate restructuring and layoffs. The company began discussions with employees in 1993 with a frank description of the old deal: the company provided paternalistic management, promotion from within, seniority-based pay, training, and job security. In return, employees offered compliance, loyalty, willingness to be directed (to relocate or change careers), and a lifetime of service. GTE then put forward a new deal that promised some key differences:

- The employer will provide candid leadership, pay linked to performance, a learning climate, the *offer* (my emphasis) of training, opportunity for development, and information on where the business is headed.

- In return, employees will provide superior performance, initiative and opportunism, commitment to business success (not loyalty), and readiness to change.[19]

Not all of the new deals had the same features, of course, because not all companies had the same set of problems. But the central components of virtually all of them include the following:

- At least an implicit acknowledgment that the employer can no longer offer job security. Not even career security, a long-term relationship in which jobs might change, can be guaranteed. The most honest of the contracts go further and offer the obvious caveat emptor: Because we cannot guarantee your future, you have to start taking charge of it yourself.

- The most important thing the company needs from you is your skills. But the company can no longer be responsible for identifying and developing those skills. You, the employee, have to take on that responsibility. Some of the deals go on to argue that the company also expects employees to follow the values of the organization, to embrace them as long as they are in the company's employ.

- In return, the company offers several things. Implicit is that it will try to keep employees with the company as long as the economic environment makes that possible. Virtually all of the deals go on to say that the company will also provide employees with the means and opportunity to develop their skills in ways that will help ensure that they can have career advancement, even if it takes them away from their current employer. Most of the deals add that the company will also offer the employees more challenging and exciting work than they have had in the past and reward them for good performance.

These contracts reflect genuine concern for the human problems caused by the enormous changes in the way employers now must operate and acknowledge the need to talk straight about the changes that have taken place. And they reflect the main human resources problem facing companies through the mid 1990s, the need to shed workers. The documents themselves, however, are problematic along several dimensions. While they are quite honest about what the employer can and will no longer do for employees, they cannot deliver on the promise of reconnecting the workforce to the employer. What they end up reinforcing is a vision of a highly contingent deal at work that causes some significant problems for companies. Here is what these deals really say—and don't say—about the new relationship.

They outline a new set of obligations that employees must now bear, such as managing their own careers and developing their own skills. They make it clear that the company will keep them in jobs only as long as the relationship works for the company. No matter how these new deals are sliced, they make the employee feel like an independent contractor who has a very contingent relationship with his current employer.

Employees are encouraged to direct their attention for career management outside the firm, to the market, where they are frequently told that their long-term prospects lie. Some of the contracts explicitly say that employees should be benchmarking their skills against the demands of the market and thinking about careers that will eventually move them to better positions at other companies. A positive spin on this message is that employees need to think more like professionals whose ultimate allegiance is to their skills and their careers. The negative but equally appropriate implication is that employees have little reason to identify with their current, no doubt only temporary, employer.

At the same time, the contracts explicitly require that employees "live our values," which implies something much deeper than a professional relationship. It strongly suggests commitment. This statement generally comes right after one telling the employees to identify with their own careers and look to the market for career guidance. It also comes after the mention of how company offerings such as job security which helped create employee commitment in the first place, will be no more.

The new deals say little about how the employer might help employees reconnect with the workforce at large. The economic commentator Robert Kuttner observed that "without a reciprocal commitment by management to a long-term relationship, the employee who buys into the partnership model is being romanced for a one-night stand."[20] The offer of more challenging work and greater pay for performance is always phrased as "in return, we will offer . . ." to suggest that these changes are a quid pro quo for employees taking on the greater risks and responsibilities of managing their own careers. In fact, the changes in these practices are not really a quid pro quo but something that the employers would do in any case, simply reflecting new ways of work that increase performance. As outlined in Chapter 3, systems of empowerment and increased responsibility have gained tenure because they cut costs. Greater rewards for organizational performance create incentives for individual effort and also shift risk onto employees. While these changes may benefit employees, the companies have made them not because they benefit the employees but because they increase organizational performance. They would make them even if the employees would not buy the new deal.

The most crucial part of the deal—and the one apparent element of reciprocity—is the promise on the employer's side to help support the development of employee skills. This does seem like an explicit quid pro quo for the charge that employees take on the responsibility for managing their careers and developing their own skills. If the new deal has any real meat to it, any reciprocity, it turns on this offer of help with skill development. Most of the new deals refer to this as the "employability" concept: We cannot offer you security with our company, but we can help you to secure skills that will keep you employable, that will lead to some security in the labor market by helping you find other jobs.

But can the employers actually deliver on this? It depends on what is meant by "developing employee skills." To the extent that it means making investments in employees, it confronts serious obstacles. The chapters that follow articulate how the pace of change has made it much more difficult for companies to make any long-term investments in employee skills pay off, even when the company is directing those skills. As described more fully later in this chapter, other aspects of the new deal will make it even more difficult for employers to overcome those problems than it has been in the past. To put it bluntly, will companies really be willing to make investments in skills that they know will walk out the door? The new deal has internal contradictions that result from companies' efforts to be honest about what they need from their employees and will be able to offer in return while at the same time trying to give employees some grounds for optimism. But there is a bigger and much more fundamental problem that undercuts the whole notion of a new deal with the workforce. The problem is that a deal or contract cannot be set unilaterally by one party. It takes two to make a deal.

What companies have done with their new deals is to make an offer to employees: This is what we want the deal to look like. How closely their offer resembles the deal that ultimately results depends on bargaining, negotiations, and the relative power of the parties. Think about some analogies. You post a help-wanted ad that lists what you want in an applicant: someone who is smart, qualified, responsible, hardworking, committed to your organization, and, oh yes, willing to work cheap. There is a very good chance that you will not find anyone who fits that description. What you might find is someone who meets many of those characteristics but is not willing to work cheap. And so you bargain and compromise. The deal you end up with is very different from the deal you propose.

It may seem obvious that management cannot impose a deal unilaterally on new applicants, but what about current employees, especially those with long service who may find it difficult to leave? Consider another analogy. You have a long-term relationship with a friend or a spouse that you would like to change. You put forward a new deal: From now on, I'm expecting you to take more responsibility for our relationship, to pay for more of our entertainment, to go to more of the places I like. If your friend or spouse is really committed to the relationship, he or she might try to accommodate your needs. But you might also find the person changing the deal in other ways. He or she might come back at you with his or her own set of demands. Or you might find the person telling you to take a hike—relationship over.

So, for companies, announcing the new deal is only the beginning of a process of arriving at a new employment relationship. One of the characteristics of the deal is that it is difficult to tell in the short run whether employees have bought it. There may be many aspects of employee behavior associated with the new deal that are difficult to monitor, such as "living our values." Other aspects may take a long time to observe, such as whether employees develop the skills that are useful to the employer (as opposed, say, to some future employer) or whether they leave as soon as a good option appears. As a result, it is very possible that employees have not bought the new deal and that their employer just doesn't know it yet.

The extent to which employers will be able to implement their version of the new deal and to which employees will force drastic revisions depends on power. And power in a negotiation depends almost entirely on one thing: options. The most crucial principle in the science of negotiations is what many observers refer to as the best alternative to a negotiated agreement, or BATNA. If I do not accept your deal, what are my options? If I have only one job offer and really need to work, I have little power, and the employer making that offer, with other candidates waiting in the wings, has lots of it as we negotiate a final deal. Once I start receiving other offers that I like just as well or better, the power in the negotiation process shifts to me. If I seem to be the only really qualified applicant for a given position (that is, the employer has no real options) and I have lots of other offers, then I am in a position to dictate the terms of the deal.

Consider the recent experience that employers have had in recontracting employment relationships. The most straightforward of these has been the collective bargaining experience in securing concessions from trade unions beginning in the early 1980s. I described the process at the time as one in which management found itself under extraordinary pressure to cut costs and approached unions with its version of the new deal: Take lower compensation and reform work rules or watch jobs disappear. Unions generally took that deal because they had no option. If they resisted with a strike, then the company would likely fail altogether. Later on, however, the unions realized that the companies had no option, either: If the unions did not agree, then the companies would fail and their managers would be out of work. Then the unions were able to negotiate changes to the deals that were more beneficial to the unions.[21]

During the period from 1981 through the mid 1990s, described in more detail in Chapter 3, when companies were unilaterally changing the terms and conditions of employment with downsizing and other restructuring trends, employees bought it because they had no choice. Because all companies were going through roughly the same trend, there were few other job options. Companies may well have been able to recontract the employment deal unilaterally for managerial employees, especially middle managers who had worked their way up the ranks in the same company. Where could they go when their knowledge base no longer had value in that company? Unionized employees wanted to stay largely because they would lose crucial seniority benefits by moving.

But that world is long gone now. And one of the factors that changed it has been these efforts by employers to communicate the new deal to their employees. Now the incredible contradiction of the new deal in the workplace is clear. At the same time that employers are seeking to impose a new deal on their employees unilaterally, they are actively encouraging those employees to get the kind of information and skills that will allow them to pursue better options in the market. It is difficult to imagine an equivalent analogy. Suppose a car dealer gave you a price that was much worse than you wanted and at the same time gave you information and training on how to get competitive bids from other dealers. Or your lover told you that while he or she was hoping to stay with you, more would be expected from you from now on. What's more, your lover was going to help you become more attractive to other partners and help you figure out who else might like you. It is hard to imagine anyone staying with either deal.

The most important aspect of the new deal, in fact, is not the new obligations demanded of employees or any of the implied quid pro quos. It is the message conveyed indirectly by every aspect of the deal that employees are now operating in the market. The suggestions that employees think of their career as going beyond their current employer, that they benchmark their skills against the changing requirements of their field, that their current position may be at risk for a variety of reasons all send the message that the most important connection they have is not to their current employer but to the market. No doubt a great many employees got that message, even before these efforts at drafting a new deal, from the waves of downsizings, the outside hiring, the market-tested compensation systems, and the other changes in practice that effectively unraveled the old system.

To recap, the new deal that employers have presented to their workforce represents an honest effort to limit the expectations of their workforce and articulate what management currently believes it can provide and what it needs from employees. But that is simply an opening bargaining position in the negotiation over what ultimately becomes the real deal. The fundamental characteristic of the real deal between employees and employers is that the relationship is no longer defined inside the company or described by internal development policies such as training, compensation, and promotion practices. It is now much closer to a market relationship in which the governance is outside the firm, in the market. That does not mean that the relationship has to be short term. We are not all temps. Long-term relationships can also be governed by the market. Suppliers and customers can and often do have lifelong relationships with each other. But even in these relationships, the prices charged and the characteristics of the deals change depending on relative bargaining power, which is ultimately determined by the market.

Perhaps the most immediate and powerful evidence that the market is now in charge of employment even in large corporations is the relatively short lifespan various new deals are having. Leading companies like GTE, GE, Xerox, Merck, Pitney Bowes, AT&T, and others began thinking intensely about redefining their deal with employees in the early 1990s, when it became clear that the churning of their workforces was not a temporary phenomenon and that the old arrangements were gone for good. By 1994, they were beginning to talk through new deals in their workplaces. By 1995, the efforts went public. By 1996, the discussion was full-blown, with conferences and consultants weighing in on how to draft a new deal.

By the end of 1996, however, the labor market began to tighten, especially for technical skills. And by 1997, while companies were still interested in the issue, the attention of these leading companies had shifted to new policies designed to make them "employers of choice." What "employer of choice" means is simply that its policies and practices, the terms and conditions of employment in its workplace, are at a high-enough standard to attract employees away from competitors and to keep their own employees from leaving. "Employer of choice" is simply a way of saying that the employment relationship is market based, the labor market is tight, and we have to respond—by benchmarking to learn about and then match compensation packages, offers of training, work, and family accommodations, whatever it takes to recruit and retain employees. The "new deals" as articulated in company pronouncements just months earlier are essentially dead. The real new deal is whatever it takes to get and hold the skills we need in the market. This kind of deal making is on the rise.

GTE was one company ahead of the pack in understanding this change. By 1996, it had essentially put its "new deal" on hold, recognizing that its main problem had already shifted from the need to get rid of employees to that of attracting highly skilled new ones and retaining those it already had. Even at the middle-management level, where most companies were cutting, GTE anticipated skill shortages because of the rising job requirements created by flatter organizations and more specialist knowledge. GTE's "new" new deal accommodates a larger role for the human resource function as an advocate for employee concerns as a way of recruiting and retaining the talent needed to run the organization and as a way of trying to reconnect employee loyalty. Career development, for example, is no longer seen as an employee responsibility but as a shared responsibility between employee and employer.[22]

So the real new deal is simply the market. What employers have to offer in order to recruit, retain, and ensure adequate levels of performance from employees will change based on the relative bargaining power of the parties. That power, in turn, is shaped by their options, by the relative pull of supply and demand.

It may be tempting to think of the new relationship as something like free agency as in professional sports or the workings of temporary help agencies, where employees hop from employer to employer, doing essentially the same work at each stop and moving whenever they receive a better offer. There are some jobs—in which the tasks are self-contained, short term, and common across organizations—that fit this model. But they are few and far between. Management positions in particular do not fit this model. A manager's tasks are by definition interdependent with others in the organization, are relatively specific to each organization, and take some considerable period to complete. These jobs do not lend themselves easily to free agency or contract-style relationships. They are much more suited to open-ended relationships in which the obligations and tasks need to be adjusted as situations change. Performance can then be observed, and rewards allocated accordingly. Some level of mutual commitment and trust is needed to facilitate changing needs, as are some skills that are unique to the organization.

At the same time, the pressures from markets and the need to restructure organizations and competencies mean that truly long-term employment relationships are largely dead. The pressures to shed obsolete skills (compounded by the uncertainty of knowing which ones will be obsolete) and the problem of poaching skills from other employers make it difficult to maintain commitment and trust, develop skills internally, and retain important skills. The defining problem of the new relationship, therefore, is how to graft the model of the market onto those occupations for which it is poorly suited.

So the new employment relationship represents an uneasy balance between a long-term relationship and a spot market, an open-ended relationship that is shaped by pull of the market. As explained in the introduction, it is less like marriage or dating than serial monogamy— several long-term relationships that either party can end unilaterally, each shaped by possibilities. The parties are constantly negotiating their commitments in light of uncertain future needs and opportunities. Pressures from outside the relationship, from the labor market in particular, are now the important forces shaping the nature of the relationship. When labor markets are slack and jobs are difficult to find, employees become more loyal to their employer and bear most of the costs of restructuring; when labor markets tighten, employee commitment falls and employers become more willing to make investments in their employees. The relationship may well turn out to last a long time, but it is continually being redefined by the power of the market.

Analogies with marriage in particular and personal relationships more generally make many people nervous because in those cases a temporary relationship suggests a failed relationship. But consider the relationship that alumni have with their schools, a relationship that is clearly temporary in that students leave—one way or the other—in short order. Yet many alumni have a deep commitment to their alma mater, often much stronger than to their current employer, despite the fact that their experience with their school was only temporary, often long ago, and they had to pay for it. Temporary relationships are not necessarily bad relationships. The commitment and loyalty seems to be driven by whether their experience exceeded their expectations. If they came out with more than they expected, then they feel good about the relationship even though it was temporary. In the case of institutions like schools or military service, the fact that people know going in that the relationship will be temporary may actually make it easier to limit and then meet their expectations. A great many people seem to have more attachment and loyalty to their first employer than to their current employer because they expected so little and got so much from that experience.

There is evidence that employees understand the nature of this new deal at work, perhaps better than their employers.[23] A survey of employee views about what they expect from work, based on internal company surveys or feedback, finds that "secure employment" is ranked fifth in importance out of ten attributes that employees expect from their companies. Interesting work, open communications, and opportunities for development took the top three spots.[24]

Focus groups conducted by Towers Perrin report that employees believe that their efforts on behalf of company goals have helped make the waves of downsizing possible, doing more with fewer people. While employers put commitment and trust as the two most important things they want from the new deal, employees want professional development and training, investments that make it possible for them to reduce their dependence on their current employer.[25]

A survey of 3,300 employees by Towers Perrin asked respondents about their perceptions of the new deal in the workplace. Only 45 percent felt that they had the opportunity to advance in their current organization. They also recognized that lifetime employment with one company is unrealistic—and may also be undesirable for them. Interestingly, there were few differences in responses between those earning more than or less than $80,000 in salary. Middle managers and hourly workers now see that they have essentially the same relationship with their employer.[26]

On the other hand, employees now seem to have rather positive views about their work situation. Seventy-nine percent believed that their company had treated them fairly and felt a sense of personal accomplishment from their work. Seventy-five percent felt motivated and believed they could have an impact on company success. The contrast with much more negative survey results just a few years before no doubt reflects several developments: the day-to-day experience in the workplace has changed as growth replaced downsizing, extensive hiring means that a large percentage of the respondents had no experience with either the restructuring period or the old deal, and employees recalibrate their perceptions over time as they focus on the present.[27]

WHY THE NEW DEAL MATTERS

The fact that the nature of the deal between employers and employees has changed is interesting to historians of the workplace, but does it matter for anyone else? It clearly matters for employees who find that they must adapt to a world where employers have little responsibility for them. It also matters for employers in equally profound ways, although most have not thought through exactly how. As described in detail in Chapter 3, employers so far have paid a relatively small price for breaking the old deal. Unemployment and the fear of layoffs basically kept employees from quitting or acting out their frustration with the broken employment relationship. But the deal that has taken its place raises a series of new challenges for employers.

One important aspect of the real new deal is that it has eliminated many of the human resource practices, based on internal, administrative principles, that essentially buffered both employers and employees from the pressures of the outside labor market. Practices like predictable promotion and career paths and compensation formulas directed at achieving internal equity meant, for example, that when unemployment rose, employees did not see their wages or job security collapse. Similarly, when labor markets tightened, employers did not necessarily face bidding wars for their best workers. The decline of internalized employment systems has reduced these buffers between employees and the labor market, making the effects of the market much more important. The efforts at drafting a new deal in the workplace, which explicitly tells employees to focus their attention on the outside labor market, exacerbates this development. The central theme of the market-based employment contract is that the most important determinants of employee behavior and attitudes are now outside the firm, in the labor market. And the most salient characteristic of the labor market is the balance of supply and demand. When labor markets are tight and jobs are plentiful, the behavior and attitudes of employees are very different from what they are when those markets are slack.

Pretend that you are a marketing manager in a large company like GE or AT&T in the 1970s. Your career has been directed by superiors and the human resources department over the past two decades, and you have changed jobs several times. Each move was to a higher-level job, sometimes in a different functional area, in which case you received extensive additional training. Subject to adequate performance, you anticipate retiring with a good pension in another twenty years. While you have a reasonably good idea what marketing managers in other companies are paid, you do not give it that much thought because you do not see yourself as being a marketing manager for long. And while you have a lot of connections to your New Jersey community, the state of its labor market is of little concern, in part because you expect to be moving to another position in a few years. What really has your attention are the changes in the organizational chart that affect your promotion prospects, the company's plans for expansion and the opportunities associated with it, and the new employee development and training criteria for middle managers.

Ten or twenty years later, the same company has downsized several times and restructured into a much flatter, leaner organization. While your performance has been good and you have survived several rounds of cuts, it is clear that there are no guarantees. Promotion prospects are slim not only because there are many fewer top jobs but also because the company increasingly fills positions from the outside. You have worked hard to build a network of contacts in northern New Jersey and have done a lot of work with professional associations in the area. You have at your fingertips not only the going salaries for marketing jobs but also the characteristics of candidates that are in demand. You have been negotiating within your company for work experience in information technology because you know that it is the hot area in the outside market. Wednesday evening is spent taking a class at the community college on local area network systems.

While the company was downsizing, as were most of the companies in the area, it sure felt good to have a job. Despite the fact that support went down and stress went up, you put on an amazing display of company loyalty—working late every night, pitching in on projects in other areas—crimping your family life in the process. This past year, the market really picked up. When a major software company moved into the community last month and started hiring experienced managers at salaries 20 percent higher than yours, it got your attention. It's been harder to find the motivation to stay late to finish projects, and you have been returning all the calls from headhunters since then.

In both obvious and subtle ways, the manager's attitudes and behavior twenty years later are driven by the market—looking inside the company when opportunities are slim but following the signals from the outside when opportunities pick up. What we know about how the market affects the way employees think and act can be summarized briefly as follows.

WORK ATTITUDES. The attitudes that employees hold toward their jobs and their employers are obviously relevant to employees, who care about being happy and satisfied, but they are also relevant to employers interested in their performance. For frontline workers and service employees, attitude is part of the service they provide for customers and colleagues. While the "happy worker" model may no longer be valid, employee attitudes still influence behavior, especially when labor markets are tight.

There is ample evidence that even one's attitude toward one's job and employer is shaped by the labor market. Studies find, for example, that job satisfaction and the like are affected by the availability of alternative jobs.[28] Comparisons between one's wage and prevailing wages in the market affect not only satisfaction with pay but also satisfaction with other aspects of work.[29] Other research shows that workers living in poorer communities are more satisfied with a given job and pay level than are those elsewhere.[30] The high levels of job satisfaction during the Depression and the widespread discontent with jobs in the 1960s can be traced in part to slack and tight job markets, respectively.

The issue of commitment to the employer, a concept considered at length in the following pages, also has clear ties to the labor market. A number of studies have found that the degree to which an employee is committed to his employer depends on the availability of other job options.[31] In one of the clearest illustrations of this phenomenon, researchers asked graduating MBA students about the number of job offers they had when leaving the program and then followed up a few years later to see how committed the graduates were to their employer. Those who had lots of options were substantially less committed. Those who had only one job offer? They felt they had found just the right job for themselves. They were highly committed.[32] Other studies support the more general relationship that the more difficult and costly it is to move, the more employees feel an emotional commitment to the interests of their employer.[33] And occupations that offer greater mobility also are ones that exhibit lower commitment.[34] We also know that more educated workers are less committed to their employers,[35] in part because education creates opportunities and enhances mobility.

Some of the survey data described in Chapter 3 suggests that professionals are the least committed to their employers, no doubt because their skills are among the most transferrable. Professional and technical workers have more than doubled their share of the workforce since 1950 to more than 17 percent. Together with craft work, these jobs share the characteristics of being organized horizontally, along occupational lines in external labor markets. These workers have professional associations and craft unions that help define how their jobs are performed and that help shape their labor markets. And they account for about 30 percent of the jobs in the economy.[36] They are more oriented toward the market outside the firm than are people in other occupations, and their numbers are growing.

TURNOVER. The rate of voluntary turnover, sometimes known as the quit rate, is a very costly matter for employers. In many cases, employees who leave represent the distinctive competency of an organization, and the acknowledged cost of finding and training replacement workers only approximates the true cost to the organization, which some observers place at about one year's salary for managerial jobs. Voluntary turnover is very closely related to the pull of the outside labor market because virtually all employees who leave voluntarily do so to take jobs elsewhere. Vacancies in one organization and industry have been shown to create turnover in others.[37] Whether employees trickle or stream out of an organization depends, therefore, on the state of the labor market. Despite all the attention given to human resource practices, the two most important factors driving turnover in firms are the availability of opportunities elsewhere and the relative wage paid by the current employer.[38]

In cases where both an industry and its occupations are organized around an external labor market, such as craft work in construction (carpenters, plumbers, etc.) or professional work, turnover is higher because both opportunities elsewhere and information about them are

greater. The professionalization of the workforce should therefore contribute to greater turnover.

Large organizations generally have lower turnover in part simply
because employees have room to move within the organization, seeking
better matches and new opportunities as their skills develop. As organizations shrink and decentralize, therefore, we might expect turnover
rates to rise because there are fewer opportunities inside the same
organization. The flattening of organization charts, reducing internal
promotion opportunities, also increases turnover.

ABSENTEEISM AND DISCIPLINE. Problems with employee performance
within the firm are affected by opportunities outside in two distinct
ways. The first concerns employee assessments of inequity. If opportunities elsewhere appear better, then it is easier for employees to feel
aggrieved at their current treatment and feel the need to restore equity
by reducing their performance. When opportunities elsewhere deteriorate, the opposite happens. Second, the more conservative view of
human nature suggests that the fear of being dismissed is one of the
factors that maintains good performance. Those costs vary with opportunities in the labor market. There is ample evidence, for example, that
absenteeism inside firms varies with the unemployment rate outside.[39]
In my own work studying the effects of the labor market on company
discipline rates, I've found that workers were more likely to handle their
complaints internally through grievance systems, as opposed to quitting,
being absent, or causing other discipline problems, when opportunities
in the outside labor market were worse.[40]

WORKLIFE. The state of the labor market also affects levels of stress,
health problems, and employee well-being. In particular, increases in
the unemployment rate exacerbate these problems, as those who do
have jobs fear they, too, will lose them. The extent of employee commitment to employers seems to buffer employees from these labor
market problems. Less committed workers are more affected in their
well-being by the state of the labor market.[41] The move from lifetime,
internal employment relationships to ones that rely more on markets and less on employee commitment will make aspects of employee well-being more dependent on the market, particularly on the
downside.

CONCLUSIONS DRAWN. Two overall conclusions can be drawn from this list of findings that are important for managers to remember. The first is that by moving to this new, more market-mediated relationship, employers have lost a substantial amount of control and influence over the attitudes and behavior of their employees. Internal employment systems were designed in large measure to buffer employees and, in turn, the organization from the pressures of the outside labor market. By abandoning those systems, we also lose their buffering effect. When labor markets tighten and outside opportunities increase, expect turnover and discipline problems to rise, morale and attitudes to decline; when labor markets slacken, expect employee performance to improve, the quit rate to decline, and attitudes to rebound.

Some might argue that this greater sensitivity to the market is a good thing for organizations and draw a parallel to the quality movement in manufacturing. There, explicit efforts were made to bring the market into the manufacturing process through systems like just-in-time manufacturing, eliminating internal inventory buffers. The presence of slack capacity or buffers served to hide and then cover up quality and design problems and also cost money. Internal employment systems, one might argue, do something similar. Because they insulate the organization from the outside labor market, it is easy for the firm to get out of touch with outside standards in areas like job performance, skills, and pay. Bringing the labor market inside forces the company to stay current and up-to-date in its employment practices.

Certainly this analogy seems right on issues such as skills and performance, where bringing the market in can reveal the need for improvement. But ultimately it breaks down because in employment we are dealing with people, not just systems or equipment, and because the process does not stop there. People are free to leave, something that other assets cannot do, and people's behavior and attitudes can actually worsen as a result of this process. To illustrate, when we bring the market inside in an area like IT services through a contractor or a benchmarking study, we might learn that our software is inferior or our networking capabilities need improvement. In that case, we might simply change those systems. Or we might learn that our systems are pretty good and do nothing. When we bring the labor market in, we might learn that the skills of our workers are inadequate and work to upgrade them. But it may also panic our employees, who fear that they might be replaced and start looking for other jobs. And if it turns out that our skills are good and pay levels below average, expect morale and possibly performance to decline and employees to start walking. Many companies are finding, for example, that when they bring in consultants and vendors, some of their key employees leave with them, having been recruited by the vendors. In short, there is a downside to bringing the labor market inside that does not exist for other aspects of the firm.

The second general conclusion to be drawn from the above shortlist of findings is that the way in which the new employment contract is defined for workers, in particular how much emphasis is given to the market, now matters a great deal. Most employers now point out to employees the difficulty they have in making long-term commitments to workers and the need for employees to keep their skills up-to-date. Suggesting that employees need to think about their careers as extending beyond their current employer, on the other hand, to develop networks of contacts outside the firm, and to benchmark their skills against the market is more than a subtle extension of the argument. It goes beyond pushing responsibility onto employees and instead shoves them directly into the outside labor market, with all of the consequences noted above.

It may well be that the only fair response an employer can make is to tell its employees to get into the market. Their current job may be so insecure and transient that they will soon end up there anyway, and it is only fair that they be prepared. The extent to which an employer makes that argument is something to consider carefully. The stronger it is made, the more one should expect these consequences for attitudes and behavior. What can be done to manage the consequences of the move to the market on employee attitudes and behavior is the next issue to consider.

THE BIG THREE PROBLEMS OF THE *REAL* NEW DEAL

Any change in a relationship comes with a new set of pluses and minuses, creating new winners and losers. The new, market-based deal has some real advantages for employers. It gives them flexibility, helps the organization respond quickly to a changing environment, and limits their long-term liabilities. In the short run at least, it has reduced costs and pushed many of the risks and problems of managing people onto employees, who, as described in Chapter 4, have borne the brunt of

corporate restructuring. But the new, market-based employment relationship also comes with its own problems for employers. These problems may not have been especially noticeable during the restructuring
era of the 1980s and 1990s. They are becoming much more of a problem
now that labor markets are tighter. The most important of these problem
areas are the need to retain key employees, the need for employee
commitment, and the need to develop employee skills, particularly
those unique to an organization.

RETENTION. Even employers who are complaining about attrition problems would be panicked at the thought of having *no* turnover in their
workforce, with everyone staying until retirement. Most companies will
find that they need to downsize some operations or will no longer have
the need for certain skills, and positive rates of turnover, including quits,
can be an asset in such an environment. The real problem is not
turnover per se but retaining key skills. That problem is complicated by
the fact that what constitutes key skills changes over time.

The ability to retain those key skills has deteriorated, and the new
deal in the workplace is only part of the problem. By eliminating many
of the arrangements that bind employees to the firm and encouraging
them to look outside, the new deal makes it easier for them to leave.
But the real problem comes from the other side of the equation, from
employer hiring practices. Companies increasingly look to the market
to meet their skill needs. Part of the explanation is tied up with the
training issues noted earlier. The pace of change makes it difficult to
anticipate skill needs, and the pressure to raise wages or risk losing
workers makes training investments hard to fund. As headhunters, temp
agencies, and other intermediary organizations get more efficient, it also
becomes easier to find the skills one needs on the outside market. So
new hiring practices are really the force behind the attrition problem as
they increasingly pull employees out of companies.

The J.B. Hunt trucking company, one of the nation's largest, found
that it was having a hard time getting the quality workforce it wanted.
The manager hired a lot of applicants with little experience and trained
them. But the washout rate was quite high. Accidents were common,
and annual turnover averaged 140 percent. To address this problem, the
company raised its entry-level wages substantially. It now had a much
better pool of applicants and was able to meet its needs by hiring
experienced drivers. Training costs fell, as did turnover, accidents, and

other related problems. The wage increase paid for itself. The strategy of hiring experienced workers solved lots of problems for this company. The flip side of this strategy, however, is that it raises problems for other companies, whose experienced drivers are quitting for jobs at J. B. Hunt.[42]

Most employers are now trying to pursue the twin goals of hiring key skills from outside and then keeping them in the company. While it's possible for an individual firm to do both (at the expense of its competitors), it is not possible for a broader set of firms, such as a regional labor market or the economy as a whole, to do so. Economic planners in Sweden tried to address this issue during the peak years of the welfare state system by preventing employers from advertising job vacancies in the belief that doing so would interfere with their efforts to operate the economy with low unemployment. In their view, employers would simply be hiring workers away from each other, causing attrition in some firms and bidding up wages.

There are solutions to the challenge of retaining key skills, even in the face of the new deal at work. They should begin with the understanding that not all skills are crucial to retain. Arrangements for binding certain workers to the firm, even in the absence of internal employee development systems, are described in the following chapters.

LOYALTY AND COMMITMENT. The evidence presented above suggests that the major casualty resulting from the dismantling of the old employment contract is employee commitment. Research studies find that the characteristics of internal employee development (promotion from within, clear promotion paths, and opportunities for advancement) make employees more committed to their organizations[43]; and the dismantling of that system will make them less so. The more we emphasize the message that lifetime careers in the same company are unlikely and encourage employees to seek information on opportunities elsewhere, the less committed they are likely to be.

The first issue this raises is the "so what?" question. Does it matter if employees become less committed to their organizations? Most executives—96 percent in a recent survey—believe that commitment and loyalty are an important factor in determining whether a company succeeds or fails.[44] Another survey of employers found them reporting that commitment was the most critical employee behavior—the one their efforts at fashioning new deals were most intended to address.[45]

Whether they are right in thinking that commitment is critical is a crucial question. Certainly there is evidence that more committed employees have higher performance on a range of dimensions. For example, they have lower quit rates[46] and lower rates of absenteeism and tardiness.[47] And they are more likely to act in the interests of the organization, to exhibit the kind of selfless behavior that makes an organization function behind the scenes.[48] These selfless actions, what psychologists refer to as extra-role behavior, are especially important in the new work systems that are reducing the supervision and direct monitoring of employees, increasing employee empowerment and input, and generally relying much more on the employees to act in the interests of the organization.

One of the biggest and most fundamental dilemmas of the modern firm is this combination of empowered employees and reduced commitment. As firms increasingly adopt high-performance work systems (described in Chapter 3) that rely on employees to act in the interests of the firm, they are also changing the employment relationship in ways that sharply reduce employee commitment to the employer. And many commentators see this as the fatal flaw of the new employment relationship. There are methods of maintaining employee commitment—substitutes as it were—even in the face of this new deal.

SKILLS. Professor Gary Becker at the University of Chicago won his Nobel Prize in Economics in part for insights into the very practical issue of the financing of investments in skills—or human capital, as it has become known. There may be many reasons why individuals acquire skills. One of them is certainly to earn a return on them. Individuals make those investments much as they would any other investment, by assessing the costs against the stream of benefits that will flow from them. The problem is rather more complicated for employers who are considering investments in their employees.

Employers initially see the incentives the same way. They weigh the costs of investments made in worker skills against the stream of benefits they expect from having more skilled employees. As Becker noted, employers earn the return on their investment in training because the value of the employee's work rises as their skills increase, while the wage they receive is less than the value of their work. The greater the difference between the value of work and the wage, the greater the return, and the more training that can be funded.[49]

The complication comes from the fact that employees are not fixed assets. Unlike other "investments," they can leave and take their skills with them. To the extent to which those skills are useful elsewhere, the employee's value to other employers also increases. As an employee, I am interested in pursuing jobs that offer me the highest wage, other things being equal. As my skills and value to other employers rises, so does the wage that I can command in the market. To keep me from leaving for a job elsewhere, my employer will have to raise my wage to match the offers in the market. But if my employer does that, its ability to earn a return on my training diminishes.

One of Becker's insights was that employers would find it very difficult to fund investments in training for skills that were general— that is, skills that were useful to other employers—for the reasons noted above. Employer investments in training were more likely to be limited to those skills that were unique to that employer, skills that were not useful outside and would not lead to an increase in market wages. Skills that are purely specific to the employer help create lifetime employment relationships. Visiting Thailand recently, I stumbled on what may be one of the last truly lifetime employment relationships: elephant trainers. A young man is assigned to work with a single young elephant through years of training and then becomes the "driver" of that elephant in logging operations until both the driver and the elephant together retire. The relationship between the handler and the elephant is based on such completely specific investments that it lasts a lifetime.

Another insight is that employee turnover kills the incentive to provide training, other things being equal, by reducing the period during which the employer can earn a return on the training investment. Recent surveys of training by the Bureau of Labor Statistics illustrate the relationship between turnover and training: establishments with "medium" levels of turnover invested 12.5 hours of training per employee compared to establishments with "high" levels of turnover, which invested 7.2 hours.[50] Any efforts that bind employees to a firm or make it difficult for them to leave increase the period during which employers can earn a return on investments in skills and their ability to fund training.

Contemporary organizations already face disincentives to train and develop employees because the pace of change makes it difficult to know which skills will pay off in the future, reducing the amount of time during which they will be valuable. Other aspects of the new workplace also hinder the ability to develop employees internally:

1. The "flattening" of organizations, which reduces the layers of hierarchy, also reduces the ability to move employees into gradually more challenging roles.

2. The associated reduction in direct supervision reduces the ability of supervisors to instruct and guide their employees.

3. Similarly, the move away from simple, more narrowly defined jobs toward broader, "high performance" work systems makes it more difficult for employees who are unskilled to enter a workplace and to acquire the skills to advance at their own pace, making a contribution in the meantime.

4. The reduction of the functional orientation in organization structures (that is, departments organized around functions like accounting or marketing) toward more cross-functional models vastly increases the skills and information employees need to know.

The new deal in the workplace also exacerbates these problems, creating additional and independent disincentives for employers to provide training. By dismantling the internal arrangements for managing employees, the new deal erodes mechanisms that bind employees to the employer. By encouraging employees to look to the market, the new deal makes it easier for them to leave. These trends make it difficult for employers to fund even the training investments that they believe are useful to the organization. By making employees more mobile, the new deal forces employers to pay trained workers a wage equal to their value in the market or see them walk. Both options kill the ability to recoup training investments.

Employees still need skills, however, many of which are unique to their organization. And employers still have to find ways of providing those skills. There are ways to develop employee skills even in the context of the market-driven new deal, however, and we explore them in Chapter 5.

Before outlining solutions to the challenges that the new deal creates for managers, it is helpful to take a step back and see what led to the new deal. The place to begin is with a brief historical tour of employment practices in the United States, where it becomes clear that the new deal is in fact not so new after all.

CHAPTER 2

The Arrangements We Left Behind, and How We Got Them in the First Place

REPORTS OF corporate life over the past decade suggest a historic break in the social contract between employers and employees. One cover story after another has advertised how the traditional relationship in the workplace has been overthrown.[1] Following is a sampling of the trends that have been covered.

Job security for all workers has declined and become much more contingent on performance. Middle management in particular has gone from one of the most secure occupations to one of the least as organizations continue to downsize their ranks. Employers routinely tell workers that their only real source of security is "employability," their ability to find a job elsewhere.

Companies worry less about developing skills and rely instead on hiring from the outside market to meet their skill needs. For jobs that require general skills, some employers rely in part on temporary workers with no real attachment to the firm. Others maintain a pool of workers that they hire on a short-term basis to fit in with changes in product demand.

Pay has also become much less secure, varying now not only with individual performance but also with the performance of the organization. Seniority in the job plays much less of a role in determining pay, and efforts to maintain a wage structure in which the rates of pay between different occupations in the organization are adjusted to maintain the perception of equity are virtually dead. Top executives increasingly see their compensation based on the stock price of their firm.

Entire functions and departments are routinely outsourced to contractors. Often the contractors hire the old employees, who then perform the same tasks within the same facilities, sometimes alongside the owner's direct employees. The contractors hire and manage their own work teams, negotiating pay and employment terms, sometimes independently for each worker.

Line management increasingly makes personnel decisions. In some establishments, autonomous work groups of skilled employees decide by themselves who gets hired, how to allocate work, how to train new workers, and, in some cases, how to distribute pay increases among members of the group.

What all of the above developments have in common is that they represent a weakening of the traditional relationship between employer and employee, one that had seemed to serve both parties well. In their place, market forces increasingly govern the employment relationship.

We see these developments today as being revolutionary, as breaking down historic barriers around the way employees should be managed and companies run. Many thoughtful observers of the workplace are deeply disturbed by these developments because they see them as violating fundamental and long-standing social conventions.

In fact, all of these practices were widespread in American industry a hundred years ago. And all of the developments above are taken from more than century-old examples. We think of the system of long-term employment relationships and related practices that is now being overthrown as having always been in place, but in fact it is a relatively recent invention in place not much longer than a generation. The recent cover story accounts of virtual companies run by venture capitalists who outsource operations, hire contractors to do the rest, and use temporary employees to do their work may in fact be as good a description of the business world at the beginning of the twentieth century as at its end.

A look at why market-based practices were prevalent in earlier periods may shed some light on why they are making a comeback now and on how they operate.

BACK TO THE FUTURE?

The historian Alfred Chandler, Jr., describes the typical firm of the 1800s as being a single-unit operation that carried out only one function. These firms were masters of the 1990s advice that companies should pare themselves down to their "core competencies"—those few tasks that they truly performed well—and either outsource or get rid of everything else.

William Durant was the man who brought General Motors together as a giant, vertically integrated corporation in 1908. Before the rise of the automobile, he headed one of the largest carriage companies in the country. His original company, the Durant-Dort Carriage Company, was strictly a marketing company, much like the modern Subaru automobile company in the United States. Just as Subaru has its cars built by Fuji Heavy Industries, Durant-Dort contracted with a local builder to produce the carriages that Durant-Dort put its name on and then distributed and sold. When its business expanded beyond the capacity that its builder could meet, Durant-Dort took on the problem of building carriages itself. Here, again, it tried to keep its tasks as simple as possible. The company only assembled carriages, contracting with local suppliers to provide all of the components.[2]

The internal organization of early, streamlined companies like Durant-Dort was equally simple. At the top, as Chandler observes, were executives who "were either partners or major stockholders in the enterprise they managed." In other words, the executives were the venture capitalists. They handled finances and managed the distribution and sale of goods. There were no managers beneath them. "As late as 1840," Chandler notes, "there were no middle managers in the United States."[3] The authority for producing goods was pushed down to the foremen and workers who actually did the work. The organizational chart of these early firms, as a result, was almost completely flat.

What is most striking about these firms from a contemporary perspective is how little they did inside and how much they pushed off to suppliers and contractors. It is no surprise to find them taking a similar approach with their employees. The earliest and perhaps the most extreme example was the "putting-out" system in which each worker was essentially an independent contractor producing products, generally at home. The firm played the role of coordinator—providing workers with materials and paying them based on finished product (minus material costs). There were no production employees in these organizations.

While the putting-out system was dominant in England, it was important in the United States mainly in clothing and shoemaking. The introduction of more productive and expensive manufacturing equipment helped bring about its demise as jobs moved inside of factories.[4] Still, it persisted for some time in England even after the rise of factories, in part because it was more flexible. The system made it easier to adjust output to changing market demand—the overhead costs were lower, and what fixed costs existed were pushed off onto the workers.[5] These arguments in favor of flexibility and reduced fixed costs are the same ones used by advocates of outsourcing today.

There is considerable debate as to the sources of inefficiency inherent in the putting-out system. Embezzlement was clearly a serious problem. Because the relationship between raw material inputs and cloth outputs was variable, the contractors had some scope to divert materials to their own purposes, especially the better quality materials. Battles between owners and workers over rights to scrap material—and over how much was scrap—were commonplace. The other problem was the variability of effort and production generated by the home workers. If other opportunities came up, such as the periodic demands of farm labor, these workers could well stop their contracting work altogether. While the owner did not have to pay them, his capital in the form of material costs was tied up, and his production and business also ground to a halt. These problems make clear that an arm's-length contracting relationship based on payment per unit of output did not eliminate management problems for the owners.[6] Contemporary critics of outsourcing arrangements point to exactly the same problems of monitoring quality and performance and ensuring reliability when work moves outside the firm.

It would be a mistake to think that these arm's-length relationships existed only for products that could be produced off-site. In the mining industry, for example, it was typical well into the twentieth century for coal miners to contract separately for the mining of each rock face. The lead worker, or hewer, would negotiate a rate of pay on behalf of the group and contract again when moving on to a different rock face.[7] These arrangements persist into the present and are typical in U.S. uranium mines, for example.[8]

Even inside the more complicated arrangements of factory production, early relations with employees were dominated by arm's-length relations and contracting. In the steel industry, for example, before 1890 skilled workers were paid like contractors, a given rate per ton of steel produced, with the added twist that the rate varied with the price of steel. These skilled workers, in turn, hired their own less skilled "helpers" and paid them out of their own pocket.[9] At some iron works, the organization of work was like a modern "autonomous work team," where the skilled workers had complete autonomy to make all the employment decisions, such as hiring, wage setting, and training.[10]

In the most complex manufacturing facilities, elaborate contracting relationships were common, and they bear more than a passing resemblance to contemporary outsourcing practices. The "inside contracting system" had contractors taking the entire responsibility for some aspect of the production process and doing the work on the owner's premises. They received payments from the firm for each unit they produced and, in turn, had virtually complete autonomy over how production occurred. Arrangements differed across contractors despite the fact that they all worked in the same facility. Contractors hired their own workers, paying them piece rates. In fact, to deal with the problems of employees wasting materials, noted above in conjunction with the putting-out system, each employee was in turn treated like a contractor. At the Springfield Armory, what many consider to be the prototype of the modern American factory, separate accounts were kept on each worker, detailing scrap and wastage rates, tools, units of product in process, and materials used. Workers had to pay for any excess materials used, and they also had to place their personal stamp on each piece they completed so that parts found to be defective could be deducted from their earnings.[11]

The advantages of these arrangements for the owners and operators of the firm were many, and the list sounds much like one that might be presented in favor of outsourcing operations today. Perhaps the most important advantage was that the owners did not have to involve themselves in the details of production. They did not have to be expert in the production process, and they did not have to worry about personnel matters associated with getting the work done. They could concentrate on their own competencies, which concerned finance, and not have to worry about monitoring production for performance, quality, and costs. In short, the internal control function was unnecessary.

Further, many of the risks of doing business were pushed off from the firm and onto its contractors—and, in turn, onto the contractors' employees. For example, if sales eroded, the firm did not have to keep paying its contractors. The practices described in the steel industry went even further toward arrangements paralleling modern gainsharing. Here, if production is steady but prices decline, the firm is protected because the payments to skilled workers also decline, limiting substantially the firm's liability. Particularly with the inside contracting model, capital costs are significantly lower for the firm because at least some of the equipment is owned and financed by the contractors and their workers, not by the firm.

All of those factors made it cheap and easy for the manufacturer to use contractors. A representative example comes from the early years of the Pratt and Whitney machining company. Like most manufacturers, Pratt and Whitney had its own employees who worked side by side with the internal contractors. If a contractor was too busy to take on a new order, it went to Pratt and Whitney's employees, who would do the job for a total cost of about 70 percent more than if it had been done by the contractor. The higher quality of work and the higher wages of Pratt and Whitney employees were only part of the explanation. The rest was related to the greater managerial expertise of the contractor, motivated by his more direct interest in the outcome. An illustrative story comes from the Baldwin Locomotive Works in Philadelphia, where a contractor's operation relied on one of Baldwin's elevators. When the elevator broke, it usually took the company about two weeks to fix it; when the contractor was relying on the elevator, he managed to get it repaired by his own crew in two days.[12]

The fact that the contractor relationship was something like a market transaction meant that market pressures forced the contractors to share at least some of the gains of their innovations with the owners. When contracts were renegotiated, generally once a year, the owners were typically able to cut the prices paid to the contractors. A dramatic example of the declining costs to owners comes from the Winchester Repeating Arms Company, where the prices paid to its contractors fell by half over the space of twenty years.[13]

But there were also costs to these arrangements. A cottage industry has developed around the debate over what caused their downfall, but something of a consensus has developed around the following factors. The economist Oliver Williamson has been eloquent and exhaustive in arguing that these arm's-length, market-based transactions had inherent inefficiencies. For example, when William Durant's carriage business expanded rapidly, he found that his suppliers were not always reliable. They often had other customers whose needs had to be met as well. And so Durant-Dort Carriage Company eventually got into the business of making its own components to ensure supply. The owner was very vulnerable to mistakes that the contractors might make, such as defective parts or poor delivery. Trying to create incentives for the contractors to meet the interests of the owners was a very difficult exercise that eventually required the owners to monitor their contractors more carefully on matters of quality, a burdensome exercise. As technology advanced and became more integrated, it became more difficult to identify discrete products that could easily be turned over to contractors and more difficult to coordinate them.

Perhaps the most important difficulties, and the ones around which there is the most consensus, concerned labor and the need to improve its efficiency. In steel, the skilled workers who had something like contractor status resisted productivity improvements that made them work harder or took some of their control away. In manufacturing, the contractors could be forced to innovate and improve productivity by means of pay cuts, but other problems remained. The historian John Buttrick observed that "difficulty with the labor force was almost the sole reason for the abandonment of the [inside contracting] system."[14] Among the labor problems were high turnover and difficulty in securing adequate supplies of skilled labor, driven in part by employee concerns about inequitable treatment across contractors. Some were paid and treated much better than others for doing essentially the same work.

The most immediate issue for the owners, however, was the sense that the contractors were making too much money. Because contractors were working inside the owner's facility, it was very easy for the owners to learn what the contractors did. The setup of machines and equipment, the workflow, the management of employees, and so on could easily be duplicated, especially if the workers remained in place. It did not take long for the owners to ask themselves why they could not get rid of the contractor and replace him with a much cheaper foreman. Now that the design and setup work had been done, all the foreman had to do was to manage the employees, and a foreman cost only about one-third what a contractor earned.[15]

The experience at the Singer Sewing Machine Company illustrates the pattern. When the company's own employees could not master assembly operations using interchangeable parts, the owners brought in contractors who took over the operations and got the process to work. Once the company learned how to duplicate what the contractors had done, it became unhappy with the level of profits the contractors were receiving and replaced them with foremen.[16]

Owners across the country moved rather quickly to replace inside contractors with foremen who were direct employees of the owner. Buttrick reports that efforts to convert individual contractors to foremen were not always successful, and about half quit rather than suffer the decline in income and status.[17] This is a contrast with outsourcing efforts in contemporary companies, where direct employees are sometimes forced to either become contractors themselves or work for contractors of the company, performing the same tasks they had as direct employees. In the contemporary examples, the move from employee to contractor is generally seen as a step down.

With the new arrangement, both the foreman and the contractor's workforce became direct employees of the company. Internal contracting soon went from being a central feature of American industry to an artifact as the companies converted the contractor's role to a management function. In many ways, though, the actual practice of managing employees changed little. The workers were paid based on piecerates, much as before, and they were for all intents and purposes working for the foreman.

Piecework was a very imperfect mechanism for managing workers. In addition to all the monitoring of output and quality that it required, it left the pace of work to the individual workers. Some worked faster, some slower, and slow performance meant that capital was sitting idle. Because workers had the very real belief that the piecework rates would be cut if they worked fast and earned lots of money—just as the contractor's rates were cut—they typically held back effort. As a result, the main task of the foreman was to get that effort up.

The technique foremen used became known as the drive system. One might think of this in contemporary terms as motivating through stress. Speaking before a congressional committee in 1912, a steel industry expert explained the role of foremen in that industry, where they were known as pushers:

Q: Who does he push?
A: He pushes the gang.
Q: Explain how he does this.
A: It is done in various ways, through motions and profanity.[18]

In other words, the foreman yelled at the workers, threatened them, and sometimes hit them to make them work faster and harder. Harvard Professor Sumner Slichter's investigation of factory work in 1919 reached the following conclusion about the drive system: "The reason why coercive 'drive' methods have prevailed in the past has been that the central management has been indifferent to the methods pursued by foremen in handling men but insisted rigidly upon a constantly increasing output and constantly decreasing costs."[19]

Put simply, it worked. Despite its unpleasantness, "driving" boosted performance. What made it work was the fear of getting fired at a time when jobs were scarce, worker savings minimal, and unemployment insurance nonexistent. Historian Sandford Jacoby reports how this fear was manipulated in a typical plant. The assistant superintendent asked, "Has anyone been fired from this shop today?" When told no, he replied, "Well, then, fire a couple of 'em. It'll put the fear of God in their hearts."[20]

The only real connection between the company and its workers in this period was between workers and their foreman, and that relationship was typically transient. Slichter's analysis concluded that turnover of industrial workers in the early 1900s averaged around 100 percent *per year*. A representative from ARMCO steel described how their typical foremen addressed the problem raised by so many workers leaving: "He went to the gate, looked over the crowd, picked out the man he wanted, and hired him."[21] The foreman would set a rate of pay on the spot, one that might well vary from what workers hired the day before were paid or what those hired by a different foreman received.

THE NEED FOR A DIFFERENT SYSTEM

Reformers argued long and hard about the inequities of the drive system, about the costs of turnover and poor morale, generally with little effect. The real challenge to the drive system and to the arm's-length employment system came indirectly, from innovations in industrial engineering. Because the drive system was so similar to internal contracting, it had many of the same problems, particularly a lack of coordination across workgroups that made it extremely difficult to manage the flow of work across an organization. The simple problem of finding where a breakdown in the flow of production was occurring was beyond most operations because they lacked any basic cost accounting.

Alfred Chandler describes how early leaders of the Society of Mechanical Engineers wrestled with this problem by developing systems for tracking components and products as they moved through the work process. Even these primitive internal control systems revealed bottlenecks, suggesting where efficiencies could be achieved. In the process, these systems challenged the control and power of the foremen.[22]

Frederick W. Taylor was perhaps the most creative of the early engineers working on internal control systems, and the famous system he proposed created a separate planning department to determine scientifically the optimal flow of work through the system. The best-known aspects of "Taylorism" concern the way it looked at task performance, breaking tasks down into simple components based on time and motion studies. At the Ford Motor Company, for example, about two-thirds of the workforce were skilled mechanics in 1910. Four years later, after Ford had adopted assembly-line techniques with single-purpose tools and standardized production, the skill level of the workforce had declined dramatically. Half of the workforce now consisted of recent immigrants with little or no previous industrial work experience.[23] But the implications for management were equally important. Under systems like Taylor's, the task of supervision became much more complicated, too complicated for a single foreman, Taylor thought. So instead of a single foreman, workers now had several bosses responsible for different aspects of the work, such as inspection and quality, the flow of product on the shop floor, and the pace of work.

With respect to employment, there were two fundamental outcomes associated with these new internal control systems and, in particular, with the arrangements suggested by Taylor and his followers. The first was the need to take control over work decisions away from the foremen and to coordinate it within the firm. Authority over individual workers was dispersed across supervisors, and managers with authority were put in place above the foremen to control and coordinate the decisions of these foremen. The second outcome, a consequence of the first, was to create a cadre of professional middle managers who stood between the executives and the workers. Historian Hugh Aitken quotes a supporter of Taylor who nevertheless warned other employers that a consequence of these techniques was to create "an astonishing number of 'non-producers'" in the form of these new managers.[24]

THE GROWTH OF MANAGEMENT EMPLOYMENT

While the shock troops of these new techniques were consultants like Taylor, who moved from company to company, the ranks of engineers, clerks, supervisors, and other "non-producers" began to grow as soon as the new accounting and work organization practices were introduced. The phrase "scientific management" was proposed by Louis Brandeis to describe these new practices, particularly Taylor's system, for which Brandeis became a powerful advocate. He saw in these new approaches a more objective set of rules for running business and a counter to the personal power and often arbitrary business decisions made by the robber barons.[25]

The other, perhaps more important factor fueling the growth of management jobs was the change in the structure of business enterprises, from the small, single-unit operation to the large, multiunit enterprise. Chandler defines the modern U.S. business enterprise as having two important characteristics.[26] The first is that it internalized the business transactions that previously had been performed by the market. Whereas the Durant-Dort Carriage Company bought carriages in market transactions and then sold them, the General Motors Corporation that Durant later ran produced components, assembled them into cars, and distributed them to the market all under the same corporate umbrella.

Chandler's second characteristic of the modern enterprise is that it was run by a hierarchy of middle and executive managers. In addition to the managerial jobs that were necessary to run production systems along the lines dictated by scientific management, the demands of multiunit enterprises created an additional cadre of managers. Their function was to coordinate the transactions that had previously taken place in the market. Rather than going to the market to buy some component such as steering wheels, taking whatever combinations of price and quality were available, the managers in the modern enterprise had to design and produce the components inside the company to meet cost and quality targets that contributed to the overall design of the final product. Then they had to produce just enough and by the appropriate deadline to fit into the production schedule for the cars being produced.

As it became more efficient to internalize the business transactions that had in the past been performed by the market, it also became more efficient to transform the employment relationship, moving from an arm's-length relationship that relied on the labor market for governance to one that was internalized in the firm. Meeting these tightly defined production and cost targets required a reasonably predictable supply of skills and human resources, and that was difficult to obtain by relying on the labor market, where both the price and quantity of available skills were highly variable. Companies internalized employment, moving away from the market, to make the supply of skills and labor more predictable.

Perhaps the best known of the pioneers in the effort to transform the employment relationship and bring it more within the control of the company was Henry Ford. In 1913, the Ford Motor Company had a turnover rate among its employees of 370 percent, with daily absentee rates as high as 10 percent. A company study of employee concerns led to some significant reforms. The foreman's ability to hire and fire was eliminated and transferred to a central employment department. A new pay scheme was introduced based on seniority and objective performance measures, taking away the foreman's control over pay as well. And wages were essentially doubled—the famous $5 per day plan—for eligible workers: married men with at least six months of seniority whose home life had passed the scrutiny of the company's sociological department, thereby ensuring that the new wage bonanza would not be squandered on drink or other wasteful habits. Turnover dropped like a stone to about 54 percent, and overall productivity rose by around 50 percent, driven in large part by greater worker discipline.[27]

The employment relationship for management positions always relied less on the outside market. As Jacoby observes, even from the earliest days of manufacturing, "The employer had a gentlemen's agreement with his top salaried employees that they would not be dismissed except for disloyalty or (under extraordinary circumstances) poor performance."[28] When managerial and white-collar employment expanded, that gentlemen's agreement expanded to cover them as well.

The employment relationship for production workers changed more rapidly as the United States became involved in World War I. The drive system was based on the fear of job loss, and its logic eroded quickly when jobs were abundant. With the labor shortage created by wartime production, employers soon reported that worker discipline on the shop floor eroded—in some cases to the point of collapse—employee effort declined, and quit rates rose.[29]

Employers responded by creating separate personnel departments that took over many of the tasks of supervisors. Following the military's introduction of standardized tests for placement, employers began using systematic selection tests for recruiting new workers. Under pressure from wartime personnel agencies and from trade unions, they worked to reduce wage inequities within and across organizations by introducing job analyses and other systems to classify jobs and set wage rates systematically.

Perhaps the most important innovations were policies to develop systems of promotion from within. These efforts began with job classification systems that arranged jobs into "promotion ladders" based on similarity of skills. The idea was that workers could learn the skills they needed for promotion to the next position by mastering their current job. These systems, it was argued, would increase skills and reduce the personnel shortage. They would also reduce turnover and make workers more loyal by giving them some longer-term incentive to stay with the company.[30]

By 1920, leading companies had installed many of the personnel practices that are common among progressive employers today. For example, their employees were evaluated for promotion not only based on their current performance but also on a range of attributes such as interpersonal skills. Many paid attendance bonuses and had a range of pay for performance plans.

As Jacoby documents, however, these programs came under attack as soon as the wartime labor shortages subsided.[31] The foremen resisted these innovations from the beginning because they took away their control and power. As the example at Ford Motor Company suggested, in many cases the innovations were designed precisely to do that. Line management generally aligned itself with the foremen and saw these personnel innovations as interfering with getting production out. The recession in 1920 triggered deep cuts in personnel departments. Some companies, like International Harvester, took personnel out of the central office and made it a line function that reported to the production department. Labor discipline and productivity improved as unemployment rose, and the drive system made something of a comeback that accelerated during the Great Depression.

Pressure from industrial unions and, once again, wartime labor shortages during World War II finally cemented the new employment practices in place. By 1947, Sumner Slichter examined how the employment relationship had changed and concluded that "millions of jobs which previously had been held on a day-to-day basis [were converted] into lasting connections."[32]

The pattern of moving toward market relationships as the basis of employment when labor markets were slack and then moving sharply back toward internalizing employment within the firm when markets tightened has important lessons for the present. It suggests, first, that there is nothing sacred or even stable about a particular relationship between employer and employee. What many still see as the traditional lifetime employment relationship may well have been a transient phenomenon. The back-and-forth movement between market and internalized employment relationships may well go on in the future as well. Second, the contemporary trends that have moved employment toward the market may have some important parallels with the earlier drive system and its offshoots. In particular, it may be cheaper and easier for management to use such arrangements when labor is abundant, as when companies all seemed to be downsizing, but it is an entirely different matter when labor is in short supply. Then it raises a series of fundamental problems for the organization that demand sophisticated and complex responses from management.

MANAGING EMPLOYMENT RELATIONSHIPS

To describe and analyze the changes in contemporary employment relationships, it is useful to outline in more detail the older system against which these changes are a reaction. The system of internalized employee management that was put in place in most corporations after World War II had several defining characteristics.[33]

- *Work organization.* As noted above, work tended to be organized around the principles of scientific management, in which each job had a narrowly specified description and tasks were sharply differentiated across jobs. Supervision was intensive not only to enforce effort but also to help train workers. Extensive use of middle management ensured compliance with company procedures and policies. This system of work organization created low-skill, entry-level tasks for both production and managerial workers and also provided opportunities to learn skills on the job. This arrangement helped create well-defined job ladders for promotion.

- *Job security.* For practical purposes, managers had jobs for life, subject to minimally acceptable performance. Production workers were subject to temporary layoffs associated with business cycles. But the system of seniority-based layoffs helped tie workers to the firm by conferring tangible benefits to greater seniority. Older, more senior workers were essentially insulated from most layoffs, and seniority-based recall rights tended to keep workers from taking permanent jobs elsewhere when they were laid off.

- *Wages.* Shareholders, not employees, were the ones taking the risk with respect to business outcomes. The piecerate systems of scientific management gave way to arrangements like the measured "day work" (what a worker should be expected to perform in a day), which varied far less with performance. Pressure from unions helped tie pay to job titles and seniority rather than to individual attributes. While managers often had bonus plans, the bonuses tended to be paid on the basis of achieving targets that were not typically missed. The lack of association between wages and firm performance became such a "stylized fact" of economic life that special theories were developed to explain it.[34] While many organizations had merit pay for managers, in practice, performance evaluations tended not to differentiate employees, and differences in merit-based pay were often trivial.[35]

- *Seniority.* The discretion of the foreman in employment decisions gave way to systematic rules and a personnel bureaucracy to enforce them. Seniority became the single most important criterion governing employment decisions such as pay increases, but especially promotions.[36] This was explicit for most production jobs as part of union contracts or personnel handbooks but was implicit for management jobs as well.

These arrangements helped insulate employment from the pressures of competitive product and labor markets. Promotions and seniority-based systems helped create incentives for employees to stay with the organization, reducing turnover. Promotion-from-within in particular helped create incentives to keep performance up, and the on-the-job nature of training ensured an adequate flow of skills, especially firm-specific skills, up and through the job ladders. The result was a kind of exchange-based psychological contract—employee loyalty and adequate performance in return for security and predictable improvements—that maintained positive employee attitudes such as commitment.

The divisions that were always in place between managers and workers were exacerbated by these new arrangements, however. Scientific management moved discretion and many of the "thinking" tasks from blue-collar workers to managers. Legislation like the Fair Labor Standards Act of 1938 (governing wages and hours) and the National Labor Relations Act of 1935 (outlining unionization procedures), which sought to protect blue-collar workers, created clear distinctions between the policies governing blue-collar and white-collar jobs. The phrases "exempt" and "non-exempt" workers come from this legislation; white-collar jobs are exempt from the requirements of the Labor Relations Act, and this distinction continues to divide the workforce in fundamental ways.

THE ORGANIZATIONAL EMPLOYEE

The gentlemen's agreement of lifetime security in return for loyalty and adequate performance that governed executives in the early years of American business now applied to a much larger group of managers, and it was possible in these large, integrated organizations to think of an entire career made up of increasingly important jobs within the same firm. The prospect of lifetime careers in a managerial hierarchy helped produce a workplace culture and a set of management practices in corporations that we now think of as being the norm, and the contemporary challenges are seen as revolutionary. The nature of the psychological contract between employer and employee that existed in that system is where we turn next.

An important part of the new system for managing employees was driven by academic research and thinking about the importance of social relations in the workplace, about the key role that group identity plays in determining workplace satisfaction. The research began in the late 1920s with efforts to understand why piecerates and scientific management were not improving productivity at Western Electric's facilities in Hawthorne, Illinois. What improved performance, the researchers found, were changes that involved the workers in decision making and other interventions that helped meet their need to feel part of a group.[37] Elton Mayo and other scholars took these arguments and helped create the "human relations" movement, which based its recommendations for management on the employee's need for identification with a group. In 1953, the sociologist C. Wright Mills described this new method of managing as an attempt to find something in addition to money to increase an employee's will to work: "It is advice to the personnel manager to relax his authoritative manner and widen his manipulative grip over the employees by understanding them better."[38]

The norms and values of the workplace turned away from individual achievement toward group and organizational performance. William H. Whyte described the new style of manager in this culture as the "Organization Man." Describing the greater importance given to job security that occurred as a result of the Depression, Whyte argued that "the younger generation of management haven't been talking of self-reliance and adventure with quite the straight face of their elders."[39] Larger, more stable companies were preferred because they offered greater security.

In these organizations, Whyte argues, the personnel department was now "the glamour one"—a complete reversal since the 1930s—as it had the responsibility for ensuring the predictability of the organization. He cites research showing that personnel departments were growing at a rate of 15 percent per year by 1955. Whyte surveyed personnel executives and asked them what kind of leaders they thought their organization needed—adaptable administrators or executives with strong convictions, unafraid to challenge existing paradigms for making decisions, what we might think of in the 1990s as "bold" leaders. Seventy percent reported that their organizations needed adaptable executives more. They argued that the days of individual pioneering were over as the organization and the group were now the real source of innovation. Leadership should come from staff management, not individuals.[40] Surveys of corporate recruiters indicated that aspects of personality, such as the ability to get along and to cooperate, were more important than a candidate's academic achievement. A study at Purdue University found that the bonuses associated with personality characteristics like these were six times greater than the bonuses associated with greater intellectual ability.[41]

The typical corporation recruited its managers straight from college campuses. And what graduates were looking for in a job, Whyte argued, was first and foremost an extensive training program. The *basic* training program at large companies in his study was about eighteen months long. To put the size of this investment in perspective, these corporations were pouring resources into these trainees as well as paying them for a good year and a half before there was an expectation of getting any productive work out of them. The idea was to give the trainees a broad experience with the organization that would make them good general managers. After that, they could move on to more specialized training, much like pursuing a major in college.[42]

Once these recruits were in the company, they stayed put. Studies during this period report that job hopping between companies was minimal—about a third of executives had never changed companies, and another quarter had been with only one other employer—and was declining.[43] A study by Booz, Allen, and Hamilton found that the main cause of job switching was the perception that opportunities for advancement within one's company were blocked.[44] Promotion was the most important reward, and the companies believed that commitment and performance were better where there were possibilities for promotion.[45]

When Rosabeth Moss Kanter looked at life inside corporations twenty years later, in the mid-1970s, she found the organization-centered approach to managing people even more thoroughly in place. The expectation continued to be that careers would be built around a single employer. Company officials reported that all job candidates were evaluated in terms of their potential for promotion, and if they did not indicate an interest in becoming a higher-level manager, they would not be hired.[46] The central characteristic governing promotion prospects was loyalty. Kanter relates the story of an executive promoted to a personnel job who fell out of favor with his superiors because he became actively involved in the professional aspects of personnel—joining associations, serving on their boards, etc. Because his interests and loyalties were seen as flowing outward, away from the company and toward the profession, he was passed over for promotion.[47]

The psychological contract in companies like these was an explicit exchange of loyalty and commitment by employees in return for economic security in the form of predictable promotions, wage increases, and employment security from the company. Twenty years earlier, William H. Whyte had described the emerging rationale of the Organization Man as an understanding that it made sense for the organization to reward you if you did a good job because the goals of the individual and the organization would then work out to be the same. As the rewards increased and deepened, so did employee loyalty. Kanter observed that "Nothing seemed to be too good for valued exempt employees, and they came to believe that this was a very special organization that cared deeply about its people."[48]

In fact, so protected and secure were managers in these large companies that observers began to wonder whether economic incentives were still a factor in motivating employees. Writing in the mid-1970s, the pollster Daniel Yankelovich reported that employees were no longer very worried about the risk of job or income loss or motivated by the potential for gain. "[T]he carrot—the lure of material well-being as defined by money and possessions—is subtly losing its savor. And the stick—once a brutal club labeled 'economic insecurity'—has thinned down to a flaccid bundle of twigs."[49] Employment had become too secure for the good of the organization.

Obviously, not all employers had abided by these secure practices. The majority of establishments in the United States currently have fewer than twenty-five employees, too small a number to cobble together elaborate arrangements such as job ladders and seniority-based promotion systems. Some researchers have calculated, for example, that organizations need a minimum of five hundred employees to make formal, job-evaluation-based compensation systems feasible.[50] One of the arguments for these arrangements is that they make it easier to recruit new employees, but some experts have calculated that only about 40 percent of U.S. employees are in firms large enough and old enough to have clear reputations among new recruits.[51]

But for larger firms, these practices became increasingly described as "best practices" for managing employees. Companies like IBM extended the arrangements with virtually lifetime employment security and "cradle-to-grave" career development exercises. The efforts to internalize employment received a further boost in the late 1970s and early 1980s when the apparent success of Japanese companies was attributed to their employee management practices, which emphasized long-term relationships, investments in employees, and job security.[52]

Less than a decade later, however, we see this entire system coming unbundled across virtually every dimension of the employer/employee relationship. Companies like Volkswagen win praise for returning to the system of internal contracting, unbundling their vertically integrated systems and employment relationships. *Fortune* calls for the outright abolition of the human resources function and the administrative practices that go with it, just as others in the business press had done more than sixty years earlier.[53] What could possibly have happened to turn this system around in such short order?

CHAPTER 3

The Pressures to Restructure Employment

For the employees caught in the change, the restructuring of the employment relationship in the United States has been a very painful process. Especially from their perspective, it is tempting to label these developments as morally wrong because of the damage they did, to blame the changes on the executives who initiated them and see their decisions as the result of character flaws. Executives do have choices about how they restructure their companies and the jobs within them, and some of their decisions have been more praiseworthy than others. As with most important developments in the economy, however, the forces behind the restructuring of employment are so powerful that they overwhelm much of the discretion that employers have. There are options as to how to restructure the employment relationship, but whether or not to respond is not an option.

Until the mid-1980s, most U.S. companies strove for long-term, career relationships with their employees. And the company most clearly associated with the lifetime employment relationship was IBM.[1] Understanding how that relationship worked at companies like IBM, how it served their corporate interests, and then how those interests began to change helps explain what caused the lifetime relationship to unravel.

THE OPPORTUNITY OF A LIFETIME AT IBM

The lifetime relationship at IBM began in the 1950s with a distinctive approach to hiring, looking for general aptitude, teamwork skills, and "character." Specific skills associated with a particular job were much less important in hiring than at other companies, first because IBM was willing to invest extraordinary amounts of resources into developing those skills, and second because it expected to rotate people in and out of different functions over time, making the skills needed for a specific job less relevant. IBM looked for bright graduates right out of school, academics interested in making a career change, and fast-track junior executives from other industries.

Once hired, these employees began a training regimen that never ended. Initial training in IBM procedures at the Armonk training center in Westchester County were followed up by three weeks of formal training *each year* at Armonk as well as by training programs and organized learning experiences in the field. Management employees spent about two years working in staff positions at headquarters in Armonk, generally early in their careers, to become familiar with its procedures and operations.

Employee development was a goal on every manager's performance appraisal. IBM also had among the most sophisticated employee morale and climate surveys in the world, and managers were held accountable for the scores turned in by their workforce. Any decline in morale would surely show up as a negative mark on a supervisor's performance appraisal.

Because IBM was so big—its divisions were among the largest companies in every country in which it operated—it was important to have clear and reliable plans for the business. And because it had few competitors in the mainframe computer market, it was relatively easy to plan for the future. IBM had one of the most sophisticated strategic planning functions in industry. Its business plans often extended a decade or so and were generally accurate. Human resources was an integral part of the planning function both as an input (whether business plans were sustainable given staffing levels) and as an outcome (staffing needs that had to be met to support business plans).

These long-term human resource plans were the bedrock of IBM's entire lifetime employment concept. Because IBM knew what it needed years in advance, it had the time to develop skills and talent internally, to observe who had which abilities and interests, offer them the right experiences, and then move them from declining areas into growing ones.

IBM was justly proud of the fact that it had never had a layoff in its forty-year history as a modern computer company and advertised that fact to all of its new hires. Some companies, like Hewlett-Packard, achieved job security by avoiding the sharp ups and downs associated with rapid hiring to meet peak demand and then layoffs when demand falls. HP did this by producing for the general market and avoiding contracts with individual customers that would cause demand to spike up to fill the order and then down when the project was finished. IBM managed employment security in a different way by accommodating internally the swings in demand produced by the outside market. The strategy it used is sometimes known as a "core-periphery" strategy: when demand shot upward, IBM would meet it by taking on more interns, part-time workers, retirees, and subcontractors with whom it had no long-term relationship. When demand fell back, it would drop these workers, who were on the "periphery" of the IBM relationship. Careful readers no doubt see that these practices do not create job security as much as they redistribute it across the organization, from the periphery workers, whose jobs are highly insecure, to the core, or permanent, employees, whose careers were safe and predictable.

Sometimes, however, the market would surprise IBM's planners, and the company would have to take some extraordinary measures to restructure operations without breaking that lifetime commitment. Harvard professor Quinn Mills documented the adjustment process that brought the company around without layoffs and described how it served IBM's long-term goals. IBM managers were persuaded to pick up and move voluntarily from one region to another and from one functional area to another because of their interest in staying with IBM. Mills describes managers who "made a career in IBM out of not having to pick a career" because the company routinely moved them across a range of functions, from production to accounting to marketing and then on to something else. They were willing to move because doing so helped them work their way up the company hierarchy.

These moves across functions and regions left these managers with relatively weak functional skills, but they were accumulating a key asset, the asset most valuable to their future: knowledge of the company as a whole and its systems. This was a huge, far-flung, and vertically integrated company in which coordination was the key challenge. Mills reports an IBM executive describing why these internal rotations were better than hiring from the outside market, even if the outside applicants had better skills: "An IBMer may not know the job well, but he or she knows the company."[2]

The central characteristics of IBM's human resource practices followed from the fact that knowing the company was the key asset for executives. Even massive redeployments could be credibly sold to employees as a development exercise: moving from finance in Westchester, New York, to human resources in North Carolina really was a career-building exercise that would improve their knowledge of the company and their personal networks. An explicit employment security policy made sense for the company because managers became more valuable the longer they stayed. And because this knowledge was much more valuable to IBM than to anyone else, it made sense for the managers to stay. Given that both the company and its managers had the expectation of staying put, it made sense for the company to make investments in training, typically massive investments, that might otherwise walk out the door. The human resources department was also able to justify highly elaborate efforts to monitor and maintain employee morale as a means to reduce turnover.

IBM got important benefits from these practices. In addition to reducing turnover and smoothing redeployments, even first-level managers were committed to carrying out the company's goals because they understood that their long-term interests lay with the corporation, not their division or their function. IBM had compliance with corporate policies at the supervisor level that was unheard of at other companies and made the internal coordination of its far-flung operations possible.

THE LAST GASP OF LIFETIME EMPLOYMENT

The market surprised IBM's planners most dramatically in 1985–1986 when the first wave of personal computers began displacing mainframes. In hindsight, the adjustment process that Mills was describing in this period turned out to be the last of IBM's lifetime employment contract.[3] IBM redeployed 21,500 people during that restructuring, equivalent to about 5 percent of its global employment and 10 percent of its jobs in the United States, moving them from areas of decline to areas of potential growth, or at least to business units where they might contribute. For example, IBM shut down its Boulder, Colorado, manufacturing facility and converted it into an information systems operation in the space of eight months, redeploying and retraining its workforce in the process.

Mills reported that Wall Street investors during this period thought IBM's commitment to employment security was a mistake, that it cost too much. Their sense was that stockholders had borne too much of the burden of restructuring IBM.[4] And, unfortunately, that restructuring never did the trick. Shortly thereafter, the company had to cut its workforce. It doubled firings for poor performance but mainly relied on attrition. Because IBM-trained employees were highly sought after in the burgeoning computer industry, it was easy to get employees to leave by offering financial incentives. In 1992 alone, the company cut 20,000 jobs, then 50,000 in the first half of 1993 followed by 35,000 more that July. CEO John Akers resigned under pressure from the investment community. The attrition was no longer keeping up with cost-cutting pressure, and IBM announced its first bona fide layoffs in 1994. So deep was the concern about the shock to employees and their communities that when the layoffs were announced in the Poughkeepsie area, IBM's home community, local officials asked gun shop owners to close.[5] By the time the layoffs had stopped, IBM's workforce had fallen to 225,000, down from a peak of 405,500 a decade earlier.

When the new CEO Louis Gerstner, Jr., took over in 1993, he discovered two problems that were particularly surprising given the nature of IBM's long-standing human resource policies. He found enormous problems with coordination across the company. He especially noted turf battles between divisions, manifested by units overcharging each other, and widespread difficulty getting departments to cooperate.[6] This was despite IBM's elaborate policies designed to foster corporate loyalty and the overall goal of leading managers to act in the interest of the company as a whole.

Even more pointedly, IBM now found it extremely difficult to retain key talent. The lifetime job security and other human resource investments designed to build commitment and retain employees apparently mattered little once headhunters arrived and the pull of the labor market took over. Gerstner noted that "Competitors are coming after my high-talent people. . . . Some of them have lists of our key people."[7] And when IBM's stock price fell, reducing the value of employee stock incentives, employee attachment to the company evaporated. Gerstner complained that he had "an employee group with absolutely no incentive to stay here because every one of their options is under water."[8]

As with most other large companies that were restructuring in the 1990s, the downsizing and layoffs at IBM were only partially about operating with fewer employees. They were also about changing the employment relationship for those who stayed. Some estimates suggest that as many as one in five of the employees who were laid off came back to IBM as consultants.[9] These workers moved from being in the core of a lifetime employment relationship to being a variable cost item operating in a spot market.

IBM also moved to outsource more of its operations and more of its employment relationships. All of the clerical jobs below the rank of executive secretary are now staffed by employment agencies like Manpower. Their terms and conditions of employment can be kept closer to market rates and below those offered to other employees without disrupting the "common culture" of the company as much as if they were actual employees. In technical areas, such as systems integration, IBM has pushed tasks to vendors. The rate at which system requirements are changing makes it virtually impossible to develop the skills necessary to perform those tasks within the company.

As in other restructuring companies, IBM continued to hire even in the midst of layoffs. Hiring on the one hand and laying off on the other was designed to change the skill mix inside the company rapidly. IBM was no longer interested in hiring raw talent that it would develop into general management skills. Now it sought employees who already had "market value skills." In sales, for example, it wanted representatives with prior experience in the industry in which they would be selling.[10] Insiders say that IBM now encourages all of its managers to develop functional skills, to define their occupational identity around fields with clear analogues in the market, such as finance or marketing. The days of the IBM general manager who made a career by never having to choose a career path are over.

The pressures that caused IBM and the companies like it to abandon their long-term employee relationships have deep and powerful roots that begin with changes in the structure of the economy but continue all the way down to the way work is organized on the shop floor.

FAT AND HAPPY

American management after World War II was in the driver's seat. Being the only industrialized country other than Sweden to survive World War II with its productive capacity intact was, to put it mildly, an extraordinary advantage in international competition. U.S. companies grew and prospered, often with little competition from abroad. Within the United States, competition in some industries was fierce, but in others it was far more genteel. Many industries, like finance and transportation, had extensive regulation restricting competition. Others, like autos, rarely competed on price and saved their rivalries for advertising. Government antitrust initiatives were a constant and necessary presence in many industries to prevent the competitive process from suffocating. In an environment where competitive pressures were not the focus of everyday attention, many companies found their operations being driven by other imperatives, often those that reflected the interests of managers. Critics referred to this as managerial capitalism, operating to serve the needs of the managers rather than the stockholders.[11]

A lot of good things came out of this period—corporate leadership in civic activities, charitable giving, investments in employees and the community. But it also led to acquisitions and growth for big, stifling corporate cultures, and declining performance.

The pressures to restructure employment arrangements began in earnest with competitive developments in the world economy. Following the OPEC price increases, especially the second round of increases in 1979, fuel-efficient Japanese cars began taking market share from the U.S. producers. U.S. auto sales declined, and so did the related demand for steel and components such as tires. U.S. consumers noticed the rising market share of imports in a range of products. The share of imports as a proportion of gross domestic product (GDP) rose only about one percentage point per decade from 1960 through 1980, when imports averaged just under 8 percent of GDP. But by 1994, imports had about doubled to more than 14 percent of GDP.[12]

Meanwhile, foreign companies were becoming increasingly likely to operate in the United States. From 1981 to 1986, new foreign direct investment in the United States annually averaged $21.4 billion. From 1987 to 1990 it more than doubled, averaging $57.1 billion annually. Similarly, the total stock of direct foreign investment in the United

States in 1980 stood at $83.0 billion, and by 1990 it had reached $403.7 billion. Direct investment by American firms abroad also rose during the 1990s, though not as rapidly. The stock of direct foreign investment by U.S. companies outside the country in 1980 stood at $220.2 billion; by 1990 it had reached $423.2 billion.[13]

The growing international competition from lower-cost, more effective competitors put tremendous pressure on U.S. firms to cut costs and become more competitive. It also created new opportunities for learning from these new competitors and, in turn, for organizational change. A survey of large companies during this period found that those with a larger share of their workforce outside the United States were more likely to have restructured employment relations, including downsizing and redesigning work systems.[14] Such companies not only were under greater pressure from international competition but also had more exposure to alternative models for organizing work from which to learn. And within the United States, companies that faced highly productive international transplants in their home market were far more likely to adopt the improved organizational designs pioneered by the transplants.[15]

On the domestic side, the deregulation of airlines in 1978 and of trucking and railroads in 1980, along with the gradual easing of regulations in financial services and telecommunications, produced the most obvious and dramatic increases in competition. In industries where domestic competition had always been fierce, such as meatpacking or tire production, the rise of lower-wage, nonunion operations inside the United States provided yet another form of competitive pressure. One immediate effect of this competition was a sharp increase in business failures (see Figure 3-1), plant closings, and reductions in capacity in firms that survived.

How business failures and regrowth played out in a single community illustrates something about the growing pace of economic change in the United States. In 1970, about 6.8 percent of all the businesses operating in Dallas, Texas, failed. By the mid-1980s, about 21 percent of the businesses in that city were failing each year. Twenty-seven percent of all the private sector jobs that existed in Dallas in 1986 were gone three years later, replaced by new ones.[16] The turnover of companies and jobs facilitated the restructuring of the entire economy. To paraphrase John Stuart Mill, change and history were proceeding from the back of a hearse: the old ways died with the failing companies,

Figure 3-1. Business Failures, 1927–1996

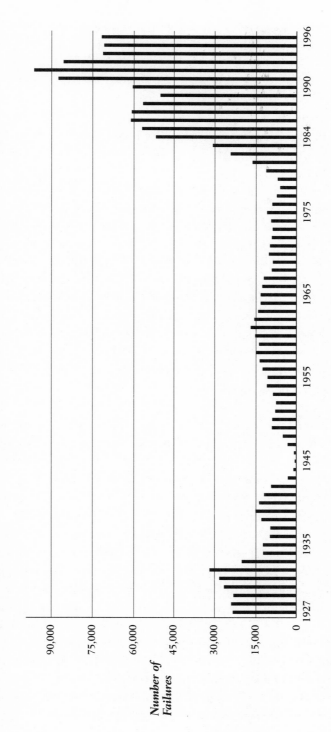

Source: Business Failure Record, Dun & Bradstreet, a company of The Dun & Bradstreet Corporation, 1996.

and the new companies began life with few precedents and a new model of the employment relationship.

Financial Restructuring

The businesses that survived the new competitive environment faced additional pressure for change that was driven by developments in finance and the governance of firms.

Developments associated with the financing of firms have driven several waves of restructuring in the past, each of which led to bigger and bigger companies. The first, between 1896 and 1902, was characterized by horizontal mergers and acquisitions that later drove concerns about monopoly power in the marketplace. The second, between 1926 and 1933, was mergers and acquisitions based on vertical integrations that reduced transaction costs and uncertainty. The third wave, concentrated between 1965 and 1969, was the creation of conglomerates, putting together unrelated businesses to achieve financial synergies by smoothing out variations in corporate revenue. All of these trends were driven by the notion that bigger is better and that there were scale economies to be achieved by putting organizations and functions together.

The most recent wave, which began around 1981 and is continuing through the present, represents an entirely different development driven by the opposite notion—that there are gains to be made from "unbundling" existing operations. Research on conglomerates found that diversification that took corporations away from their "core," or basic, business interests hurt overall performance. For companies that acquired new businesses, the closer the new operation was to their existing operations, the better the overall corporate performance was; for corporations selling off businesses, the less related the sold operation was to their core functions, the better the corporation's subsequent performance was.[17] These results helped persuade conglomerates to spin off divisions that were not related to the core functions of the business.

My Wharton colleagues have examined the data on about two thousand companies that have restructured their business portfolios. The companies most likely to restructure are generally those in some financial distress, and the returns are greatest—about 5 percent—for spinning off operating divisions as new companies owned by the current stockholders. The return rises by a factor of five or six if the spun off operation is subsequently merged into another company. Selling off divisions or operations leads to returns about half as great—about 2.4 percent.[18]

An important component of this restructuring trend began with innovations in debt financing, junk bonds in particular, which made it possible to raise large amounts of cash for speculation. Even small groups of investors could purchase publicly held companies and take them private through leveraged buyouts that used funds raised from junk bonds to buy out stockholders and acquire companies. Of the 500 companies on the *Fortune* list of top manufacturers in 1980, one-third had experienced a hostile takeover threat by the end of the decade, and one-third no longer existed as an independent entity by 1990.

After the buyouts, the acquired companies had to generate higher profits to pay off the high interest on the junk bonds and make the transaction financially feasible. Some researchers argue that higher debt forces companies to run more efficiently.[19] One reason why so many of the leveraged buyouts were led by a company's existing management, the argument goes, was because they already knew how to make the companies more profitable.

Where do the performance gains come from when these operations are sold off? Economists Andrei Shleifer and Lawrence Summers argue that an important source of these gains comes simply from breaking long-term employment relationships, particularly those which implicitly deferred compensation. Because labor accounts for the vast majority of operating costs, even small savings in labor costs translate into large improvements in financial performance. Shleifer and Summers calculate, for example, that the value of the union concessions secured by Carl Icahn as part of his 1985 acquisition of TWA accounted for all of the post-takeover improvement in the company's financial performance. In fact, the value of the concessions exceeded the value of the takeover premium by 50 percent.[20]

Other studies find that about 27 percent of the stock price premium associated with takeovers across firms can be attributed to the cost savings of layoffs.[21] The empirical research on leveraged buyouts suggests that firms involved in such transactions cut substantially more jobs—12 percent more—than do other companies.[22] The cuts associated with takeovers are especially deep in white-collar jobs.[23] Other studies find that more senior workers suffer especially under hostile takeovers; fewer of them are employed proportionately after the take-over, and the wages associated with seniority are significantly reduced.[24]

The new techniques for delivering improved performance concentrated on restructuring the companies through cutting jobs. Many observers believe that downsizing does not pay off for companies, basing their conclusions on reports from managers inside the companies about the problems in making it work. Or they observe companies that are already in serious financial trouble downsizing *because* of their poor performance, assuming that the downsizing contributed to the crashing of the company. More systematic studies suggest a more nuanced story, at least for financial performance. One study of share price reactions to company layoff announcements found that stock prices rose an average 4 percent when layoffs were announced as part of a restructuring program. Downsizing announced simply as a cost-cutting measure, however, depressed stock prices an average 6 percent. Investors like restructuring *and* job shedding but not cuts without a plan for running the company thereafter.[25] A more recent study that looked at the effects of downsizing over three years found that while companies that did so did not earn higher profits as measured by return on assets, the downsizing did seem to yield higher stock prices, which is the ultimate financial goal for publicly held companies.[26]

Consider the experience of the Xerox Corporation, which was generally seen as a very well-run company in 1993. Investors still reacted extremely positively in late 1993 to its plans to slash about one-tenth of its workforce as part of an effort to make the organization more effective. By day's end, Xerox stock had soared by 7 percent.[27]

At the end of the 1980s, corporations were selling off divisions and companies and buying new ones at a rapid rate. While the pace of mergers and acquisitions slowed somewhat during the early 1990s, it has accelerated since then. Merger and aquisition activity around the world has risen every year since 1992, and estimates indicate about a 25 percent jump in 1997 over 1996 figures, continuing to rise at record levels through 1998 (see Figure 3-2). Firms that wanted to sell operations needed to raise their profitability, and the easiest way to do that was to cut costs. Similarly, the best way to avoid being sold off or, for publicly held companies, being acquired through a hostile takeover was to show that it would be difficult to raise profitability, that there would be no obvious gain for the acquiring company. And the best way to do that was to cut costs in advance of a takeover. The possibility of a hostile takeover was generally more than enough of a threat to force companies to restructure.

A related pressure for change came from the growing concentration of ownership among large institutional holders (see Figure 3-3). In they past, they followed the "Wall Street rule," avoiding any direct involvement in management and expressing any disappointment with a company's performance by selling their holdings. But the largest institutions are no longer able to dispose of their undesirable stocks so readily. One reason is that a greater proportion of their holdings is now indexed—that is, tied to the market as a whole—and not actively man-

Figure 3-2. Global Merger and Acquisition Activity, 1991–1997

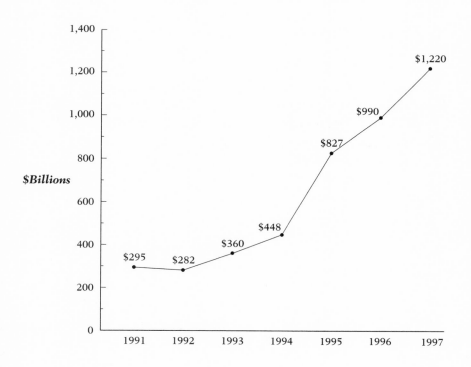

aged. About one-sixth (15.9 percent) of all institutional stockholding is indexed, much of it allocated among the widely used Standard and Poor's 500. About one-third of the equity managed by banks (33.4 percent) and corporate pension funds (35.9 percent) is indexed, and more than half (51.7 percent) of the equity managed by public pension funds is indexed.[28]

If an investor owns a portfolio based on an average of the entire market, it is difficult to sell shares of individual companies. Even if it could be done, it would defeat the principle of holding the market average without having to manage the fund. And where portfolios are actively managed, it is often difficult for the largest investors to sell off major holdings without depressing the price.

An alternative to disposing of ever larger blocks of a declining stock is to pressure management for company changes to improve performance. The techniques used include voting against a company's directors, supporting unfriendly acquisitions, and pressing for changes in governance, such as confidential votes and the creation of shareholder advisory committees. These efforts got management's attention even when the investors failed to get them implemented.[29] Restructuring-re-

Figure 3-3. Percentage of Shares of 1,000 Largest U.S. Companies Held by Individuals and Institutional Investors, 1985–1995

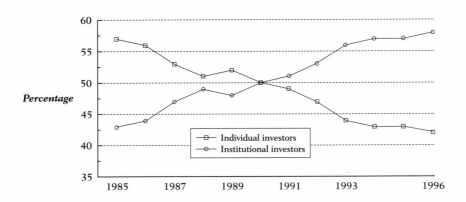

Source: Professor Michael Useem, The Wharton School, University of Pennsylvania.

lated job cuts, for example, were bigger at companies whose shareholders were organized into larger blocks, as in institutional holdings.[30]

Boards of directors for publicly held companies have a legal obligation to one stakeholder only, the shareholders, and investor lawsuits directed against companies and their directors over the course of the 1980s and 1990s drove that point home in ways that were difficult to miss. Corporate boards responded to investor complaints about poor performance by replacing the chief executives at a wide range of companies—including American Express, Digital Equipment, Eastman Kodak, IBM, General Motors, and Scott Paper—that had previously been characterized by decades of stable leadership and succession in the executive ranks. The new CEOs were committed to corporate change and often pushed through extensive financial changes. IBM's new CEO, Louis Gerstner, for instance, ushered in stringent financial controls that were similar to those used after hostile takeovers at other companies during the 1980s.[31]

New accounting and control techniques, such as economic value added (EVA), create measures of financial performance at division and operating levels that have helped drive the restructuring trend. They include the opportunity cost of capital and related fixed assets when measuring performance, creating incentives for managers to cut fixed investments of all kinds.[32] Not only are employees often tied to these fixed assets, in many cases they *are* the fixed assets.

One immediate consequence of the application of techniques like EVA has been the effects on office space and employee accommodations. Ten years ago, a typical office had 250 square feet per employee. New office buildings give them 200, and some areas, such as phone centers, are down to 100 square feet. The trend is also away from high-rise buildings toward low-risers because the latter are cheaper to build. And with fewer layers of management in the new restructured organizations, office architects report less need for corner offices, facilitating the trend toward shorter, broader buildings.[33]

Perhaps the ultimate adaptation to the pressure to cut accommodation costs for employees is the move toward "hoteling," or temporary offices, for permanent employees. This trend was pioneered by professional service firms such as Arthur Andersen, which initiated it in 1989. Now, at companies like Ernst and Young, a concierge directs the incoming manager to a desk he or she has reserved along with a check-in and check-out time. The space preferences of each manager are noted on file, and they have a locker for their files and personal effects. Within fifteen minutes, the phone is hooked up, files are on the desk, and the manager is ready to go. The Chiat/Day advertising company goes a step further and issues their arriving managers walk-around phones.[34] The immediate goal of hoteling is to cut real estate costs dramatically, but it also pushes managers to spend more time in the field, with clients, and in relationships away from their own organization.

Another common reaction to the pressure to squeeze fixed costs out of the organization are efforts to outsource entire functions, moving them from fixed to variable costs. J. P. Morgan, for example, recently outsourced the management of its data centers to the Pinnacle Alliance, a consortium it created with four major technology companies. One of the main advantages of this arrangement, the company argues, is to push the fixed costs of information system employees and hardware out of the company and onto the Alliance. Nine hundred J. P. Morgan employees moved to the employ of the Alliance. The risks associated with employing these workers, including the fact that their skills will rapidly become obsolete, are now the problem of the Alliance. Instead of large, up-front, and fixed investments in technology, J. P. Morgan now has monthly charges that vary with its demands.[35]

Shareholder pressure also helped change the arrangements for compensating executives, which in the past created perverse incentives for them to take actions that were not in the interests of stockholders, such as diversifying the portfolio of the company to smooth out the variance in corporate earnings and, in turn, their own compensation packages.[36] Between 1982 and 1993, the variable fraction of total compensation received by the top seven employees at a sample of 45 large firms rose from 37 percent to 54 percent, with long-term incentive pay—mainly stock options—rising from 17 to 38 percent of total compensation. (See Figure 3-4). When George Fisher took office as CEO at Eastman Kodak, for example, he received options to purchase more than 750,000 shares of Kodak stock, of little or no value unless the stock price increased substantially, but potentially worth $13 million to $17 million if it did so.[37] Most other CEOs have similar arrangements.

Because the additional compensation appeared to be "free" in the sense that it came from new earnings, it is easier to justify what are often huge payouts. Contingent pay plans worked their way down into the middle management ranks as well, albeit at substantially lower amounts, increasing the incentives for managers to cut costs but also putting more of their own pay at risk.

The trend toward making compensation contingent on shareholder value has also expanded to boards of directors, helping to turn their attention away from other priorities and to maximizing stock prices. In 1985, only 8 percent of companies offered stock to directors as compensation. By 1995, almost two-thirds did so, including many for whom all of the compensation is in the form of stock. And the trend appears to be continuing.[38]

Nowhere did these pressures to maximize shareholder value have a more dramatic effect on a company—and its employees—than at Scott Paper.

THE SCOTT PAPER EXAMPLE

Brothers E. Irvin and Clarence Scott founded Scott Paper outside Philadelphia in 1879, and for the next 115 years, it was a pillar of the

Figure 3-4. Senior Management Compensation, 1982–1997

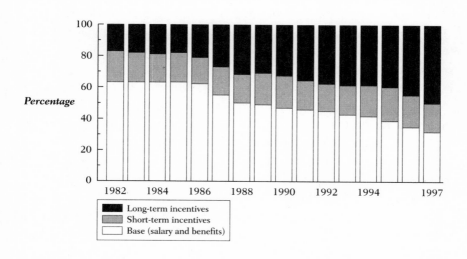

Source: *Professor Michael Useem, The Wharton School, University of Pennsylvania.*
Note: *Data for top seven executives at forty-five large industrial companies.*

area's business community. Scott invented the paper towel, went on to pioneer other innovations in the consumer market, and soon became a household name. Under Phillip E. Lippincott, CEO from 1982 to 1994, the company became the largest tissue producer in the world, with consolidated operations in twenty-one countries. As an employer, Scott offered good-paying production jobs, especially important in depressed communities like Chester, near its headquarters, and the company pioneered joint union-management committees in its plants. Scott was also a generous contributor to civic and philanthropic projects in the community.

But the early 1990s were not kind to paper companies, and especially not to Scott. A notoriously cyclical business, the paper industry suffered its worst recession since the Great Depression beginning in 1989. A 15 percent decline in tissue prices cost Scott $275 million from 1990 to 1993 as overcapacity in the industry combined with growing customer reluctance to pay more for brand-name paper products. To make matters worse, Scott had just added substantially to its own capacity right when the downturn hit. Other paper companies began restructuring in the 1980s, but Scott waited. The company finally responded by reducing debt and capital expenditures and cutting its workforce in 1990, but the bleeding continued. Sales had been flat since 1989, and by 1994 the dollar losses were in the hundreds of millions. Scott was paying about $190 million in interest charges on its debt, and there was concern that its bond ratings were about to be downgraded. Two more restructuring efforts failed to turn the company around. In early 1994, Scott announced a more drastic three-year plan to cut its workforce by 25 percent.

Twenty-four North American paper companies got new CEOs between 1993 and 1994, so it was no surprise when Lippincott announced his resignation as Scott's CEO in 1994. What did come as something of a surprise, however, was the way Scott's board of directors sought to replace him. For the first time in the company's history, an outsider was brought in to run the company. Alfred Dunlap, a former paratrooper and West Point graduate, began his career as a trainee at Kimberly-Clark but soon joined Sir James Goldsmith's financial empire, where he helped reverse the fortunes of as many as eight troubled companies, most recently the Lily-Tulip paper products firm. His management style was notable for its ruthless cost cutting.

Dunlap's appointment "surprised a lot of people," says one senior executive in the industry. "The company had already announced massive cutbacks. I'm surprised that they didn't get someone who's known as a morale builder. . . . The thinking in the industry was that Scott would hire somebody with expertise in consumer packaging. . . . That's why some people were shocked when [Dunlap] got hired."[39]

Dunlap was already a wealthy man from his previous stints in corporate leadership. Why would he come out of retirement in Boca Raton to head Scott? "He wants to show people, this time, that he is more than Rambo in Pinstripes," said one insider, that he can build a company and not just cut it up for sale.[40] Other observers were not so sure. The day Dunlap's appointment was announced, respected Brown Brothers Harriman & Company analyst Kathryn F. McAuley said to herself, "'Well, the board sold the company.' When you looked at his background, you realized that what he had done best was sell companies."[41]

What followed after Dunlap was appointed in April 1994 was an extraordinary transformation of the old Scott company. Dunlap proclaimed that "The Scott story will go down in the annals of American business history as one of the most successful, quickest turnarounds ever."[42] He made it clear from the beginning that he felt the old management at Scott had failed to deliver value to shareholders. In his words, Scott was "a stodgy old company which had totally lost its way. . . . Its shareholders would have been better off captured by terrorists. They'd have been treated better."[43]

The most important part of the turnaround plan was to consolidate operations around Scott's core business, making tissues. Scott was far and away the world's leading tissue maker. The first step in that direction was to sell the company's S. D. Warren unit, which made printing paper, for $1.6 billion. Other sales, primarily real estate and woodland reserves, would realize $3 billion, which would repay part of Scott's $2.3 billion debt and provide its global tissue business with new investment money.

The most dramatic part of the restructuring plan was a 34 percent reduction in staff, including an astonishing 71 percent cut in headquarters' staff, resulting in total layoffs of more than 11,000 employees. This reduction may well be the largest single downsizing of any major U.S. company. It differed in important ways from an earlier plan to cut 25 percent over three years. In addition to cutting more jobs, taking them out all at once put the savings up front and the trauma behind the company, so that it could go forward. For the employees, however, a more gradual rundown that relied in part on attrition and early retirements would have significantly reduced the personal trauma.

Dunlap was particularly unapologetic about the cuts in management, which included most of the board of directors: "When you do a turnaround, you must by definition get rid of the top people. They're the people who got it wrong, and if they did it once they'll do it again. Every corporation has a culture. In a corporation which is not doing well, you must eradicate the culture."[44]

And he made it clear that shareholder value was his concern, period. As to whether the interests of employee and community stakeholders should be considered in management decision making, Dunlap argued that "Stakeholders are total rubbish. It's the shareholders who own the company."[45] To reinforce his point that the company should be run to benefit shareholders, Dunlap bought $4 million of Scott stock with his own money, had his compensation and that of his executives leveraged highly on Scott's stock price, and compensated his board of directors entirely with shares in the company. He also eliminated all corporate contributions to the community and reneged on the last payment of a $250,000 gift that Scott had committed to the Philadelphia Museum of Art. Managers were forbidden from involvement in community activities, as that would take time away from their work. Memberships in industry and business organizations were also scrapped. Scott's fifty-five acre headquarters was sold—too extravagant—and arrangements made to move what was left to Boca Raton.

The financial community was uniformly positive about Dunlap's moves. Wall Street analysts concluded that "since Dunlap took over he has dramatically, very dramatically, turned the company around and refocused it."[46] Reports from line management indicated that decision making inside the company was quicker and more decisive than in the past. Despite the layoffs, at least some part of the remaining workforce seemed inspired by Dunlap's personal vision for the company. Its financial performance soon exceeded the wildest dreams of the investment community. Scott went from losing about $300 million to a profit of $200 million within a year. Most important, its share price rose from $18.6 when Dunlap arrived to $51.6 in the space of about a year, an incredible increase of 225 percent or so. Accolades poured in from investor groups and shareholders, including employees whose 401(k) plans had doubled in value.

In July 1995, fifteen months after he arrived as CEO, Dunlap announced that Scott Paper would be sold to Kimberly-Clark. This was only two weeks after Scott's headquarters had been moved to Boca Raton and the company received a $280,000 grant from Palm Beach County for bringing jobs to the area. With characteristic chutzpah, Dunlap indicated that he had no problem with Scott keeping the incentive money because he only promised to bring the jobs to Boca Raton, not keep them there indefinitely.[47] (When Kimberly-Clark announced that Scott staff positions would be consolidated at its Texas headquarters, it let the county keep the grant money.) Dunlap walked away from Scott $100 million richer, including $20 million from Kimberly-Clark for signing a noncompete agreement. His team of executives, most brought in from outside, also did well. His marketing chief, for example, earned $17 million from his leveraged compensation.

Kimberly-Clark CEO Wayne Sanders praised Dunlap's performance at Scott, saying that it "has been a wake-up call to a lot of CEOs, and he has been good for American business."[48] While there is little doubt that Dunlap's performance got people's attention, it is more difficult to tell what lessons should be learned from it. Shareholders gained enormously from the turnaround at Scott, but could other companies succeed in the same way? Did Dunlap really "create value" in a manner that is good for the economy?

The end of the recession in the paper industry in 1995 and the significant rebound in tissue prices certainly contributed to the company's improved finances. Beyond that, Dunlap's own calculations suggest that the $3 billion he raised from selling off Scott's assets was equal to about $40 per share of stock,[49] accounting for some significant part of the run-up in share price. Cost cutting also contributed to that improvement, albeit at the expense of employees. Critics like Sarah Teslik, executive director of the Council of Institutional Investors, wonder about the long run: "Dunlap holds himself up as a role model, but any company is apt to have significant stock run-up if current costs are reduced by a huge amount. That's no guarantee it will do well in the future."[50]

Some observers wonder whether Scott could have continued its profit performance for long if it had not been sold, whether the cuts had gone beyond fat and deep into muscle. Its budget for R&D was cut by half, not a good sign for the long term. Scott began losing market share to its competitors in key products during 1995. An executive at a rival company suggested before the merger with Kimberly-Clark that Dunlap's massive cost cutting may have come down to an effort in "polishing up the company to show it off to potential buyers."[51] Only months after the restructuring program began, Dunlap's team retained Salomon Brothers to begin looking for a merger partner. By definition, not all companies could succeed with this strategy, because someone has to do the buying.

Nonetheless, the pressures to focus on shareholder value are increasing. Institutional investors like CALPERS, the California public pension fund, maintain a well-publicized "hit list" of companies that it believes are underperforming shareholders and deserve a management shakeup. Company takeovers, many driven by efforts to replace management teams seen as not maximizing profits, are at record levels.

REENGINEERING

When maximizing shareholder value became the goal, reengineering became the means through which costs and jobs were squeezed out of the organization. *Reengineering* refers to the systematic effort to redesign specific organizational tasks, usually white-collar functions, with its focus on the level of jobs and tasks. Some observers suggest that it is to white-collar functions what industrial engineering was to production tasks. An example from the insurance industry illustrates the concept.[52]

In a traditional insurance company, a customer who has an accident or some other claim calls his agent, who then sends the claim into company headquarters. There it is assigned to a claims representative who verifies whether the customer's policy is paid and in effect. If it is, the claim may be passed on to a company investigator who determines whether the claim is fraudulent and, if not, whether the insurance company or some other party is liable for the damages. The claim then goes to an adjustor who determines the total damages and attempts to settle with the claimant. In all, the claim has passed through at least four offices and may take as long as six weeks to complete. From 10 to 15 percent of the total costs of insurance claims are associated with the administrative costs of processing them.

The reengineering of this process relies heavily on new MIS (management information system) technology. In reengineered systems, agents call up an information system on their computers that immediately verifies whether the customer's coverage is valid. They then call up an expert system that looks at the customer's previous claims, assesses the nature of the current claim, including the dollar value, and estimates the likelihood that the claim is valid and should not be contested by the company. If it passes that threshold, then the agent simply pays the claim. If not, then the claim goes to headquarters for more traditional processing. The cost and overall time required to process claims falls dramatically. The job of claims representative disappears because coverage is now verified by the agents using their information system. The number of investigator jobs falls precipitously, as does the number of adjustor positions, because the expert system now decides whether claims should be investigated and pays most without a fight. The organization structure, or "chart," gets dramatically flatter as the administrative functions that constitute the middle of the organization are cut out.[53]

No expert system is so perfectly automated that it leaves employees with no judgment calls, and the companies need to find ways to guide the judgment of the agents without being able to supervise them directly. In this example, it's done with financial incentives—contingent compensation—that rewards agents for reducing errors and catching fraud. And the agents are made directly accountable for all issues associated with claims.[54]

Related developments that help squeeze employees out of the system, especially managerial employees, include various quality programs, such as total quality management (TQM), which transfers responsibility for quality from managers to lower-level employees. Developments that push decision making down to lower levels in the organization and substitute incentives and corporate culture for administrative controls also squeeze managers out of the system. Hierarchies are flatter and spans of control are broader. Operations are less functionally divided and more "organic," organized around products and markets. Organizational form itself becomes more flexible and more responsive to customer demands and to the market. Vertical charts yield to more horizontal networks.[55]

A picture of how these changes in organizational design are altering the shape of firms emerges from a study of 140 major companies from 1986 to 1992.[56] The exempt, white-collar jobs in these companies were classified into four main management categories: the lowest level, for people with no supervisory responsibilities, the next level supervisors, the third-level managers who direct supervisors (for example, directors of divisions), and the highest-level executives with strategic decision-making responsibilities (vice presidents and above). The change in the distribution of jobs across these four levels of hierarchy, as illustrated in Figure 3-5, is dramatic. It demonstrates a major flattening of the organizations and a sharp reduction in the number of management jobs.

To illustrate how these changes played out in a single company in the beginning of the restructuring era, consider one in which the total number of corporate managers, including the heads of all major divisions and functions, fell from more than three hundred in 1984 to less than two hundred by 1990. General managers with staff functions dropped from 31 percent of the total in 1984 to 18 percent by 1990. In 1984, this corporation employed about one general manager for every four hundred employees. By 1990, there was one general manager for every six hundred employees. In 1984, the general managers of the company's twenty-three business units (divisions that carried profit and

Figure 3-5. Change in Number, Skill, and Compensation of Management Levels, from 1986–1992

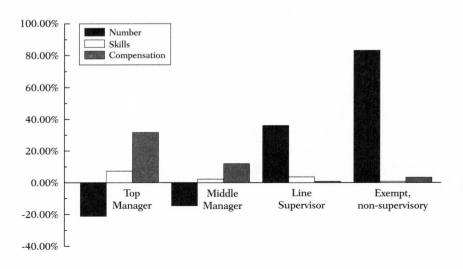

Source: Author's calculations from data collected by Hay Group.

loss responsibilities) had a buffer of thirty-seven managers between themselves and the chief executive. By 1990, following the elimination of almost an entire layer of management, heads of the company's sixteen business units had only eighteen managers between themselves and the CEO's office.

The flattening of corporate hierarchies dramatically reduces the opportunities for promotion. In the above example, the number of jobs above general managers fell by half, cutting the odds of being promoted (other things being equal) in half in just six years. Combined with increased hiring from the outside, the reduction in the hierarchy so sharply curtails the prospects for promotion as to change the orientation of employees and their relationship with the employer. Earlier in the book I described how promotion prospects were the key mechanism behind the lifetime employment relationship because they provided a flexible mechanism for settling up in the long run with employees who pursued the firm's goals. Promotions also drove the psychological process of modeling the behavior of superiors. Without a reasonable prospect of promotion, the focus of the employment relationship can no longer be a career, which spans several jobs. The focus is now on individual jobs. Employees may still be motivated to perform well in their jobs because they expect bonuses or, more likely, better job offers elsewhere. But they are no longer thinking about advancing the long-run interests of the company employing them in their current position.

Attempts at producing alternatives to promotions push the relationship toward a more contractual basis and further reduce the employer's flexibility. "Golden handcuffs" and other arrangements that reward employees for staying with the company, for example, end up becoming complicated legal documents that provide greater motivation for retention than performance. Stock options work somewhat better for senior executives whose performance can have a direct effect on share prices, but they do less to ensure the performance and commitment of lower-level employees whose jobs have very indirect effects at best on share prices.

PRESSURE FOR ARM'S-LENGTH RELATIONSHIPS

The developments noted above have clearly contributed to massive cuts in jobs, especially managerial jobs, and to the end of lifetime careers for workers in them. But, critics might ask, isn't this a one-time reduction, a change that is behind us now? After companies have adopted these new systems and cut positions no longer thought necessary, won't they return to a more traditional, long-term relationship with those who remain?

The answer is no, and the reason is because of related pressures that drive companies to restructure continually. Several of them relate to the changing nature of competition in product markets and, in particular, to the greater need for flexibility.

Employment relations in the motion picture industry played out the theme of a breakdown in internalized arrangements and a move toward more arm's-length, market-mediated arrangements decades before the rest of the economy. In its early years, the film industry was organized much like any of the leading manufacturing facilities of the day. Companies like the Universal Film Manufacturing Company turned out movies according to standardized formulas, as if they were producing cars, pricing them per foot and turning out a huge number of films every year. A single studio produced as many movies in a year as the entire industry does today.[57]

The "studio system," as it became known, was a vertically integrated operation where all of the component functions took place within the same company. Scriptwriting and location scouting, casting, set construction, filming, editing, distribution—every aspect of the process took place inside the studio. That included the development of the actors who played the parts and might eventually become stars. Virtually all of the workers were full-time employees, and mass production principles were used to push films from department to department, something like an assembly line, and then quickly into the theaters, which were also owned by the studios.[58]

In the 1950s, competition in the form of television, aided by antitrust action, led to a sharp decline in the industry and a shift in strategy toward fewer, more novel feature films. The studios turned to outside contractors not only to cut fixed costs but also to find new ideas. Employment contracts also shifted from long-term relationships to a project basis. The internal development of movie stars also declined, just as it would later for managers in industry, because the up-front investments made in their development and the fixed costs associated with carrying them became burdensome. Given the rapid changes in tastes driven by competition from other media, the studios could no longer be sure that certain stars could be used in a long series of movies, and so long-term contracts with those stars became a burden.

Once a network of production companies and specialized suppliers developed, it was both cheaper and easier to unbundle the firms— push particular functions off onto smaller subcontractors—and move the employment relationship toward a more contingent model. Even the subcontractors then begin to unbundle, hiring skilled workers only when they need them to avoid being stuck with fixed costs in a downturn.

One consequence of the increasing competition described earlier is that companies must work harder to find markets where they can enjoy some protection, no doubt temporary, from the grinding pressure of competitors. One of the few opportunities for finding such protection is in market niches with products that are so finely tailored that they appeal to only a small segment of the marketplace, small enough that competitors may not see the costs of entering them as worthwhile. Again, developments in the auto industry provide good illustrations.

In 1960, the best-selling car in the United States was the Chevrolet Impala, with about 900,000 vehicles sold that year. By the end of the 1990s, the U.S. car market had about tripled in size. But the best-selling model in any given year now sells only about 400,000 vehicles, less than half the number from earlier decades, because the variety of models has increased enormously. Ford has begun marketing models that it believes will sell only about 5,000 cars per year. Subaru, an entire company based on the four-wheel drive market niche, now has advertising strategies that target even smaller segments of buyers within that niche, such as the lesbian market.[59] The immediate consequence of this strategy is much smaller production runs and the need for more flexible operating principles to produce the cars efficiently.

The expansion of international markets has increased the speed at which product markets change, a development that has direct consequences for the way work is done and the relationship with employees. One example of these changes is that the novelty—and competitive advantage—of new products no longer lasts for long. One reason, especially where matters of taste are important, as in fashion, has been the globalization of consumer preferences. It was common in previous decades for U.S. producers to transfer products to consumer markets in developing countries for a few years once they had fallen out of favor in the United States, significantly extending the life and production runs of those products. As television and other media become increasingly global, however, advertising campaigns follow, and trends in tastes become much more common across borders. Designs now fall out of fashion in Mexico City at about the same time they do in Chicago, making it much more difficult for firms to extend product lives by shipping the goods abroad. In the 1970s, new products accounted for one-fifth of corporate profits in the United States; by the 1980s they accounted for one-third.[60] Shorter product lives translate into shorter production runs. And that, in turn, makes fixed investments in production systems obsolete more quickly.

Another factor involved in reducing the novelty and life span of new products is the increasing ability of competitors to copy them. Studies of "reverse engineering" find that for about 70 percent of all new products, modern competitors can learn just about everything they need to produce it themselves within one year. Even about 40 percent of the idiosyncratic "process learning" associated with understanding how to produce a new product is eventually acquired by competitors.[61]

Driven by lessons from Japanese companies, U.S. firms began searching for new ways to meet these challenges by getting closer to customers, tracking changes in consumer demand more closely, and adjusting products to those changes. The epic battle for market share in the motorcycle industry between Honda and the smaller but more aggressive Yamaha taught Honda a lesson that spread throughout Japanese industry and then to the United States: after being initially caught out of position by Yamaha's new product lines, Honda reorganized its product delivery and introduced a staggering 113 new models in the next eighteen months, making the Yamaha lines look old and dated and effectively burying Yamaha's challenge.[62] In the 1980s, compared with U.S. producers, Japanese car companies introduced new models twice as quickly.[63]

These lessons were soon adopted by U.S. companies. The time from conceiving to producing and marketing a product has dropped dramatically across a wide range of goods—by half for those like cars and telephones.[64] Reducing time delays in production, for example, not only cuts time to market but also reduces the costly overshooting of production that occurs when product demand is changing because of the time lag in adjusting output. Product variety has also increased as producers find that market share and profitability both benefit from broader product lines. This has forced producers to develop "flexible factories" where costs do not rise when variety expands.[65]

Nathan Myhrvold, the chief technology officer of Microsoft, explains the challenge that these market developments pose for business: "The implementation technologies change so fast that you are always at an incredible risk of becoming obsolete. It is very hard to change a manufacturing business fast enough because of the large investment in tooling up for what will soon become yesterday's technology."[66]

To reduce the lag time between assessing consumer needs and getting products out the door, dedicated equipment and procedures had to be replaced with more flexible ones that could be rearranged more easily. Empirical studies find that an important way to cut development time is to change traditional, functionally oriented systems of work organization and replace them with cross-functional teams, cutting managerial jobs in the process.[67] Another technique for speeding development time is to rely on external sourcing and subcontractors, especially where product markets are uncertain.[68]

But the most important effect of these developments in competition is that they make fixed investments obsolete more quickly. Internalized employment structures and all the long-term commitments associated with them are among the most substantial of those fixed costs, as they often imply lifetime employment for skills that may become obsolete. The competencies and skills needed must change when products change, and the old ones become obsolete much more quickly. How firms get the new skills they need in a hurry is a central question for the employee relationship. Hiring workers with general skills and abilities and developing them over time inside the firm is rarely an option because it takes too long. If the skills are truly new to the firm, it is difficult to learn them inside. Even if they are simply in short supply, the market may have moved on by the time the current workforce learns those skills.

Instead, firms look outside for the new skills, from subcontractors, joint ventures, or outside hiring, in part because it now takes too long to develop them inside the firm. And the cost of carrying employees with obsolete skills often pushes employers to break the employment relationship, pushing the existing employees out the door.

An example of this kind of turnover could be seen in the Philadelphia radio market in the 1990s. Radio station WFLN in Philadelphia played a classical music format for fifty years. Its monopoly on that format gave it a comfortable niche that helped the station become an important patron of the Philadelphia Orchestra and a pillar of the broader arts community. New owners acquired the station in 1997 and saw a more profitable audience for its frequency, abandoning the classical music format and moving to urban contemporary music. The announcers, programming staff, and other employees, with their deep experience in classical music and its audience were now obsolete and shown the door.

Now there were no classical music stations in the nation's fourth largest market. The classical music audience, while small, is also a wealthy one, highly prized by advertisers. WRTI, a station with an all-jazz format, saw that it could make better use of *its* frequency by shifting to an all-classical music format during the day, and it moved to take over the niche previously held by WFLN. WRTI hired many of WFLN's key staff to secure a classical music competency. Now that Philadelphia has no radio station with a pure jazz format, no doubt some other station will move to that niche, rearranging the staff's competencies and employees in the process.

The radio programming in the community may look no different to the consumer at the end of this process than it did at the beginning; the same music is being played, often by the same announcers, but at different locations along the radio dial. A single strategy initiative set off a series of adjustments by competitors that caused workforces to be reshuffled across the local industry. What is new about this process is that more frequent changes in ownership and more rapid changes in markets have caused firms to change their business strategies—and, in the process, their employment practices—more frequently.

A study of electronic firms in southern England found that these successful companies knew that their engineers were the key assets in their organizations. And they managed them much more like short-term than long-term assets, hiring and laying off to rearrange their competencies as an organization and keep them current. One of the main reasons companies took this approach to employment was that they were frequently restructuring and changing product lines. In the process, they were changing the competencies and assets that they needed for the new products. And the engineers were part of those assets. While they were in many ways the core of the capabilities of these firms, that core was always changing. And the companies made continual use of the market as a means of getting the new skills they needed.[69] Evidence from corporate surveys in the United States suggests that companies are now much less likely to relocate their employees to new locations (there was a 9 percent decline in the number of relocations between 1997 and 1998), which is consistent with the view that they are going outside for skills.[70]

Through the 1980s, firms like IBM argued that their *internal* employee management systems gave them flexibility by reducing resistance to restructuring. But they had a different notion of restructuring, associated with relatively modest and predictable changes in product mixes that could be accommodated by rearranging existing workers around existing operations. Knowing that in five years one mainframe computing product will be replaced by another is an example of the more modest restructuring that can be accommodated within the firm. Finding that the market for mainframes has declined sharply and shifted to personal computers is something else. In the pharmaceutical industry, for example, the shift from physical chemistry to biochemistry as a basis for new drugs means that existing research and development competencies based on physical chemistry are largely obsolete. Retraining a physical chemist to become a biochemist is a prohibitive undertaking for employers who cannot wait for the new skills.

Especially in service industries, competencies often reside within individual employees, as opposed to within an organizational system. Software development, accounting, or legal services, for example, are largely individual rather than organizational skills. And rearranging the competencies of such firms may well require rearranging its employees.

New Management Techniques

New ideas about how firms should be managed have provided additional arguments for moving employment to an arm's-length relationship. Many of these ideas were driven in part by academic research.

Movement to "Core Competencies." The arguments noted above that conglomerates should concentrate on related businesses to become more successful have their parallel in the management of individual operations. Here the argument is that successful firms have a "core competency" or distinctive capability, such as superior product design or marketing skills, that differentiates them from competitors and drives their competitiveness. Such competency cuts across individual product lines.[71]

One implication of these arguments is that firms should get out of business lines that do not exploit their competencies. Companies on the Fortune 500 industrial list were active in only half as many product sectors by 1990 as were their 1980 counterparts, in part because they had already begun to focus their attention on what they did well.[72] Outsourcing functions that are not among a firm's core competencies is another implication.

The notion that a firm should restructure itself around its core competency creates continual pressures for change because a firm's core competency changes when consumer tastes and preferences change. And whether a competency continues to create a competitive advantage depends on what one's competitors are doing. Product development was a core competency for Japanese auto companies selling in the United States precisely because they were much faster to market than U.S. companies. But now that Chrysler is able to get new models out even faster than the Japanese firms, those companies may have to look for a different competency, just as they shifted from their original reliance on cost as a source of competitive advantage in the 1980s toward innovative product development.

Companies that follow the core competency notion restructure in significant ways when those competencies change. Sarah Beckman, a former executive at Hewlett-Packard, describes how that company's difficulties in finding qualified vendors in its early years led to a tradition of backward integration and highly vertical integration. By the 1980s, however, the burden of staying on the edge of technology in so many different areas became overwhelming, and HP began the painful process of vertical disintegration in order to concentrate its resources on a few core competencies. The process began by allowing divisions to outsource to vendors that offered better specifications, causing the internal suppliers to atrophy and eventually die. As the vendor market became more sophisticated, outsourcing moved from functions fairly distant from HP's core, such as sheet metal, to those central to HP's business, such as the making of integrated circuits.[73] When tasks move out of the firm, so do the skills and employees that had performed them. While companies have always restructured, the difference now is that the pace of restructuring cannot be accommodated by normal employee attrition or other adjustments within the existing workforce.

The most radical examples of the reduction in formal structures and their replacement by market relationships are the so-called "virtual" organizations. They take the concept of a flexible organization structure even further by eliminating fixed investments in permanent structures altogether. The Clos LaChance winery in California, for example, leases space from an existing winery, purchases grapes from growers, has its bottling done by a mobile operation, and stores its bottles at another warehouse. Independent brokers are retained to distribute the wine. Clos LaChance owner Bill Murphy also works in marketing at Hewlett-Packard, and his contribution to the wine venture is limited mainly to directing its marketing, which happens to be the company's "core competency."[74] Companies like the Global Business Network take this concept to its extreme. This virtual consulting firm assembles teams of independent experts from around the world for different project assignments. With essentially no overhead and a potentially limitless pool of "partners," it has considerable advantages over its more integrated competitors.[75]

It is probably fair to say that virtual organizations have remained something of a novelty for small, start-up operations. The only real source of competitive advantage is the aspects of business that remain inside the organization, and virtual organizations have so little inside that there is not much on which they can earn a return.

An additional aspect of the effort to restructure companies has been to decentralize operating control through new organizational structures. Strategic business units (SBUs), with full profit and loss responsibilities, are increasingly the dominant organizational form, and they in turn can be divided and subdivided on much the same principles. For example, when the Asea corporation merged with Brown Boveri to form Asea Brown Boveri (ABB), the multinational power engineering company, it reorganized its workforce of 240,000 employees around roughly 5,000 profit centers—one for approximately every fifty employees—and cut its corporate headquarters employees to 150. With these new arrangements, each employee feels inextricably tied to the performance of his or her unit and no longer insulated from the market but very much a part of it. Organizing companies around particular product markets as opposed to functional areas, as the Xerox Corporation did in the early 1990s, also helps bring the product market orientation inside the firm.

Once profit and loss and market pressures more generally become the mechanism directing the inside of the firm, the need for corporate-level control and oversight diminish dramatically, and with them, corporate staff. During its 1993–94 restructuring, for example, IBM reduced its corporate staff from 5,100 to 3,900, with further reductions expected. "Our view of corporate headquarters," offered its new senior vice president for human resources and administration, "is that there should be as little of it as possible."[76] Bringing market pressures inside the organization also means that those pressures and risks get translated more directly to the employment relationship. Once a business unit becomes accountable for meeting performance targets, it is no longer insulated from business risk and bears the costs of failure when markets change. That makes the operating divisions much more wary of fixed costs and other long-term investments that can cost them when markets change, a development that is reinforced by new accounting techniques such as economic value added.

These changes in organizational structure squeeze more management jobs out of the organization, but their most important impact on the employment relationship concerns the sharp reductions they represent in the governance of organizations by administrative rules. Product market discipline, more focused performance measures (and monitoring of them), and financial incentives based on those measures are the mechanisms that govern organizations.

The fact that markets are more volatile greatly increases the risk of being caught with capabilities and investments out of sync with market requirements. As a result, companies now have a strong preference for investments and capabilities that can be adjusted to changing markets. This preference plays itself out in a much greater reliance on contracting out functions, on hiring contingent workers, and on putting those workers on contingent pay schemes.

INFORMATION TECHNOLOGY. Another contributor to the restructuring of employment comes in the form of new management information and control systems made possible by cheaper computer power. Information technology has transformed the workplace, first by transforming companies themselves, sharply reducing the need for internalized management systems and, in turn, internalized employment systems.

When William Durant began acquiring and integrating the various components of carriage production, he did so to ensure a predictable supply of components and, ultimately, of carriages. The theme of vertical integration required purchasing suppliers and then creating a corporate staff to control them. In vertically integrated corporations, middle managers from headquarters had the job of coordinating the operation of these suppliers, ensuring quality production, and alerting headquarters to any bottlenecks or problems as soon as they appeared.

With modern information systems, however, it is possible to ensure quality, predict supply, and integrate planning without middle managers and, in fact, without owning suppliers. GM's Automotive Industry Action Group illustrates this point. GM requires all of its suppliers to conform to a common specification of computer and information systems and monitors the systems itself. These systems contain virtually all of the internal accounting, quality, and performance measures used by the suppliers. GM knows virtually everything about its suppliers, but without having any corporate staff or ownership stake in those suppliers.

In the retail sector, companies like Benneton have been able to develop enormously responsive capabilities with very little in the way of formal organization by using information technology to link up with the market and suppliers. The company's 4,000 shops are outfitted with information systems that send daily sales data to headquarters, where it is analyzed to predict trends. The information is then fed through Benneton's information systems to a collection of vendors who use it to adjust the styles of clothing they produce. Benneton's ability to react to changing consumer demand is the envy of its competitors. And it gets by with only 1,500 employees. Its subcontractors, however, employ 25,000.[77] A key advantage of using a common information system in this case is the sharp reduction in costs and problems associated with information transactions. To take an obvious example, errors are reduced considerably because the data are entered into the system only once, at the source.

Information systems like these obviously make outsourcing easier. Complicated arrangements like "just-in-time" inventory, where components must be continually delivered in small batches, can be coordinated between independent companies. Even in financial services, the tasks required to manage complex financial instruments can be unbundled and distributed to the market. For example, self-directed financial annuities are a major product for many life insurance companies, but they now outsource trading, billing, customer complaints, and other key aspects of the relationship with their customers to companies like Delaware Valley Financial Services, which perform those tasks more efficiently.

Information systems also help reduce the distance and time between suppliers and their customers. American Hospital Supply's ASAP system, begun in the late 1970s, was one of the pioneering efforts in this area. It kept track of a hospital's inventory electronically, reordering supplies automatically. This system cut inventory and ordering costs, which had been almost *equal* to the costs of the supplies themselves, down to almost nothing. In the process, it eliminated middlemen suppliers as well as inventory managers in both the hospitals and the supply company while still ensuring compliance with corporate policies.[78]

These systems have indirect but powerful implications for employment relationships. The first and perhaps most obvious is that firms and the employees in them can be more easily "unbundled," with components pushed out to suppliers. When a large purchaser like GM deals with a variety of vendors, it can easily move work across them. Because GM knows virtually everything about its vendors through shared information systems, including their cost structure, the pressure to squeeze costs to expand their vendor's business—or retain it—can be quite powerful. Research suggests that the use of information technology systems is associated with smaller firms and less vertical hierarchy, other things being equal.[79]

The coordination power of information technology and this ability to unbundle complicated operations that had been vertically integrated inside the firm has led to the return of the century-old "inside contracting" system. As described in Chapter 2, manufacturers in the past would even subcontract aspects of complex assembly operations to contractors who then worked side by side to produce products. In Resende, Brazil, Volkswagen opened a truck assembly plant in 1996 staffed almost entirely by employees of its suppliers. While VW manages the facility and does quality inspection, the assembly is done entirely by the workers of its eight contractors. J. Ignacio Lopez, the former head of purchasing for GM and now at VW, is often credited with advancing the modern version of inside contracting. Both GM and Chrysler are opening Brazilian assembly facilities where their suppliers will provide most of the assembled vehicle.

The advantages of this arrangement are similar to those of a century ago. The host company can dramatically reduce its capital requirements and risk by pushing off production to its contractors. At the Volkswagen plant, for example, one-third of its capital requirements were met by Volkswagen's suppliers. The management issues are also substantially reduced. These arrangements were introduced in Brazil because its business environment was open to innovations, but the goal is to transfer them to operations elsewhere. Volkswagen has already introduced lessons from its Brazilian experience to its Skodia subsidiary in Eastern Europe. Similar developments, albeit on a smaller scale, are underway at the Mercedes assembly facility in Tuscaloosa, Alabama, where, for example, suppliers are already providing finished modules, including the entire cockpit of Mercedes' new sport utility vehicle.[80]

Within firms, information technology takes over much of the internal accounting function and helps eliminate the tasks of middle management, such as internal control and coordination, and ultimately the jobs of those middle managers. Spreadsheets and financial planning software have taken over tasks that had been performed by lower- and midlevel accounting managers and made them available to virtually every employee of the company. The effects are particularly dramatic at headquarters, where the most important tasks are coordination and compliance with corporate policies and internal control, leading to a net reduction in management jobs.[81] New "enterprise-wide software" developed by SAP, Oracle, and PeopleSoft, in particular, is designed to coordinate operations across an organization, especially along its internal supply chain. These programs essentially take the place of the corporate managers whose jobs were to coordinate operations across the company to ensure synergies.

Inventory supply systems like American Hospital Supply's ASAP and McKesson's pioneering inventory system for pharmacies, which collect information directly from customers, also change behavior and attitudes in the supplying firm because they bring the product market, through those customer preferences, much more powerfully inside the firm. Information about customers, and in many cases about competitors, comes in daily and is the focus of attention. The interactive capabilities of computer-assisted salespeople had an unexpected effect on a related labor market when they were introduced in one part of the health care industry. The representatives of a medical supply company were linked by one of the earliest E-mail systems, and they soon started conveying information to the doctors they served about jobs in their specialty, creating their own well-informed and efficient employment network.[82]

These new systems of information technology change the employment relationship in three distinct ways. The first is simply that they make it possible to cut jobs, especially corporate jobs that had served the function of coordinating and ensuring compliance with procedures. The second is that they make it possible to unbundle companies, to push more functions outside to suppliers in the market without losing the advantages of predictability that came from performing those tasks inside. When firms unbundle, jobs obviously do as well. But the process does not stop when the work has moved out of the firm. Once these information systems are in place, the costs of moving work from one supplier to another fall dramatically. One of my colleagues describes a Japanese electronics company that relies on these systems to allocate projects across plants on a *weekly* basis according to cost differences. As projects shift from the firm to suppliers and then back and forth from suppliers, so, too, do the jobs.

Third and finally, information systems make it possible to bring information about the market inside the firm so that even the most bureaucratic and firm-specific areas of the company feel a connection to the market, changing the orientation of employee expectations and attitudes.

BENCHMARKING. Of all the new management practices, the technique of benchmarking may have the most direct and immediate effect on the attitudes and orientation of employees, making them feel on a very visceral level that they are no longer protected by the boundaries of the firm but are completely exposed to the market. Benchmarking is a data-gathering exercise that in its simplest form takes some subprocess or task within the organization, such as handling consumer complaints, and compares an organization's performance on that task with those of other organizations, especially those with strong reputations in that area. Beyond giving the organization an understanding of how well its performance stacks up against that of competitors, benchmarking is also designed to reveal the causes of superior performance. Entire organizations, such as the American Center for Productivity and Quality or the Saratoga Institute, are devoted to the benchmarking process.

In a typical study, the managers in charge of the process or task being benchmarked are deeply involved in the exercise and often lead it. The organizations that are most willing to share their data—indeed are eager to share it—are vendors and other providers that are interested in taking in business. The employees doing the benchmarking study, therefore, end up comparing their costs and processes with those of organizations interested in taking over their jobs. Before the benchmarking study, these workers may have understood that their employer was engaged in competition in the product market but probably saw their own operations as isolated from competition, deeply embedded within the bigger organization. Through the benchmarking study, they not only discover that there are competitors for their jobs, they stare those competitors right in the face. While information technology has helped bring a product market orientation inside the firm, benchmarking has become a mechanism for making every administrative function and process in the firm feel as if it has many competitors.

Bankers Trust began a benchmarking exercise in check-processing operations that was led by the employees who did the work. What they learned in the process was that their cost structures were as much as three times higher than that of some of their competitors, including vendors like EDS and other banks that take in check processing as contract work. They could see which of their processes were the real problem areas and what the cost items were, including their own wages and salaries. They also learned that some of their low-cost competitors were willing to take in check-processing work and so made the obvious connection that their jobs were on the line. In the reengineering exercise that followed the benchmarking study, the check-processing group managed to cut costs dramatically, below those of its competitors in the benchmarking study.

BUNDLING CHANGE

Employers have increasingly come to understand that the management practices associated with restructuring and described above are most effective when they are bundled together. An analysis of 131 studies of companies that set out to restructure their organizations between 1961 and 1991 examined the practices pursued and the resulting effects on performance. The practices included forming strategic business units, creating cross-functional teams, and pushing decision making down to lower levels in the organization. The researchers found that the largest and most sustained improvements in company performance came when the company pressed for integrated, systemic changes in both organizational design and human resources practices and when it fostered changes at the corporate and business unit level, not just at the group or individual level.[83]

A study of process reengineering at more than one hundred companies during the early 1990s reached the same conclusion. The translation of short-term process improvements into long-term gains for business units depended on the implementation of the change process across the entire unit and the inclusion of new performance measures, compensation incentives, information technologies, shared culture, employee skills, and organizational structure.[84]

Systemic change across a range of practices is required if performance is to be improved. If only one component is changed, its effects are likely to be washed out as other unchanged components undermine the intended impact. Creating a strategic business unit (SBU), for example, without simultaneously reengineering the headquarters operations to reduce administrative oversight, will defeat the decentralizing effort. Devolving authority without also tightening financial controls around shareholder value is likely to undermine any efforts to improve stock price and dividend payout. The fact that these restructuring practices are increasingly bundled together implies that the effects on the employment relationship are that much greater.

EMPLOYMENT LAW. A surprising amount of pressure for change, and one that is not well recognized, has come from the legal framework regulating employment and the legislation designed to protect employees. The array of federal legislation directed at employment is vast. It has made the U.S. Department of Labor the largest enforcement agency in the federal government. The main pieces of legislation read like an alphabet soup of regulations: the National Labor Relations Act (NLRA) governing employee representation, the Civil Rights Acts on equal opportunity in employment, the Fair Labor Standards Act (FLSA) governing wages and hours, the Occupational Safety and Health Act (OSHA) on workplace conditions, the Employee Retirement Income Security Act (ERISA) on pensions, the Worker Adjustment and Retraining Notification Act (WARN) affecting plant closings, the Family and Medical Leave Act (FMLA) providing unpaid leaves, the Americans with Disabilities Act (ADA), and a series of executive orders on similar issues whose mandates work in much the same way as legislation. This is just the federal legislation. It does not count state laws—workers' compensation in particular—which are not only complex but usually vary state by state, creating real nightmares for companies operating in many locations. Nor does it count the exploding litigation based on civil law around issues such as termination.

These laws provide protection for employees by constraining the actions of employers and, in the process, imposing significant administrative costs on them in order to comply. Much of this legislation came from the New Deal, and the model behind it was the dominant model of industrial employment in the 1930s, in which an "employee" is on site in a long-term relationship with close supervision and a narrowly defined job. If the employment arrangements are different from that traditional model, the "employees" are often not covered by the legislation. Here are some examples.

The 1938 Fair Labor Standards Act was driven by the assumption that workplaces were divided in two parts, between regular employees and management, and that those in management were "committed career employees" who did not need to be protected from the employer. They were "exempt" from the act—hence the term "exempt employees." The FLSA governs overtime, but an employer can avoid these requirements if the employment relationship moves away from the traditional model. Hourly employees who work without direct supervision can be exempt, and the compensation for certain kinds of sales jobs can be shifted toward commissions to achieve the same ends.

The National Labor Relations Act also divided the workplace into two camps—workers and managers—and does not extend the right to be represented by labor organizations to supervisory employees. In a famous case involving Bell Aerospace, the U.S. Supreme Court extended this exclusion from coverage to purchasing agents. Even though they had no supervisory responsibilities, these agents were seen as more like managers because they carried out their tasks with autonomy, without direct supervision.[85] An employer who redesigned jobs to give workers autonomy, along the lines of teamwork and the "high performance" work systems currently advocated as best practices, could effectively take those positions away from union representation and remove those workers from the protection of the act.

Employers can avoid many of the requirements of these laws, and the administrative burdens associated with them, if their workers are leased from an agency such as a temporary help firm. All of the considerable compliance burdens and threats of litigation associated with hiring and firing workers are removed from an establishment when its workers are the direct employees of an outside agency. The establishment's management can simply cancel the contract of any leased employees that they do not find acceptable, with no elaborate justifications required, and call up the agency to get new ones.[86] A great many small employers in particular use this arrangement to hire permanent employees. They try out temps from an agency until they find one they like and then offer the individual a permanent position.

Most labor laws allow some exemptions for small employers, as measured by the number of workers they employ. And most do not count workers who are truly temporary or leased as employees of the organization. Small operations can get bigger and retain their small employer exemptions by using leased workers.

The 1975 Employee Retirement Income Security Act requires that generous retirement programs for management be offered proportionately to lower-level employees as well. Employers who want to reduce the burden of providing more generous pensions for management can take low-level jobs off their own payroll and place them on a contractor's. The incentives to avoid labor law requirements by outsourcing jobs or using contract workers became more powerful once an infrastructure of leased employee companies developed. Such companies now offer every kind of specialized skill imaginable.

RESISTANCE TO CHANGE. Despite the fact that the changes in employment associated with restructuring seem to make employees substantially worse off, at least in the short run, resistance by employees seems to have been virtually nonexistent. One reason is that the ability of unions to counter management efforts to change practices declined sharply in the 1980s. The overall weakness of many organized firms left unions with little option but to acquiesce to restructuring efforts or see the enterprise fold. In other situations, management's ability to move jobs away from union representation seriously weakened union power and forced unions to accept concessions. In the past, union gains have spilled over to nonunion facilities, where management adopted practices that protected workers as a way of buying out some of the interest in unions. But as the threat of union organizing declines, nonunion companies are increasingly abandoning those practices in a kind of reverse spillover effect.

A second factor undermining employee resistance is the scope of these changes across the economy. An employer that broke lifetime employment arrangements with its employees might normally expect those employees to quit and to have some difficulty hiring new ones. But because most companies were engaged in similar restructurings, no individual company was at a relative disadvantage for doing so. And the fact that the changes tend to shed labor created an excess supply of skilled labor, especially managerial labor, in the outside market, which made it still easier to adopt these new strategies. It is relatively easy to get new skills from the outside labor market, making it costless to abandon internal development practices. And the visibility of so much job loss made remaining employees very nervous about resisting these changes.

Resistance to these changes within the employer community also erodes as more companies make them, not only legitimizing them but also making companies that have not abandoned the old practices feel old-fashioned. IBM's announcement of its decision to abandon employment security and lay off employees, for example, was followed shortly thereafter by a wave of layoffs at other large employers. Xerox was considered a highly successful company in 1993, with a strong commitment to good union management relations and to its employees. But when it announced it would slash its workforce by about 10 percent, observers reacted not with concern about the potential costs of broken commitments but with applause. An analyst with First Boston observed, "We are just starting to see these types of restructurings. These guys are ahead of the curve." (As it turns out, they were.) By the end of the day, Xerox stock had risen by 7 percent.[87] The fact that investment markets tend to react positively to downsizing decisions not only broke any norms for employment but created pressures to cut.

At the beginning of the 1980s, employers were still advocating long-term commitments to employees and internal development of skills as the best practice model. A decade later, the business community had organized itself to press for the opposite. For example, the Labor Policy Association, an employer group concerned with employment policy, produced a study in 1994 arguing that the key to improved corporate performance is greater management discretion in employment decisions of the kind that come from reducing employee protective legislation, union contracts, and due process rules in company handbooks.[88] In other words, the ability to dismiss current workers and hire new ones. The report was widely disseminated and had considerable impact.

CONCLUSION

The restructuring of firms that has occurred since the mid-1980s was initially viewed as a one-shot phenomenon, a kind of overdue corporate correction. But the developments in the economy, in corporate governance, and in management practices outlined above that have created the pressure for changing employment relationships show no sign of abating. Because integrated, systemic change is required if restructuring is to achieve its ends, the reshaping is also likely to press more deeply into more facets of organizational and work systems. In short, restructuring means more than a one-time adaptation to a new organizational model. It means continual change. And that implies an end to the long-term employment relationship of mutual commitments.

CHAPTER 4

The Magnitude of Change

To THIS point I've documented the pressures on firms to change the employment relationship and some of the responses to those pressures. But just how extensive has the change been? Along with the stories in the press about the beating employees have taken in recent years is the occasional article suggesting that all this talk about change in the employment relationship may be overblown, that the change has not been widespread or that even if it was, firms are now settling back into the more traditional model.[1]

The debate breaks down neatly as follows. Those who argue that the change is revolutionary study firms, especially large corporations. Those who believe the change is modest at best study the labor market and the workforce as a whole. While I have yet to meet a manager who believes that this change has not stood his or her world on its head, I meet plenty of labor economists studying the aggregate workforce who are not sure what exactly has changed.

The change in the employment relationship—still under way—represents a breakdown in long-term commitments and stable relationships. But not all employees had long-term, stable employment relationships to begin with. Even if we focus on the private sector alone, leaving out the roughly 9 percent of the workforce that is self-employed, farms, or works at jobs that do not fit the model of working for an "employer," organizations have still had to be of a certain size before it made sense for them to have systems of internal development and training, job ladders, and other arrangements associated with long-term commitments. Seven percent of private sector employees work in establishments with fewer than five employees, and 44 percent are in establishments with fewer than one hundred.[2] One researcher calculated that organizations need a minimum of five hundred employees to make formal, job-evaluation-based compensation systems feasible.[3] Another argued that only about 40 percent of U.S. employees were in firms large enough and old enough to even have a reputation in their community, something that he saw as necessary to make the implicit contracts behind internalized employment practices operate.[4] Even within those organizations, the lifetime commitment model was generally a phenomenon for managerial workers, who typically constituted about one-fifth of a company's workforce.

It is hard to get a precise estimate of the percentage of the workforce that belonged to the lifetime, career employment system described thus far. But if we define the population as managerial employees in firms large enough to have reputations, a ballpark estimate would be about 10 percent of the private sector workforce. If one looks at that segment of the workforce, the changes in employment are dramatic. If one looks at the entire workforce, the changes are less so, in large part because most workers have never had the long-term, internal employment relationship associated with corporate management. Given that, it is easy to see why observers looking at large corporations and those looking at the labor force as a whole might reach very different conclusions about how much change has occurred in the employment relationship.

In this chapter we'll consider all the evidence available—both for large employers and the workforce overall—that allows us to measure the magnitude of the change. We'll then consider the effects of the change on employers and employees: how extensive is the effect on employee performance? on the balance of temporary and permanent workers in the workforce? on wages and employer-provided training? The answers to those and other questions are good indicators of the extent of the change that's taken place in the employer-employee relationship. The most recent information in particular paints a picture of a relationship that has become less secure and more contingent even for the average worker in the labor force.

EVIDENCE OF CHANGE: EMPLOYMENT SECURITY

A central aspect of internalized employment practices is the protection they afford to both employee and employer—one from the risk of losing a job, the other from the uncertainty of finding and keeping qualified employees. One way to see whether employment security has changed in the United States is to examine employer policies concerning employment security. As noted in Chapter 1, two-thirds of large employers say that they no longer offer employment security.

The authors of the book *The 100 Best Companies to Work for in America* found in 1993 that ten of those companies had an explicit "no layoff" policy; by 1997 only two still had such policies, and only one of those two was a publicly held company.[5] A benchmarking study of leading companies conducted by the Corporate Leadership Council in 1995 found that companies gave managerial jobs an average life expetancy of three or four years—that is, the jobs were designed with the expectation that the incumbents would leave in that time period.[6]

The job security that used to exist in most companies was an implicit policy never written in employee handbooks, which makes it difficult to use changes in explicit policies as a measure of the change in job security. Another, more promising approach is to look at explicit employer decisions to end job security: downsizing. There are many ways in which employment can be reduced that do not necessarily change the employment relationship. Attrition, hiring freezes, or even a decision to increase the percentage of workers dismissed for poor performance can reduce the workforce without changing the relationship with current employees. Downsizing, in contrast, refers to dismissing workers for reasons *other* than poor performance. While the term *layoffs* has traditionally referred to cutting workers in a business downturn (typically with the intention of hiring them back when business returned), *downsizing* has come to mean cutting workers to reduce costs and improve financial performance, not necessarily to respond to declines in business. In the past, firms clearly laid off production workers in response to cyclical downturns or other situations in which business declined. In fact, except for reductions in force caused by technological developments, it is hard to find any example before the mid-1980s of a case in which production workers were let go for a reason other than a sharp decline in business. And there are fewer still in which white-collar or managerial jobs were cut. In other words, no downsizings. As late as the end of the 1970s, survey evidence from the Conference Board indicated that management's priorities in setting employment practices were to build a loyal, stable workforce. By the end of the 1980s, that priority had clearly shifted to increasing organizational performance and reducing costs.[7]

The first round of downsizing began as part of the recession in 1982–83, the deepest economic downturn since the Great Depression. Those cuts began as layoffs driven by sharp declines in business and were clearly seen as a temporary phenomenon. Sixty-one percent of the human resource executives surveyed by the Conference Board in 1984 thought that the downsizing was losing its momentum.[8] By 1991, a similar Conference Board survey found that more than half of the executives polled believed that downsizing would continue to be necessary to maintain a competitive organization.[9] That year, other surveys reported that 22 percent of companies polled were planning to make cuts in their workforce. In fact, 46 percent of those companies, twice as many, ended up cutting workers.[10]

An important driver of the downsizing wave has been mergers and acquisitions, which, as indicated in Chapter 3, have once again surged to record levels and present opportunities for consolidations that lead to layoffs. A typical example of this process can be seen in the workings of the Commonwealth group of insurance companies, part of Capital Holding Corporation in Louisville. In 1987, it had 1,600 employees. It then acquired two other insurance companies with about 300 employees each. Yet consolidation and downsizing programs cut its total workforce to 1,100, with plans to drive that number down to 800, less than half its workforce before the acquisitions.[11]

The American Management Association (AMA) has surveyed its member companies about downsizing since 1990, a few years after the wave of cuts began in corporate America. It found that the incidence of downsizing increased virtually every year until 1996, when 48.9 percent of companies reported them in a trivial decline, down from 50 percent the year before. Forty percent had downsized in two or more separate years over the past six. Other surveys report roughly similar rates of downsizing.[12] The AMA concluded from its employer surveys that while workforce reductions have been a continuing theme over the past decade, they are increasingly "strategic or structural in nature" as opposed to representing a response to short-term economic conditions associated with declines in business.[13] In every year since 1991, the actual cuts that firms imposed were roughly twice as big as what they reported as their plans. Looking at the one hundred largest companies in the United States, the AMA found that 22 percent of their workforce has been laid off since 1978, with 77 percent of those cuts targeted at white-collar jobs.[14]

What seems to have incensed the public about downsizing in the late 1980s and early 1990s is the apparent callousness with which it was carried out. Anecdotes tell of the telecommunications company that laid off two hundred workers by voicemail, the executive laid off on "take your daughter to work day," with his daughter in the office, and the sharp rise in downsizings during the holiday period between Thanksgiving and New Year's Day. What is different about the downsizing programs in more recent years is that firms are hiring at the same time that they are laying off. Thirty-one percent in 1996 were adding and cutting workers at the same time, and the average firm that had a downsizing was in fact growing by 6 percent. Smaller firms were creating more jobs than they were cutting, while large firms with more than 10,000 workers were more likely to see actual declines in overall employment. The telecommunications industry provides a good illustration. At its peak, AT&T employed 950,000 people. Now it employs fewer than 300,000, with plans to cut further. Yet the telecommunications industry still has about the same number of employees as a decade ago. While AT&T has shrunk, both through divestitures and downsizing, smaller competitors have grown up around it.[15]

The causes of downsizing have also changed, with a growing number of companies reporting that restructuring (66 percent) and outsourcing (23 percent) were the causes. Virtually none now cite overall economic conditions as an explanation, and most of the companies that cut are profitable in the year they do the cutting. Both assistance to the displaced and retraining are also declining; assistance is now at its lowest level since 1990.[16]

Looking at data from the labor market on workers who are displaced from their jobs, economist Henry Farber finds that the overall rate at which workers have been permanently displaced backed down a bit in the 1980s from the peak of the recession period, 1981–83, but then rose again—despite the economic recovery—and jumped sharply through 1995. The rate at which workers were forced out of their jobs was actually greater in 1993–95, a period of significant economic expansion and prosperity in the economy as a whole, as compared with 1981–83, the worst recession since the Depression. It is difficult to imagine more compelling evidence that the nature of the employment relationship has changed than this. About 15 percent of the workforce saw their jobs go forever during 1993–95. And the cause of the job losses has shifted away from economy- or company-wide reasons such downturns in business or plant closings toward eliminating particular positions associated with restructuring (see Figure 4-1).[17]

Perhaps the most telling change in the employment relationship has come with the downsizing of white-collar and management employees whose jobs were traditionally the most protected. The AMA survey found that while salaried employees held roughly 40 percent of all jobs, they accounted for more than 60 percent of all the jobs cut. The number of supervisory positions eliminated as a percentage of all jobs that were cut doubled in 1990–91 and 1993–94, finally reaching 26 percent.[18] The rate of displacement was actually higher for managers in the 1980s than for other occupations, controlling for other characteristics.[19] It rose sharply through the early 1990s but appears to have declined somewhat in 1993–95,[20] perhaps simply because of diminishing returns: So many management positions have already been cut that it has become harder to keep finding new ones to eliminate.

Figure 4-1. Rate of Job Loss by Reason

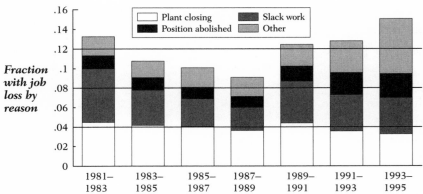

Source: Henry S. Farber, "The Changing Face of Job Loss in the United States 1981–95," *Brookings Papers on Economic Activity, Microeconomics, 1997,* 68.

The "churning" of the workforce—the occurrence of hiring and laying off at the same time—had the biggest negative effects in the AMA surveys on middle management, where three jobs were cut for every one created (see Figure 4-2). These are the positions that are the most entrenched in the internal employment system. Professional and technical jobs, in contrast, benefited, with five new jobs created for every three cut. And these jobs have the skills and responsibilities that translate easily across organizations, jobs that are more clearly in the market.

That churning of the workforce did more than simply rearrange permanent employees. A survey of five hundred human resource executives whose companies had downsized found that one-third refilled at least some of the positions that had been cut but that 71 percent did so with either temporary or contract workers.[21]

Another way to see how traditional protections have come under threat is by looking at the characteristics of the individuals most at risk from displacement. Older and more educated workers, the kind one would expect to find in "better" jobs, more buffered by the organization

Figure 4-2. Distribution of Job Cuts Across Occupations

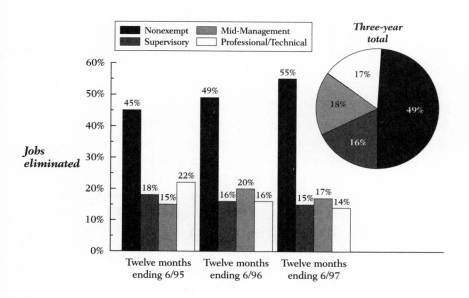

Source: American Management Association, 1997 AMA Survey on Job Creation, Job Elimination, and Downsizing (New York: American Management Association, 1998).

from market pressures, were increasingly likely to be displaced in the early 1990s compared with earlier periods. To illustrate, the Health and Retirement Survey, a national probability survey of individuals over age fifty-five, reports that 15 percent of all those in that age group were laid off from a job in which they had at least ten years of seniority. Forty-seven percent of those who left employment took advantage of an "early out" financial incentive to leave.[22] The cause of job loss for these older and more educated workers was the elimination of their position (as opposed to plant closings, slack work, or other causes)—in other words, these were job cuts made in conjunction with restructuring.[23]

The proportion of prime-age male workers (age thirty-five to fifty-four years) who were permanently displaced from their jobs almost doubled between the 1970s and the early 1990s.[24] Displacement among college graduates was 18 percent higher in 1990–91 than in 1982–83. Using data from the Panel Study of Income Dynamics (PSID), researchers Boisjoly, Duncan, and Smeeding found that the rate of job loss was higher in 1980–92 than in 1968–79, even for older and more educated workers.[25] Job losses were also somewhat higher over the period for white-collar jobs. Overall, the percentage of people laid off rose by one-third during this period, while the percentage fired doubled.

Increases in the rate at which companies fired workers, as opposed to laying them off, became an important but less visible part of the change in employment security. Before IBM announced its first layoffs, for example, it had already doubled the rate at which workers were dismissed for poor performance. Nowhere was this change more noticeable than for executives who sometimes found that they were let go shortly after taking office either because the needs of the organization had changed or, in some cases, because the company had found someone better in the meantime. The risk of being cut spared no one. Robert "Teddy" Turner, the son of Turner Broadcasting's founder Ted Turner, was a senior executive in that company when he asked his father for a sense of how secure his job would be after the company was acquired by Time Warner. "You're toast," said Dad. And he was.[26]

The typical probation period for new managers has been cut in half in the 1990s, to three months, compared with the previous decade. An American Management Association survey taken in the early 1990s found that 22 percent of companies had fired managers with fewer than three months on the job, with the most common explanation being that competitive pressures were forcing them to make a perfect match between their needs and the executive. One company head who fired a new executive even before he arrived on the job explained, "With such a tremendous pool of talented people out there, you might as well get the one who will work out best." T. Quinn Spitzer, CEO of the Kepner-Tregoe consulting firm, observed that for those hiring in previous decades, "Your reputation was on the line if your hire didn't work out. So you did everything you could to make them better. Now, your reputation is on the line if you don't get rid of them fast enough."[27]

Other aspects of the change in employment security are illustrated by changes in the unemployment rate. Perhaps the most significant development has been the declining likelihood of recall from layoff or, to put it differently, the increase in permanent as opposed to temporary job loss. Layoffs in the past were associated with downturns in business cycles, where one could be expected to be recalled when business picked up. These have given way to permanent layoffs, as indicated in Figure 4-3. Ninety percent of the increase in unemployment during the last recession, 1990–91, was the result of permanent job losses.[28]

According to the Bureau of Labor Statistics, during 1992–93 only 15 percent of those laid off could expect recall, as compared with about

Figure 4-3. Job Loss by Recall Status

Source: Peter Cappelli, Change at Work (New York: Oxford University Press, 1997), 175.

44 percent in the previous four recessions. And half of those who eventually did find new jobs had to change industries to do so.[29]

Changes in the unemployment rate for white-collar workers also tell a story about the decline in the employment relationship for these traditionally more protected jobs. White-collar unemployment, relative to overall unemployment rates, has risen steadily since the 1980s. (See Figure 4-4.)

EMPLOYEE ATTITUDES. The place to begin investigating how the new deal affects employee attitudes, especially their commitment to the employer, is in the issue of breaking the old contract. There is little doubt, for example, that the decisions to downsize and unilaterally restructure other aspects of the employment relationship have had powerful effects on employee attitudes. The S.R.A. Corporation has conducted employee attitude surveys every year since the 1950s on approximately one-half million U.S. workers across a range of industries and employers. The scores on items that included satisfaction measures with various aspects of employment and commitment to the organiza-

Figure 4-4. Changes in the Unemployment Rate for White-Collar Workers

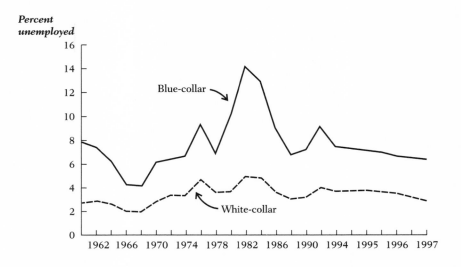

Source: Peter Cappelli, Change at Work *(New York: Oxford University Press, 1997), 174.*

tion were remarkably stable until the early 1980s when they began a sharp decline. By the mid-1980s, they were in a virtual free fall. Similar surveys conducted by the Mayflower Group, an informal collection of companies that compare employee attitude data, also registered a decline in employee satisfaction during the 1980s. The Ganz-Wiley survey of several thousand employees showed sharp declines in satisfaction with employment security between 1985 and 1996, especially among older employees.[30] Employee surveys conducted by Hay Associates also showed a sharp decline in employee attitudes beginning in the 1980s, especially in terms of commitment to the employer.[31] A national survey of approximately 1,800 employees by AON Consulting found sharp declines in employee commitment from 1995 to 1998 across jobs, industries, and demographic groups. About a quarter of the respondents in 1998 report that it would take less than a 10 percent salary increase for them to quit their current job and move to a new one.[32]

Middle managers appear to be the group that has experienced the sharpest drop in morale precisely because they appear to be the group whose contract with the organization had been among the strongest and has now been the most severely violated. They have fewer opportunities elsewhere, in part because middle managers are promoted from within, not hired from the outside. It is therefore no surprise that the surveys that break out attitudes by occupational group, such as the Hay surveys, find that middle managers have had the sharpest declines in morale, especially in areas measuring trust in the organization.

A survey of managers reported by *Training* magazine in 1997 suggests that managers do not even pretend to believe in commitment to the organization.[33] Only 2 percent reported that dedication to one's organization was now the key to success. Individual ambition, in contrast, was cited by 56 percent. Describing the sharp decline in employee commitment observed over time in his polls, Daniel Yankelovich notes that "Companies are unaware of the dreadful impact they are having. They don't realize they are violating an unwritten but important social contract they have with workers."[34]

Studies that relate management restructuring actions to measures of employee attitudes and morale, broadly defined, document the obvious, that they have a negative effect on employees. For example, a recent survey by the Wyatt company is one of many reporting that employee attitudes and perceptions of the employer across a wide range of issues were substantially lower in companies that had downsized compared with those which had not.[35] A survey of downsized firms by Right Associates found 74 percent reporting that workforce morale was low and distrust of management high.[36] The American Management Association found that 72 percent of the surveyed companies that had cut jobs were reporting an immediate and negative impact on morale. Nine percent reported an associated increase in absenteeism, and 13 percent an increase in disability claims.[37] In 1988, a survey by International Survey Research Corp. found that 33 percent of employees often did not believe what management said. By 1996, the number had risen to 40 percent.[38]

How do employees respond when these psychological contracts are violated? What are the consequences of the decline in morale? Whenever the members of one party believe that the other party has broken any kind of agreement, they not only feel cheated but feel the need for redress. With commercial contracts, the aggrieved party often seeks redress through the courts. There is no doubt that many of the lawsuits brought by workers who were the victims of restructuring programs were driven by the perception that the psychological contract had been violated, even though the actual suit is expressed in some other way consistent with the framework of labor law, such as age discrimination.

A vast body of research shows how employees react to perceptions of injustice in the workplace, especially when there are no legal or administrative avenues available for redress. They try to reestablish a fair exchange or a sense of equity themselves by changing how they work. A classic illustration was reported by the psychologist Jerry Greenberg in an insurance company when agents were assigned to new offices during a remodeling project. In this corporation, as in most, offices were an important symbol of status and a reward for good performance. But the temporary offices were assigned randomly, and some superior performers found themselves in low-level offices. Greenberg reports that the performance of these superstars tumbled after the assignment. They withdrew effort and performance to reestablish equity: "If you're going to treat me badly, I'm not going to perform."[39] Other studies also show that quit rates and virtually every measure of performance suffer when employees perceive that they have been treated unfairly.[40]

A series of studies by Professor Sandra Robinson and her colleagues examine perceptions of psychological contracts and their breach.[41] Among recent MBAs hired into their first job after graduation, for example, she found that they see their employers as having substantial obligations to them, and they trust that those obligations will be honored. When those obligations were breached, the employees responded by reducing their own obligations and self-reported measures of performance and commitment. (The more trust the employees had in their employer initially, however, the less likely they were to perceive breaches in the employer's obligations.)[42]

Studies like these examine cases in which the breach of an employer's obligations was at the level of an individual employee, in which the employer did something direct and immediate that changed an individual's job. The likely reaction of employees to a breach of implicit contracts that govern the workforce as a whole, such as an end to implicit job security, is a different issue. What is the experience of surviving employees after a downsizing or other restructuring efforts, for example?

It would be reasonable to assume that employees would withdraw their voluntary cooperation and implicit support of company goals if they perceived that the psychological contract had been broken. The effective operation of company management could very well grind to a halt. Employee resistance is thought by executives to be far and away the most important barrier to change in organizations, cited by 58 percent of respondents in a recent Wyatt survey.[43] And, some critics argue, that is the Achilles heel of the whole trend toward restructuring companies.

In one study, researchers surveyed 597 employees of a national chain of small retail stores in the early 1990s that had closed many of its outlets during the previous twelve months. Those employees experiencing the most intense distress from the restructuring had the greatest decline in work performance.[44] Other research suggests that restructuring undermines employee attachments to the firm and makes recruiting and retaining employees more difficult. One early 1990s study of managers at seventeen Fortune 500 companies, for example, reported that managers who had survived a restructuring process focused more on their own careers and less on organizational goals.[45] Anecdotal reports of sabotage and especially theft seem tied to the employee sense of injustice associated with changing employment relationships. Frank Johns, the managing director of Pinkerton Risk Assessment Services, describes the growing problem of hi-tech theft: "It's a lot easier for [an employee] to say, 'Hell, they aren't paying me a lot. These chips are going by me, and they're making those SOBs rich. Why shouldn't I take a few?'"[46]

Despite these specific examples, however, the more aggregate data suggest that on average firms did not pay much of a price for downsizing or restructuring their companies in terms of decreasing employee performance. Not all studies even find that employee attitudes suffer. One examined the relationship between different aspects of restructuring and employee reactions and found that none of them were associated with reduced loyalty to the organization, not even downsizing. In general, restructuring made employees focus on their careers and made them identify more with a career that extended beyond their current employer, but that apparently did not lead to any reduction in loyalty toward their current employer.[47]

While most studies do find declines in morale and attitude when companies restructure, it is much more difficult to find evidence that employee and company *performance* decline when companies break the old employment contract.[48] The 1994 AMA survey on downsizing, for instance, found that while 86 percent of companies that had downsized reported a decline in employee morale, employee productivity rose or held constant in 70 percent of downsized companies, and profits rose or held constant in 80 percent.[49] (See Table 4-1.) A Wyatt Company survey of employers that had restructured found adverse effects on workloads (62 percent), morale (56 percent), and commitment (52 per-

Table 4-1. Consequences of Downsizing

- After-effects of downsizing
- Reported by 870 HR managers in firms that experienced one or more spells of downsizing during 1988–1993

	Declined	Remained constant	Increased
Operating Profits	20%	24%	45%
Worker Productivity	22%	38%	34%
Employee Morale	80%	13%	2%

Source: *American Management Association, 1994 AMA Survey on Downsizing (New York: American Management Association, 1994).*

cent) but sharp reductions in costs (68 percent of those who saw this as a goal of restructuring), increases in productivity (59 percent of those seeing this as a goal), improvements in service levels (77 percent), and increases in the competence of the workforce (72 percent).[50] (See Figure 4-5.) Another AMA survey found that short-term profits were either constant or increased in 85 percent of downsizing companies.[51] Only 1 percent of managers reported that they were dissatisfied with the results of downsizing, while 79 percent were either very or somewhat satisfied.[52]

The apparent absence of performance effects has led to a certain amount of revisionism of what's been called the "happy worker" model—which is based on the idea that happy workers are more productive—as some psychologists begin to question whether there are links between worker satisfaction or stress levels and performance.[53] Presumably because there has been so little impact on organizational performance,

Figure 4-5. Consequences of Restructuring

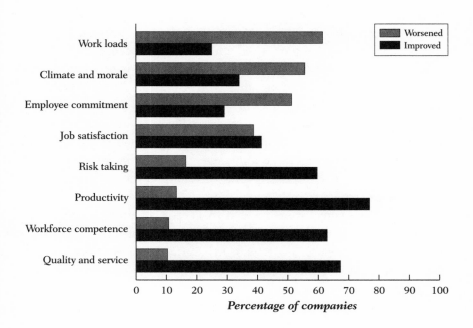

Source: Peter Cappelli, Change at Work (New York: Oxford University Press, 1997), 57.

management does not generally seem worried about the decline in worker attitudes. Employee morale ranked eighth out of a possible nine management priorities for the future in a Conference Board survey of executives.[54] In the Kepner-Tregoe survey, while executives reported that the most troubling issue for the future was "people issues," such as commitment (50 percent), less than 4 percent reported that these issues were among their goals for the next year. Human resource executives admit in private that concerns about declining morale had little effect on top management decision making. Indeed, some suggest that if employee attitudes had not suffered, there was a sense at the top of organizations that painful restructuring had not gone far enough.[55]

PERFORMANCE COSTS, AND WHY THERE SEEM TO BE NONE

The obvious question is, why did the performance of employees and their organizations not crumble given the massive and unilateral breach of the employment contract represented by more than a decade of downsizing and restructuring?

Part of the answer is that what employees experience when these contracts are broken seems to depend not simply on what happens to them—a downsizing or a plant closing—but also on why it happens and how it is carried out. Employees are more willing to accept the breaking of agreements like psychological contracts if the pressure to do so comes from outside the organization—that is, if it appears to be beyond the control of employer and employee.[56] An employer that abandons life-time employment security is much more likely to be forgiven if the reason is a collapse in the demand for its product than if it is a goal to achieve a higher return on an equity target set by the board of directors. At IBM's Endicott, New York plant, for example, the employees were willing to accept downsizing when the company as a whole was struggling and cost savings were needed to keep it financially afloat. But when downsizing was directed at creating space for new skills, a purely internal concern that also cut against the prior norm of internal development, it led to a union organizing campaign.

Columbia professor Joel Brockner found that the experience of surviving layoffs does not necessarily translate into decreased performance. It seems to depend on how downsizings and related changes are carried out: If they are perceived as being fair, if the procedure for selecting those let go was equitable and their severance is reasonable, then employees remain committed to the organization and can be just as responsible as they were before the restructuring.[57]

Two other, no doubt complementary explanations are also given for the apparent absence of a relationship between the breaking of the traditional employment relationship and performance. The first concerns other changes that occur in the workplace as part of these restructuring efforts. Employers clearly abandoned job security, employee development, and long-term commitments to employees, but the process of restructuring seems to have made the remaining jobs themselves more satisfying to employees.

A survey of 12,000 managers worldwide found a sharp decline in loyalty and commitment to employers from early 1980 to the mid 1990s. Interestingly, the respondents were more satisfied with their work than with their employer.[58] While about two-thirds of employees in another national survey were satisfied with their jobs, 60 percent reported that they were less committed to their organization than they had been ten years earlier.[59] And the Wyatt survey in Figure 4-5 found that despite employee perceptions of insecurity, greater workloads, and reduced commitment, their job satisfaction in the restructured companies on average increased.[60] Another survey found that companies that had restructured and downsized were more likely to have introduced work redesign measures.[61]

The downsized General Electric engine plant in Lynn, Massachusetts, illustrates how downsizing and new work systems can go together, how job satisfaction can increase even while other attitudes seem to get worse. Employment had been cut by half during the early 1980s, and those still on the payroll feared additional rounds of layoffs. At the same time, they found the reorganized work system, with its flatter organization, increased teamwork, and increased employee empowerment, to be more engaging and collegial. While they worried about the decreased job security, they appreciated the new work arrangements that helped make them more productive.[62]

A detailed study of restructuring at one of the regional Bell operating companies produced a similar conclusion. A survey of employees revealed that the company's extensive restructuring had led to increased workloads and reduced job security but also to expanded work responsibilities and job discretion. Because of competitive market pressures, this firm had undertaken extensive restructuring, including substantial downsizing of its managerial ranks. Ninety-three percent of middle managers reported that their workloads had intensified during the past several years. Three-fifths now had more overtime or take-home work than they desired. Ninety-two percent of the middle managers reported reduced job security, 89 percent saw fewer promotion opportunities, and 80 percent saw less job mobility. Fewer than two in ten now expressed satisfaction with their job security or career opportunities. At the same time, a majority reported that they had more discretion to meet customer needs, that they participated in cross-functional or problem-solving teams, and that they had substantial control over their work tasks, procedures, and pace. Seven in ten expressed satisfaction with their jobs and the work, while a similar proportion expressed *dis*satisfaction with their employment and career prospects.[63]

These studies indicate that while companies were shredding the long-term employment contract, they were also making changes in the way jobs were performed. The happy coincidence is that workers became more satisfied with their jobs as well as more productive. The negative effects of breaking that contract are still there, such as greater stress and reduced commitment, but they might be offset somewhat by the positive effects of new job designs.

The other, more important, explanation for the fact that employers apparently paid such a small price for breaking the old contract has to do once again with the market. The important mechanisms for reacting against perceived inequity, as when an implicit employment contract has been violated, are all tempered by opportunities in the labor market. There is extensive research showing, for example, that people quit jobs mainly when they can move to new ones. When the labor market is slack, as it was for managers in particular all through the downsizing period, there was little freedom to quit. There is also considerable evidence that worker discipline is tied to the state of the labor market. For example, I examined the discipline problems across auto plants in the United States, related them to local economic conditions, and found that, controlling for other factors, discipline rates were lower when the local unemployment rate was higher.[64] It may be that employees are more careful about infractions such as absenteeism when the potential costs of getting fired are greater, as when the opportunities for finding a new job are worse. Particularly when the fear of layoffs is in the air, no employee wants to risk dismissal by reducing their performance, even if they feel perfectly justified on equity grounds to do so. And it may be that employees see fewer things to grumble about when many people in their community and in their peer group are out of work altogether. Because employees feel that they have no redress against the broken psychological contract—they cannot reduce their own performance or risk being fired, yet they cannot quit—their morale falls and stress rises. They are still tied to the company because they feel they have to be, and their performance does not decline because they are afraid of being fired.

The fact that virtually all employers were restructuring at the same time further reduced employee resentment. A company violating the psychological contract might be expected to lose talented workers to other employers who maintained that contract. But are there any major employers still operating under the old contract? If other companies are restructuring at the same time, the causes seem more external and, as noted above, more easily accepted. Some part of employee attitudes is based on comparisons with their experiences before restructuring, but an important part is also based on comparisons with what they see going on outside their firm, with friends and family in jobs elsewhere. One of the more interesting anecdotes about employee relations is that the highest levels of employee morale were recorded during the Great Depression. Despite the fact that employers were cutting wages, increasing workloads, and often being arbitrary and capricious in their demands, employees could not help but be influenced by the crowds of unemployed who would be happy to have any job, including theirs.[65]

The "happy worker" model of employee behavior, mentioned earlier in the chapter, was a basic tenet of business school course work. It was based on research from social psychology, and it said, in brief, that the best way to keep workers productive was to keep them happy, that satisfied and committed employees were the key to performance. While it is difficult for many of us to admit, that model more or less went out the window in the 1980s and was replaced by what might be called the "frightened worker" model. Fear of job loss and comparisons with displaced employees have kept worker performance up and both discipline problems and turnover down. The frightened worker model is, of course, an old argument that goes back at least to Karl Marx, who observed how the supply of unemployed workers in Victorian England, the "reserve army of the unemployed," helped ensure discipline among those who did have jobs.

The sharp declines in morale may have been exacerbated because the labor market constraints prevented employees from lowering their performance standards. It is because employees *cannot* act out their frustration with the break in the psychological contract by quitting or shirking responsibilities that their perceptions of injustice, dissatisfaction, and stress continue to rise. If an organization acted alone to downsize and restructure, breaking its psychological contract with employees, one might expect those employees to vote with their feet and go elsewhere. Indeed, this is the argument used to suggest how internal labor markets counter employer "opportunism," because an employer that breaks its side of the agreement—as so many appear to have done—would suffer reputational effects that would hinder its ability to recruit and retain workers. But reputations are all relative. When most organizations appear to be downsizing at the same time, a company's reputation does not suffer from doing so. And for employees, there is no place to go. The fact that one's employer is continuing to look for jobs and for employees to cut from the rolls makes it very risky to act out one's frustrations. Empirical studies document the general point: morale and employee satisfaction matter in determining whether employees quit, but only when there are places for them to go.[66]

Do employees whose jobs are explicitly temporary or contingent have lower levels of commitment and performance? The assumption is that workers with less attachment to the employer, an even weaker psychological contract, will be less committed and less likely to act in the interests of the employer when they have some discretion. The answer is relevant, because all jobs may be more contingent now and because the percentage of the workforce with an explicitly contingent relationship to employers—such as temporary help, short-term contracts, or part-time—is now higher.

Once again, the apparently obvious relationship turns out not to be so. Most studies find that contingent workers are just as committed to the organization they work for as full-time employees (sometimes even more so) and that their willingness to act in the interests of the organization is just as great. Some evidence suggests that the contingent workers may experience conflict between their own desire for closer affiliation with company, to be a good team player, and the limitations on involvement spelled out in their employment contracts. But they still seem as committed to the company as full-time employees, despite the fact that they are much less definitely attached to the company.[67] How can this be?

Part of the explanation has to do with the fact that the contingent workers have just signed on. As noted earlier, new hires have a much greater sense that they own the company—not the reverse. I discovered something similar in my own research on pay plans: new hires brought in under lower, two-tier wage plans were nevertheless happier with their pay than the more senior workers operating under the higher wage schedule because for the new hires, this job beat all of their alternatives. They compared their jobs to jobs in the outside market, not to senior workers in the company.[68] In this case, the contingent workers are like new hires, not expecting much and glad to be there. Of course, one reason why "permanent" and "contingent" workers have similar attitudes may be because they see little difference in their situations now. In fact, a recent study found that only about 20 percent of contract employees actually see their jobs as being contingent in the sense of unstable or at risk.[69]

While it may seem obvious that breaking the old psychological contract will lead to problems from employees in the workplace, the fact is that such problems have been remarkably rare. The view that the restructuring mill will grind to a halt because of the collapse of employee commitment and the withdrawal of cooperation has proven false. The main factor mitigating these problems, however, was a labor surplus, and that situation is transient. Labor shortages that create plentiful job opportunities and relieve some of the fear of job loss might well unleash some of that pent-up resentment and a wave of quits for jobs elsewhere.

How long an employee and employer stay together is another measure of the stability of the employment relationship, one that is obviously related to downsizing. If there is an overall decline in job security in the United States because of downsizing and the churning of the workforce, we might expect to see a reduction in the average length of time that an employee spends with an employer. Only part of the changes in job tenure are driven by employer decisions to dismiss workers, however. The other and empirically more important factor is employee decisions to quit, typically for jobs elsewhere. The importance of voluntary quits in shaping average tenure makes it a poor proxy for job security, although tenure remains an important measure of how stable jobs are.

A flurry of academic research in the mid-1990s examined whether average rates of job tenure have changed and produced remarkably contradictory results that seem to vary almost perfectly with the data being used.[70] The conclusion from these initial reports was that probably not much had changed even while reports from within companies were suggesting that employee turnover was rising sharply.[71] More recent studies using data from the mid-1990s suggest that, indeed, something has changed. A simple, overall picture of job stability is hard to capture, but some of the main trends are as follows. The overall length of time that the average employee stays with a given employer was quite constant until the mid-1990s, when it appears to have eroded. The experience of particular groups within the population, however, may have changed a great deal. Because women are now less likely to quit their jobs when they get married or have children,[72] their job tenure has have increased over time, albeit for reasons that have nothing to do with employer behavior.[73] Average tenure for men is much more likely to show a decline over time. This is particularly so for those with less education and for those who have been on their job only a few years. Studies that compare cohorts over time seem to find the biggest changes—such as a 10 percent increase in the rate of job changes for younger workers—now as compared with earlier decades.[74] They also find large declines in tenure for older, white men in particular, the group most protected by internal labor markets. For example, for men approaching retirement age (fifty-eight to sixty-three), only 29 percent had been with the same employer for ten years or more as compared with a figure of 47 percent in 1969.[75] Even some of the studies that previously found little change for this group now find evidence of reasonably dramatic declines in more recent data especially for managerial and professional employees.[76] The most recent studies find that the percentage of the workforce with long-tenure jobs, of ten years or more, declined slightly from the late 1970s through 1993 and then fell sharply through the current period. They are now at the lowest level in twenty years.[77]

How much average tenure has changed may be less interesting for the purposes of understanding the employment relationship than why it has changed—specifically, how much has been driven by the employer. Figure 4-6 illustrates how permanent dismissals and voluntary quits have moved in opposite directions over the past two decades, with the former rising and the latter declining.[78]

Quits and dismissals tend to move in opposite directions: When the labor market is tight, more workers quit but fewer are dismissed. When it is slack, fewer quit but more are dismissed. That is one important reason why overall tenure rates have some built-in stability.

The studies that examine *why* a job ended indicate that, compared with earlier decades, the rate of dismissals is higher now than before the 1980s, and the quit rate, at least until recently, has been lower. Permanent dismissals rose through the 1980s and early 1990s while quit rates were falling.[79] One study found that the rate of dismissals increased sharply for older workers with more tenure, doubling for workers age forty-five to fifty-five. And while the probability of getting a new job was no different for employees who left on their own as compared with earlier periods, it was noticeably worse for those who were dismissed.[80]

When the question asks how frequently an individual employee has changed occupations, as opposed to employers, the results are very different. The attachment to an occupation now appears much stronger than that to an employer. If anything, workers seem to be staying in the same occupation longer now than in the past.[81] While workers were much more likely to change employers in the 1980s and 1990s, they were likely to keep their occupation.

The trends of declining attachment to employers but increasing

Figure 4-6. New Permanent Dismissals as a Share of Employment (Monthly)

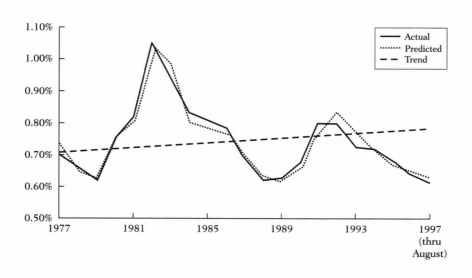

Source: Federal Reserve Bank of San Francisco. Reprinted with permission from "Job Security Update," by Rob Valletta, FRBSF Economic Letter, No. 97-34 (November 14, 1997).

attachment to occupation go together in a straightforward way. In the traditional, internal model of the employment relationship, managerial employees in particular would routinely change careers at the direction of the company. The IBM model of having a career without focusing on a functional area was typical: Moving from a staff job in marketing to plant management in the field and back to headquarters in the strategy group was a reasonably common career path that was facilitated by lots of training. The declining corporate interest in relocating employees noted in Chapter 3 is evidence of the decline in this model of employee development.

When employees leave a company for a job elsewhere, in contrast, they almost always stay in the same general occupation. When a corporate headhunter approaches a marketing manager with an offer to move, you can be reasonably sure that it is about a marketing position elsewhere and not a finance or accounting job. Employers who hire experienced workers are looking to bring in specific skills, not raw talent that they can train to do something else. As employees spend less time in a given company, there is less opportunity for them to change careers; as employees move more frequently across companies, they are more likely to stay in the same occupation. The implications of this important development for individuals and for the management of employees are considered below.

CONTINGENT WORK AND CONTRACTING OUT

Much of the anecdotal attention given to changes at work concerns the shift of work from "permanent" jobs to contractors, leased employees, and part-time and temporary workers. The term *contingent* was given to these jobs to reflect the fact that they are likely to be much less stable and secure than regular jobs, more contingent on the short-term needs of the organization. Replacing permanent workers with contingent employees has been part of the effort to squeeze out the fixed costs of employment and increase flexibility. One survey indicates that at least half of all temp use stems from spikes in demand, such as special projects or peak seasons. These efforts redistribute the job instability from a permanent workforce to the temporaries. Companies like Revcor, which makes electric fans, found that it was regularly staffing up and then laying off its workforce to meet seasonal demands. It shifted its approach and now has three hundred permanent employees whose jobs are quite secure and a hundred temps whose positions are predictably temporary, coming and going with seasonal demand.[82] Kurt Manufacturing Company, a computer industry machining company, uses the same approach and even manages to integrate the temps into TQM programs. The arrangement works because the company has been able to get the same group of temp workers every time, a situation made possible by slack labor markets.[83]

The most ironic examples of temping occur when companies hire back as temporary workers those employees they have laid off, often to do the same work they did as permanent employees. A study by the U.S. Department of Labor found that 17 percent of the temps surveyed had a "previous, different relationship" with their current employer, and an AMA survey of employers found that 30 percent brought back employees who had been downsized. Typically, they brought the employees back to work on a contract basis, although in some cases they were rehired. At companies like Pacific Bell, 80 percent of temps are former permanent employees who sometimes earn more per hour than they did before. The staffing flexibility this gives the employer compensates for the extra cost.[84] Other companies use their retirees as temps, and there are even agencies, like Retiree Skills in Tucson, which only place temps over age fifty. Even in these situations, where the temps already have long-term ties to the company, employers are cautious about keeping a temp relationship with workers for very long for fear of creating expectations about long-term employment. Companies like WorldSpan, an airline reservation company, has a policy of keeping temps for only one year. KLA Instruments, an inspection equipment manufacturer in Silicon Valley, audits its temp arrangements every six months, as in zero-based budgeting, to see if they are still needed.[85]

The expansion of temporary help from its traditional roots in clerical functions into professional and executive jobs has been rapid. (See Figure 4-7). Companies like Lab Support provide temporary scientists and technicians, Attorneys Per Diem offers temp lawyers, Advanced Technical Resources focuses on engineers and programmers, Interim Services offers doctors, and Imcor supplies executives. As the supply of temp professionals gets more predictable, the need for companies to develop and manage their own professional workforce internally erodes. As Imcor's president John Thompson observed, "What's core today can be considered contingent tomorrow."[86] It also creates new opportunities for doing business in different ways. In the United Kingdom, for example, the availability of temporary executives has helped change the way banks deal with troubled creditors. Rather than sending accountants to the headquarters of struggling client companies to monitor finances and, in the worst cases, begin disposing of assets, banks now send in temporary executives with the aim of straightening out the problems.[87]

Figure 4-7. Statistics for Temporary Professionals and Managers

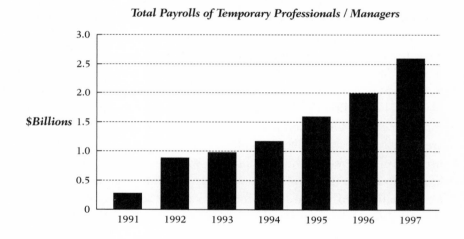

Total Payrolls of Temporary Professionals / Managers

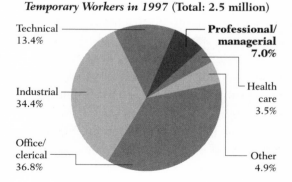

Temporary Workers in 1997 (Total: **2.5 million**)

Technical 13.4%

Professional/ managerial 7.0%

Industrial 34.4%

Health care 3.5%

Office/ clerical 36.8%

Other 4.9%

Source: *National Association of Temporary and Staffing Services.* The New York Times, *6 June 1998, D1. Copyright © 1998 by* The New York Times. *Reprinted by permission.*

The most advanced efforts to integrate contingent employees into the existing organization take place at companies like DuPont, where research and development teams, at the core of the company's competency, include temp scientists and technicians. DuPont's incentive for including temps in these teams was, once again, the need for speed and flexibility, to get the teams up and running quickly by bringing in the skills that were not available in-house and then to change the skills in the team as the project evolved. DuPont treats the temp and permanent team members as equally as possible but also makes it clear that the temp positions will not be (and never have been) a means to a permanent position in the company. DuPont argues that the temporariness of these positions helps workers focus their attention on the project instead of directing it toward longer-term career goals. The Henkel company hires temps exclusively for the technicians who work side by side with its researchers. Henkel makes a similar argument, that this is a means to acquire the most up-to-date skills and keep them current.[88] These strategies are only possible, however, because of a slack labor market that has kept the temp scientists and technicians from finding permanent jobs.

Exactly how extensive contingent work is in the economy is a subject of intense debate. Richard Belous received a great deal of attention when he estimated that in 1988 contingent workers represented from 25 to 30 percent of the U.S. labor force, a figure that includes temporary and part-time workers as well as business services that include contract workers.[89] While there was substantial criticism of that calculation because of the definition (many contract workers, such as business consultants, do not appear to be contingent in the usual sense) and possible double counting (for example, some of those working part-time are also temps), more recent studies have come up with reasonably similar figures. A 1993 estimate by the U.S. Census Bureau put the number at 25 percent, with a tighter definition of contract employees. A 1997 estimate of the contingent workforce found part-time work at 17.5 percent, self-employed at 11.8 percent, and temporary employees at 1.8 percent of the workforce, for a total of 31.1 percent.[90] Some 78 percent of employers use contingent workers—a full 72 percent use part-time—and 40 percent expect their use of these workers to grow.[91]

Part-time work may not seem to be contingent in the same sense that temporary work is, as it may often be both regular and permanent.

Such jobs are common at companies like United Parcel Service, where they are represented by unions and come with attractive wages and benefits. The Teamsters strike against UPS in August 1997 helped focus attention on the growth of part-time work at that company. A privately held company, UPS always prided itself on its internal promotion opportunities. Virtually all of the managers and executives at UPS began their careers driving trucks. It was the epitome of the internally oriented employment system. In recent years, however, it has greatly expanded the use of part-time employees. It has hired 500,000 part-time workers since 1993. These part-time jobs are cost-effective for the company because the workflow of delivering packages, particularly at the distribution centers where most are employed, peaks at very predictable times. With part-time positions, the company pays employees only when the work needs to be done. Employees in these jobs can bid to secure full-time jobs, but the queue to secure such positions is enormous. Since 1993, only 13,000 of the workers hired as part-time employees have advanced in the company.[92] What has happened at UPS, as well as at many other companies, is that a growing proportion of the workforce has been shifted to part-time jobs that are permanent and regular but that offer poor prospects for advancement either within the company or elsewhere.

Contingent workers are paid less on average than permanent employees. They account for almost 60 percent of the bottom decile of the wage distribution in the United States—that is, of the working poor. Temporary workers earn about 14 percent less than permanent workers and are about half as likely to receive any employer-provided health care. But because companies pay fees to agencies that are about 40 percent of the wages that temps receive, lower labor costs are rarely cited as reasons for using temps. In an employer survey, only 20 percent reported that their hourly costs were lower for temps, contract workers, or part-timers. Instead, they reported that their demand for these contingent workers is driven by the need for flexibility.[93]

Most of the attention to the topic of contingent work has been given to the temporary workers, because their relationship with employers seems to be the most clearly contingent and because their numbers have been rising at an incredible 11 percent per year since 1972. Unpublished data from the Bureau of Labor Statistics suggests that 2,071,200 workers were employed as temps in 1995.[94] Most estimates suggest that temps account for just under 2 percent of total employment, but

Katharine Abraham estimates that including the temporary workers employed directly by companies, not through agencies, would more than double the official figures.[95] Comparisons of the temp workforce with permanent employees suggest that temps are younger by about two years, are on average slightly better educated, and have almost four times the amount of unemployment. The biggest change in the temp workforce in recent years has been the rise of men, from 24 percent of the total in 1988 to 39 percent five years later.

Certainly some part of the rise in these more contingent jobs reflects the preferences of some workers for more flexible schedules, but the evidence indicates that most of the growth is the result of changing employer demands.[96] This is clearest for part-time workers. Three-quarters of the part-time workforce would rather have full-time jobs.[97] Researchers Leete and Schor found that all those who would like to work more hours but are unable to do so (involuntary part-time and the unemployed) as a group doubled from 1969 to 1989, when they constituted 14.5 percent of the labor force.[98] Other estimates suggest modest increases since then.[99] Approximately 4 percent of all U.S. workers are in this involuntary part-time category. Of the twenty industrialized countries that form the Organization for Economic Cooperation and Development (OECD), only the Netherlands has a higher figure, and its overall levels of unemployment are considerably higher.[100]

The National Association of Temporary and Staffing Services, the industry association, reports that customers of its firms believe that getting the flexibility from the workforce they need to compete is the key factor driving the demand for temporary help.[101] Researchers Mangum, Mayhall, and Nelson report that it was the largest firms, with more than 1,000 employees (those most likely to have internal labor markets) that made far and away the greatest use of temporary help.[102] A more recent study reported similar findings, that the firms that have less developed internalized employment systems and less firm-specific training are more likely to use temps and contractors.[103] Employers may also push jobs out to contractors or temporary agencies as a way of differentiating employment contracts without appearing to divide their own "core" workforce. Companies that have generous benefits policies and want to treat all of their employees as family find that they can keep labor costs down by contracting out low-wage janitorial or cafeteria jobs, thereby reducing the size of their "family."

For employees, temporary help in particular appears to have become the de facto entry-level position for the labor force (companies like DuPont notwithstanding). The industry reports that 29 percent of temps were getting more than twenty hours of training from their agency. A survey conducted by the National Association of Temporary and Staffing Services found that 76 percent of temporary workers believe that temporary help is "a way to get a full-time job" and was an important factor in their decision to become a temp. Thirty-eight percent have been offered a full-time job at the organization where they were assigned. This 38 percent represents those workers who were offered permanent jobs and turned them down; some other group offered such positions took them and are therefore out of the temp workforce and out of the survey.[104] Census data suggests that 57 percent of the workers in temporary jobs in a given year were in permanent jobs the next year.

It is a relatively small step from reliance on temps to handle what had been tasks performed by permanent workers to turning entire functions over to the companies that manage those temps. Companies like Pitney Bowes have long managed mailrooms for corporate clients, and Xerox and Kodak operated photocopying departments for other companies. The expansion of these efforts into new areas is a popular trend known as "Vendor on Premises," where contractors take over more central and diverse operations for clients. Companies like Norrell, for example, run entire clerical operations for companies like IBM, UPS, and Equitable.[105] Like Manpower and other large temporary help firms, they also provide company-specific training for the temp workers going on site to the bigger contractors, getting them comfortable with a contractor's systems, for example. Satisfaction with contractors has also been rising during the 1990s.[106]

The arguments presented in Chapter 3 suggest that the need to concentrate on core competencies and reduce fixed costs were the key factors in turning to outside suppliers. One study of contracting concluded that firms in high-wage industries were more likely to contract out low-wage work, while those firms in low-wage industries were more apt to contract out high-wage functions,[107] suggesting that they push off to contractors those functions which do not fit well with their own organization.

Estimates of the extent of contracting out are hard to find, but one survey conducted by the Bureau of National Affairs found 57 percent of firms used contractors to provide services that could be performed by employees.[108] Another survey found that 9 percent had contractors in management and supervisory positions. Researchers Mishel and Bernstein report that 78 percent of employers used independent contractors to do work in 1989 that would have been done by employees, up substantially from 1986.[109]

The rise of consulting firms also represents some evidence of the growing importance of outsourcing, or contract work, at the professional end of the distribution. In the early 1980s, for example, management consulting accounted for a relatively minor share of the recruiting of MBA graduates at schools like Wharton. By 1990, 26 percent of the graduating class were heading for jobs in management consulting. By 1996, that figure had grown to more than 40 percent. Employment in the "business services" industry, which includes consulting firms, has grown 6.9 percent per year since 1972, more than twice as fast as the growth rate in the economy as a whole. Across the economy as a whole over the past two decades, employers expanded their use of business services considerably faster than they brought in new employees.[110]

How contracting out affects the employment relationship in the economy is an interesting question. Certainly the decision to contract out a function affects those employees currently performing that function. And if the choice of what should be contracted out or conducted inside changes over time, then these adjustments will continue over time.

But if an employer contracts its data processing out to another large firm, for example, jobs simply move from one large employer to another. After the initial job losses have been absorbed at the parent company, has there really been any significant long-term change in employment relationships? Consider DuPont's recent decision to outsource most of its information systems work to Computer Sciences and Andersen Consulting; 3,000 DuPont information systems employees will change employers, 2,600 to Computer Sciences and 400 to Andersen. They will do more or less the same work, in many cases even in the same location. Both Computer Sciences and Andersen Consulting are huge companies with 44,000 and 45,000 employees, respectively.[111] What's the difference?

Even in examples like this one, the employment relationship has changed in important ways. Many contractors, like temporary help agencies, have very casual, arm's-length relationships with their employees. Thirty-seven percent of the employees of temporary help agencies, for example, work for more than one agency.[112] For these workers, the employment relationship is very much like an organized open market, a hiring hall. For those contractors with a more permanent attachment to their employees, the nature of the internal employment structures may still be very different. For example, a cleaning service that provides janitors for businesses has a very simple job ladder—janitor, supervisor, manager. The ability to develop a career in that company is limited; the ability to change careers and move into a different field, as is common in corporate life, is virtually impossible.

Similar arguments could be made about more sophisticated operations such as consulting or law firms. The ability to get exposure to other functions and to work one's way up a hierarchy, to learn different skills, and to essentially change careers may be very limited even in large contracting firms because they focus on only one task, such as data processing. The move toward single-purpose employers may be part of the explanation for the finding noted above that employees are now more likely to stay with an occupation even though they are less likely to stay with the same employer. The research on displaced workers, for example, shows that professional service firms have among the lowest rates of job loss of any sector of the economy.[113] Among the explanations for this may be the fact that such firms are more protected from business risks because they take in a portfolio of business from many sources. And because they are single-purpose organizations, they do not have many of the restructuring opportunities present in more typical firms, such as outsourcing options or rearranging core competencies. The partnership governance structure of professional service firms in particular reduces the pressure to squeeze fixed costs out of the system in the way that publicly held firms have experienced.

PROTECTING THE CORE

Could the move toward more contingent work and contracting out functions actually lead to greater stability for the permanent employees who remain? In this view, job security is explicitly redistributed away from a core of permanent employees toward more casual workers on the periphery. The example of Hewlett-Packard, where outsourcing is manipulated to maintain stable employment and product market strategies are chosen to reduce employment swings (for instance, avoiding contract work), has long been a teaching case illustrating how business strategy can help ensure job stability.[114] Detailed arguments about how firms can buffer employees from job insecurity have also been popular, most recently in the form of Charles Handy's arguments about the "Shamrock Organization," which has several different sets of relationships with different employee groups, including one that protects its most valuable, core employees.[115]

These arguments begin with the assertion that production systems are under pressure to change in order to adapt to new economic circumstances. Employers need a workforce that can be flexible and can adapt quickly and easily to new demands, and the best way to achieve that is to create a "peripheral" workforce of employees that can be adjusted to meet changes in demand conditions. These include employees who can be easily replaced (based on their labor supply), part-time and contingent workers, and subcontracting arrangements.

Most of the contemporary debate about the core-periphery model has been in Britain, where the contingent workforce is of significant size and has clearly been growing.[116] But these changes have been under way there for several decades and do not seem to be the result of a conscious core-periphery strategy. Less than 10 percent of the workforce is with employers that report having a conscious core-periphery labor strategy.[117] Seventy percent of U.K. employers surveyed reported that their organizations had been restructured between 1993 and 1995 alone, reshaping the workforce in the process.[118] In Australia, there is some evidence that employment relationships have shifted over time away from the permanent employment model.[119] But there is little evidence that Australian firms have moved toward the flexibility model associated with core-periphery arguments.[120] In New Zealand, part-time work increased, and the projected use of casual workers and contractors in particular rose through the early 1990s, with little evidence that employers were pursuing a core-periphery strategy.[121]

In the United States, the most compelling evidence against the notion that employers are pursuing a strategy of protecting some segment of their workforce is the fact that downsizing efforts, as noted above, increasingly strike at employees who seem to be in the "core" of the workforce—management positions and older and more educated employees are more likely to be targeted than in the past, and early retirement and related programs, which continue to be widespread, pull workers out of the workforce based on their own preferences, irrespective of their relationship to any "core." In Katharine Abraham's survey, employers were asked about their reasons for using temporary help, outsourcing, and subcontracting. "Providing a buffer for regular staff against downturns in demand" was one of the least frequently cited explanations for these changes. Of the nine options, only the inability to recruit regular employees was cited less often (respondents were free to cite more than one choice).[122]

WORK ORGANIZATION

The way work and tasks are organized creates job and promotion ladders, opportunities for skill acquisition, and other characteristics that are central features of internalized employment systems. The evidence indicates clearly that sweeping changes in these arrangements are under way that are helping to change employment relationships.

Despite decades of arguments from academics and a series of well-publicized experiments, it was still a novelty through the early 1980s to organize work in ways that differed from the traditional scientific management approach described in Chapter 2. The highly influential "America's Choice" report, sponsored by the National Center on Education and the Economy, which described skill and education challenges, estimated that only about 5 percent of the workplaces in the United States in the 1980s organized work around principles of empowering employees and reducing supervision.[123]

A survey of the Fortune 1,000 firms by the Government Accounting Office in 1987 was repeated in 1990 and indicates how quickly change was occurring. In 1987, for example, 72 percent of the firms surveyed reported that they had no self-managed work teams. Three years later, that figure had fallen to 53 percent. The percentage of firms making no effort at job enrichment to redesign the tasks of individual workers also fell from 40 to 25 percent over the same period.[124]

Two years later, Paul Osterman's survey found that 55 percent of all establishments have teams and that 41 percent have them for a majority of their "core" workers—those directly involved in producing the final product; 43 percent have job rotation; 41 percent have quality circles; and a third have total quality management.[125] Establishments that had these practices also had little or no direct supervision of employees, cutting the ranks of management. They are also more likely to have profit-sharing plans and pay-for-skill programs that make compensation more contingent and to have more cross-training, but—most important—not employment security. In other words, companies were moving toward an employment model that empowered workers but also pushed more risk onto them. And two years after the Osterman survey, a 1994 establishment survey conducted by the Bureau of the Census for the National Center on the Educational Quality of the Workforce also reported high levels of participation in these new work systems.[126]

These developments relate to internalized employment practices in a powerful way. Teams, quality circles, and other efforts that transfer autonomy to employees reduce the need for supervision. Supervisory jobs and the middle management positions that support them disappear as well. Autonomous teams and especially job rotation also break down narrow job descriptions. In the work organization reform going on in auto plants, for example, the number of job titles in production work has fallen from as many as a hundred to as few as five, a process that is often referred to as "broadbanding."[127]

These changes, in turn, break down traditional job and promotion ladders—with unskilled jobs at the bottom, semiskilled positions in the middle, and supervisory jobs at the top—which has provided opportunities for employees to work their way up the hierarchy. Where employees function in teams, especially in autonomous teams and with job rotation, they develop important skills that are highly idiosyncratic to that setting, such as learning the tasks of other jobs, developing routines unique to that team, and learning to get along with that set of individuals. But, as Osterman found, there was no effort to enhance job security where these practices were common. The combination of greater skills, including those specific to the firm, and yet declining policies for retaining them is one of the central paradoxes of the new deal at work.

The other important development associated with these new work systems is that the employee development ladder has, in many cases, essentially disappeared. Many of the unskilled, entry-level jobs in production, such as "housekeeping," have been eliminated and their tasks incorporated into other jobs.[128] Within teams, workers are performing broader, more complicated, and higher-skilled tasks. But it is not obvious how new workers will learn the work-based skills needed to get into these teams, given that the option of starting in unskilled jobs like housekeeping is disappearing. Flatter organizational structures contribute to reduced promotion opportunities in the management ranks as well. Job-level data on white-collar positions from 140 companies between 1986 and 1992 suggests the magnitude of these changes. Employment in the bottom category of nonsupervisory exempt jobs grew 22 percent over the period, while supervisory positions declined by 6 percent; middle management jobs declined by roughly 6 percent, as did jobs in the top category of executives.[129] The organizational pyramid represented by these changes suggests far fewer positions to fill from within.

WAGE STRUCTURE

A primary function of compensation systems is to allocate and motivate labor within the organization. Doing so requires insulating employees somewhat from the pressures of market forces that may pull in the other direction. The pay structures that result from job evaluations and other internalized employment systems "bend" the market wages for each job—raising some and lowering others—to create a consistent internal pay system that reinforces the promotion structure.

The extent to which wages have been tied to an employer's internal labor market can be seen by comparing the effect of tenure with an employer on earnings for managerial jobs, which are more clearly tied to a firm's internal labor market, with its effect on professional jobs, which have a clear outside labor market. Managers with medium attachment to their employer (between five and eight years of tenure) earned $30,000 less than did those with strong attachment to an employer (in eight of the last ten years), but professionals with medium attachment earned only $18,000 less than those with strong attachment (on average, professionals also earned more).[130]

Competitive pressures on firms have been found to make wages within the firm more sensitive to labor market conditions, reducing the extent to which wage structures are protected from the outside market.[131] Another study compared the career moves of employees in the same organizations with those of employees who moved across employers and found that, historically, moves within the same company tended to produce greater improvements in the form of higher wages and a better match between the attributes of the employees and the requirements of the jobs. But by the early 1990s, there was no longer any advantage to the inside moves as compared with those across employers.[132]

A stylized fact of labor economics is that an individual's productivity in jobs rises initially and peaks toward the middle to latter part of one's working life before declining, tracing out a convex pattern, like that of an inverted "U." The pay practices of most internal labor markets generally smooth over these variations in performance so that new entrants and older workers are paid much more than their productivity merits, while midcareer workers are paid less. Recent evidence suggests a reversal in these practices. For example, entry-level wages for high school graduates fell in real terms by 18 percent from 1979 to 1989, while real wages for all high school graduates—the majority of whom have been in the labor market for some time—dropped by only half as much; entry-level wages fell another 8 percent from 1989 to 1993, while real wages for all high school graduates dropped less than 3 percent. Entry-level wages for college graduates rose marginally faster than wages for all college graduates in the 1980s but then fell sharply—6 percent from 1989 to 1993—at a time when wages for all college graduates were basically flat. The relative decline in entry-level wages is consistent with a decline in internal pay structures that had operated to equalize pay.[133]

Data relating wages and years of work experience illustrates the decline in the redistributive nature of internal wage systems even more clearly. In the 1980s, workers with one to five years of work experience saw their real wages decline by 7.7 percent, those near the peak of their experience-related productivity (from sixteen to twenty years of experience) saw a slight gain, and those with more than thirty-five years of experience lost just under 3 percent.[134] These changes seem to bring the pay of individuals more in line with general performance and are consistent with a decline in the redistributive aspects of internalized arrangements.

The apparent decline in the return to tenure with the same employer is perhaps the most compelling evidence of the decline of more traditional pay and employment relationships. Traditional pay systems in large organizations seemed to keep rewarding seniority independent from performance.[135] But that relationship now appears to have changed. For example, researchers studying the semiconductor industry found that the wage premium paid to more experienced workers was declining. Among the explanations are that new technical skills are becoming more important, and those skills are learned not inside the firm but outside, typically in higher education.[136] Another possible explanation is simply that change inside these companies makes existing skills increasingly obsolete.

At the aggregate level, the returns to seniority with the same employer have collapsed in the past decade.[137] Other studies find a sharp decline in returns to seniority of about $3,000 annually between the 1970s and 1980s for workers with ten years of seniority. Putting it differently, the costs of job changing dropped dramatically; workers who changed jobs every other year saw almost the same earnings rise in the late 1980s as did those who kept the same job for ten years.[138] But this effect seems to depend on why one changes jobs. The probability that employees who quit would find a job that offers a large pay raise has increased by 5 percent, while the probability that those who were dismissed will suffer a large decline in their pay has risen by 17 percent over the previous decade.[139]

These results suggest that a good, lifetime match between an employee and a single employer is becoming less important in determining an employee's long-term success. By default, what must be becoming more important are factors outside of the relationship with an individual employer, factors associated with the outside market.

Other data also suggests greater risk and more variance in individual earnings over time.[140] This is partly because of a much stronger relationship between individual performance and pay. Hay Associates, the compensation firm, collects data from clients on the pay increases associated with different levels of individual performance as measured by performance evaluation plans. In 1989, the increase associated with the highest level of performance was 2.5 times larger than the increase associated with the lowest level.[141] By 1993, that ratio had risen to a factor of 4. A 1996 Towers Perrin survey found that 61 percent of responding firms were using variable pay and that 27 percent of firms were considering the elimination of base-pay increases altogether, so that the only increases in compensation would result from performance-contingent pay.[142] The Bureau of Labor Statistics found that the percentage of employees eligible for bonuses rose from 29 percent on average in 1989 to 39 percent in medium and large firms and 49 percent in small firms by the end of the 1990s.[143] The change in contingent compensation has been especially great for executives (see Figure 4-8).

One clear illustration of the shifting of risk onto employees associated with the new deal concerns changes in pension plans. Defined benefit plans, in which workers earn the right to predetermined benefit levels according to their years of service, covered 83 percent of all workers who had pensions in 1979. By 1988, that figure had fallen to 66 percent, a trend that experts expect to continue. The change was accounted for by growth in defined contribution plans, in which employers make fixed contributions to a retirement fund for each employee, especially in 401(k) programs whereby employees contribute directly to their retirement fund.[144] Perhaps half or more of the decline in defined benefit plans is attributable to employers switching pension programs.[145]

In defined benefit plans, the employer bears the risk of the pension by guaranteeing a benefit stream for as long as the pensioner lives. These plans also make employee turnover very costly to employers and create incentives to reduce it. If a worker quits or is laid off after his or her pension is vested, for example, the employer still bears the full pension liability for that worker but loses the benefit of their future performance, out of which the costs of the pension would be earned. Until the pension is vested, the employee has an incentive to stay with the employer. But after the pension-vesting period, the incentives for em-

Figure 4-8. Variable Pay for Management Positions

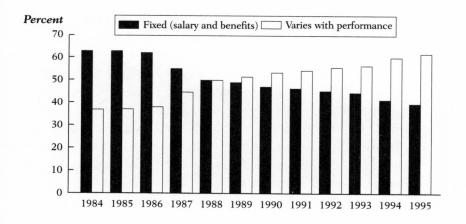

Source: Professor Michael Useem, The Wharton School, University of Pennsylvania.

ployees to quit increase, since they can then take all of the pension benefits with them.

With the shift to defined contribution plans, in contrast, the employer no longer bears the risk of guaranteeing a stream of benefits. That problem now falls to the employee. Because employer contributions and costs stop when an employee leaves, the fixed costs of employment drop dramatically. Beyond minimal vesting requirements, there are no incentives for the employee to stay or to leave. Arguably, 401(k) plans go even further in pushing the risk toward employees by allowing them to share in the contributions and, in essence, to control how large their retirement fund will be. Whether the shift toward defined contribution and 401(k) plans was part of an effort to reduce fixed costs and move away from long-term employment relationships is a matter for speculation. But it clearly facilitates that move.

EMPLOYER-PROVIDED TRAINING

As described earlier, training is one of the key components of the traditional employment relationship. It provides the means for molding entry-level applicants into career employees and for helping them adapt to changing company needs. Whether employer-provided training has changed along with other aspects of the new deal at work is an important issue.

One simple question is whether the amount of training that employers provide has increased. Reports of rising skill requirements and massive investments in training by successful companies like Motorola create the impression that training is on the rise, as indeed the measures of dollars spent on training seem to indicate. When one looks at real spending on training, however, discounting for inflation, the increases are marginal; and because the number of employees has increased, training expenditures per employee have declined somewhat.[146] Other studies find that the incidence of employer training rose slightly for prime-age workers, those aged thirty-five to fifty-four, from 1990 to 1995 but declined for all other age groups, reflecting the same redistributive pattern noted above for compensation.[147]

There have been changes in the type of training provided by employers over time. One study compares the proportion of workers in 1983 and 1991 reporting that training was needed to qualify for their current job, in particular, formal training paid for and provided by the employer. Training to qualify for one's current job refers to entry-level job skills, often general training that is equally useful to other employers. The incidence of such training was essentially unchanged for the work-force as a whole, but the length of training, a proxy for the amount of training provided, declined substantially. Declines in both the incidence and length of such training were especially sharp for high school drop-outs. For workers with less than ten years of seniority, the incidence was about the same, but the decline in the length of such training was especially great. The incidence of employer-provided training to improve skills in one's current job, on the other hand, rose over this period.[148] Other research suggests that while the overall returns to training have risen, they did not rise for informal or on-the-job training, which does not translate well to the outside market.[149]

THE MAGNITUDE OF CHANGE IN JAPAN

If this is the situation in the United States, it might be instructive to examine whether similar changes are going on elsewhere, especially in Japan. In the 1970s, the Japanese example helped persuade many U.S. employers (and even more consultants and academics) that the key to high-performing organizations was making greater investments in employees and tying them even closer to the firm than U.S. corporations had done so far. How is the model of lifetime job security in the core of the Japanese economy holding up in the 1990s, especially under pressure from a resurgent U.S. trading sector?

The perception of the Japanese lifetime employment model was always greater than its reality, applying only to the core or permanent workforce of the largest Keiretsu companies, perhaps no more than about 15 percent of the total workforce in Japan. These companies always relied heavily on subcontractors who paid wages amounting to about two-thirds of those paid by lifetime employers. The subcon-tractors were essentially captives of the larger companies, operating with long-term proprietary relationships that made them roughly the equi-valent of operating divisions of the large companies. The Keiretsus used their subcontractors as buffers to accommodate fluctuations in production to maintain stability among their own workforce. But that relationship is breaking down as the Keiretsu companies increasingly treat their subcontractors as suppliers in a competitive market and not as long-term partners. Long-term contracts are giving way to shorter and shorter deals, downward pressure on prices is replacing the notion of a fair return, and subcontractors have concluded that they can no longer rely on a single, long-term relationship. They are now in a market.[150]

The most dramatic examples of change are in those segments of the economy most directly exposed to foreign competitors. Foreign companies operating in Japan needed staff and found that they were quite able to hire away midcareer workers who, feeling trapped by the seniority system, were seeking better opportunities. Companies like Mobil and IBM were especially successful at hiring Japanese women whose advancement was blocked by the internal (and male-dominated) promotion system.

The rapid expansion of foreign investment banks in the 1980s brought an end to many of the internal labor market practices of the Tokyo finance houses. The foreign firms hired away much of the midcareer talent in the Japanese banks and finance houses, talent that was the result of the considerable investments that had been made in those workers. Once it was clear to senior executives that they could not keep such workers without matching outside offers, the investments made in such workers and the system that produced them dried up. In short, the Japanese organizations could no longer make their early investments in workers pay off. By the 1990s, most Japanese firms found that they, too, were hiring midcareer employees from the outside market. If they paid these outside hires based on the old seniority system, they could never hire them away from competitors. But if they paid them based on merit and then tried to fit them into the existing, seniority-based pay schedules, it would create enormous inequities and resentment. Many companies created subsidiaries that existed solely to hire the new recruits at market wages. Then these new workers would be sent to work at headquarters.[151]

A 1992 study by the Japan Productivity Center concluded that even in manufacturing, where Japan is the world leader, Japanese companies would have to cut almost 40 percent of their employees to reach the level of labor productivity of their U.S. competitors. Companies like TDK and Pioneer announced some layoffs, but much more common— as in the United States—are early retirement programs. Almost twice as many employees are taking these offers as anticipated. For those who remain, the employment relationship looks increasingly like that in the United States. In compensation, for example, the annual salary system with across-the-board increases and pay levels dictated by seniority is giving way to merit pay and annual performance reviews. Companies like Honda now have real salary differences between managers at the same level, based on performance.[152]

Temporary help agencies were illegal in Japan until 1985 but are now booming, with more than 11 percent of all paid employees on short-term contracts. The main factor cited for the rise in temporary work is the employers' interest in getting work done immediately without the long period of training and on-the-job learning that characterized the old model. Part-time work has also risen, up 80 percent in ten years from the 1980s. It now accounts for more than 20 percent of all paid employment, with another 11 percent working in temporary or short-term contracts.[153] In the mid-1990s, the number of temporary workers were increasing at a rate just below 6 percent in the Tokyo area.[154]

And the employees are adapting to these developments by changing their own attitudes. In the mid-1980s, for example, only about a third of workers in their early thirties said they would consider changing jobs for better opportunities. But by the next decade, that figure had doubled. In the 1980s, only one in a hundred Japanese managers left a company for other opportunities after doing a tour in the United States. In the 1990s, estimates put that figure at one in ten.[155] Leaders within the Japanese corporate community have begun calling for reforms that expand the use of stock options to reward executives, to move the focus away from seniority and toward performance, and to rely on measures of performance that are visible and easily understood by investors. In short, these changes would make Japanese executives and firms act much more like those in the United States.[156]

The extraordinary pressures that Japanese middle managers or "salarymen" are experiencing as their companies attempt to restructure have made their way into popular culture. In 1994, a hugely successful musical opened that symbolized the trials of these contemporary middle managers: *The Salary Man Who Became Naked*. In a plot that is far more respectable than the title, the demoralized executive hero gets shipped off to a subsidiary company when business turns down. His son drops out of cram school, and his wife threatens to leave him. The failing subsidiary has one chance at survival: Get the big order finished and shipped in an impossibly short time. Like Rocky Balboa pounding out his roadwork, the salary man and his colleagues work through the night, shaming their wives and children with their incredible efforts. Soon wives, kids, and executives are laboring together, the project is completed, and the final chorus reaffirms the importance of individual commitment to a company's success.[157] Even though the ending is presented as a happy one, the executive remains stuck with a second-rate job.

CONCLUSION

What the results discussed in this chapter suggest for U.S. employers is consistent with the earlier arguments on work organization—that employers now make less of an investment in the skills of new employees for the purposes of learning a job. Greater fear that the training investment will be lost—either through layoffs or quits—produces a reduced incentive to invest. Employers are likely to make a greater investment in upgrading the skills of existing workers, perhaps under pressure from the demands of changing work organization. Other research has shown how the outside labor market shapes the internal training decisions of employers—for example, that how much training a firm is willing to pay for depends on how hard it is to get applicants.[158]

Indeed, while traditional human capital theory and research suggest that employer-provided training should be higher when skills are unique to the firm (because they cannot be secured on the market), Osterman's 1995 survey found that employer training was actually *lower* in such jobs.[159] Employees contribute to the cost of general skills training through lower wages,[160] but employers must recoup the investment in specific skills training over time through improved worker performance. The fact that employers are not necessarily making that investment in firm-specific skills even when the jobs seem to demand them is consistent with the view that decreased attachment has made it more difficult to recoup the investment in firm-specific skills.

Employers have responded to the changing environment outlined in Chapter 3 by reducing the extent to which they try to manage employment inside the firm. Under this new deal at work, employees have less job security; the attachment between employer and employee has weakened, leading to reduced incentives for employer training; new systems of work organization make internal development of employees more difficult; and compensation systems are increasingly driven by the outside market. Innovative compensation and work organization practices, paradoxically, may also be mechanisms for addressing the problems created by the new deal at work that were described in Chapter 1: increased attrition, declining employee commitment, and reduced incentives to train employees. Those solutions are considered in the next chapter.

CHAPTER 5

Market-Based Relationships

ONE WAY to begin thinking about how to address the management problems created by the new deal at work is to look at the industries and settings where, for historical reasons, market-based employment relationships have long been in place. The important lessons to learn from these arrangements lie not so much in their individual details as in their common characteristics—the necessary conditions for market-based relationships. The most important of these are aspects of infrastructure that lie outside the individual firm. While it is appealing to think of markets as self-sufficient, in fact they need a wide range of supporting arrangements to operate effectively. It is also important to see what individual employers lose in terms of control with market-based employment relationships. Some of the most prominent examples are discussed in this chapter.

CRAFT WORK

When they imagine how workers might have a career that takes them from company to company, most people have a model in their mind of craft work, such as the skilled trades of the construction industry. The notion of the manager of the future as a mobile professional, like an accountant or corporate counsel, who moves from company to company doing work governed by professional norms is essentially a version of the craft model.

Craft work predates industrial systems of employment, and like any survivor in a system subject to evolution, it must have something going for it. Early on, craft-based systems found solutions to the central problems of managing market-based employment relationships: providing skills, minimizing attrition, and managing employee commitment. The solutions contain elements that are common to other market-based arrangements, and they turn on the concept of infrastructure.

Much of the infrastructure in craft work, especially in skilled trades like carpentry, plumbing, and electrical work, has been provided by guilds and unions that operate independently of employers. The guilds or unions in the past essentially owned the craft. Two conditions made that possible, and they turn on the concept of monopoly powers. For employers, the central problem with employee training is that they may not recoup their investment; an employee can pick up and take that investment to another employer. Although union training programs made similar investments, workers found that while they might very well jump from employer to employer, they could not easily leave the union because it was difficult for anyone who was not a member to secure employment in that craft. Union dues, contributed over a lifetime of work, helped repay the union for its training investment.[1] So the union provided the infrastructure that compensated for the fact that employees routinely changed employers.

Another characteristic of the union arrangement that contributed to the ability to fund training was its system of work organization. The model of organizing workers and tasks by skill and training level—apprentices, journeymen, master craftsmen—with pay levels much lower for those who were learning the craft, made it possible for trainees to help pay for their training as they went along. Another part of the answer is simply that they were doing work of real value as part of their on-the-job training. So the apprentices and journeymen were essentially paid less than they were worth to the employer, at least relative to the master craftsmen.

What about the issue of retention? Another problem for employers with new deal at work is that employees are likely to leave more frequently, often at times that are inconvenient for the employer, as their skills are equally useful in other settings.

One way in which the costs of worker turnover can be reduced is by making it easier to find replacement workers. The craft model does that by standardizing skills, creating clear credentials to certify the achievement of those skills, and essentially standardizing the tasks that each craft performs. Two licensed, master electricians will install the same electrical outlet essentially the same way. (The construction industry in particular aids this standardization through uniform building codes.) If one electrician walks off the job, another one can pick up the remaining work the next day without missing a step. Union hiring halls helped organize the outside labor market and made it easier for employers to replace workers.

The credentialing system in craft work also helps address the related problem of how to assess worker capabilities. If one of the advantages of long-term, internal employment systems is to monitor workers' performance before they are promoted to truly important tasks, then a problem of market-based systems is the risk that workers will be thrust into important roles without much careful evaluation. And greater turnover makes that likely to happen more often. Clear credentials for skills combined with standardized tasks made the problem of assessing performance an easier one to address.

Finally, what about the problem of worker commitment? Even if a long-term relationship with the employer is irrelevant, employers clearly care about the quality of workmanship and the effort put in by their employees. The fact that craft workers may be less likely to stay with any given employer makes it less likely that they will identify their long-run interests with the employer and feel committed to them. The solution pursued in the craft model is to rely on what might best be described as the culture of the craft, the norms of performance and quality that are drilled in as part of the powerful socialization process offered by apprentice programs. And, as noted above, the fact that the individual tasks performed by these occupations are standardized makes it easier to monitor compliance with them.

Efforts to mimic the advantages of the craft model for youth entering the labor force have led to the creation of youth apprenticeship programs as part of the school-to-work reform movement. These programs typically combine formal classroom training with job experience at employer sites. Their model has been the German youth apprentice system, which replicates many of the attributes of union-based, craft models through legislation and other contracts. For example, the fact that employers are bound by agreements not to hire away apprentices until after they have finished their training means that the wages of apprentices can be held down, below the level of their contributions to the employer, so as to help recoup some of the employer's training investments. Attempts to introduce programs like these in other settings without the supporting infrastructure provided by these agreements have failed. In the United Kingdom, for example, similar youth apprentice programs were introduced but without the protective infrastructure that constrains opportunistic behavior. Employers quickly hired away the best apprentices before they could complete their training, and the program ended up as little more than a government-subsidized screening device for new hires.

The professional employment model best typified in the United States by doctors and lawyers has essentially the same attributes as the craft model, which is why wags often refer to the American Medical Association or the American Bar Association as trade unions for professionals. Lawyers have the stripped-down model: students pay for the formal training out of their own pockets (or more likely those of their parents) before moving into a system with certification of skills (the bar exam), reasonably standardized procedures, strong professional norms to ensure effort and quality of work, and profession-based enforcement arrangements for dealing with trespassers.

Doctors have the much more elaborate version: while the initial formal training is paid for out of pocket, the more advanced internships, residencies, and fellowships are funded differently by having the student doctors perform work of value for teaching hospitals while being paid wages well below the value of their work. Elaborately differentiated credentials—board-certified plastic, cosmetic, and reconstructive surgeons, for example—are based on standardized exams. Medical school and teaching hospital training programs are also regulated and certified. This system of national credentials and regulations allows doctors to move easily across employers. And the fact that the standards for patient treatment are more or less uniform across teaching institutions means that the practice of medicine and surgery is conducted in a similar manner nationwide. Doctors can change hospitals or work with different colleagues without much difficulty. Once they are ready to practice, doctors are governed by strong professional norms and profession-governed enforcement mechanisms (county medical associations).

The matching of students and training programs is perhaps the most stylized and highly regulated aspect of the training. The National Resident Matching Program, begun in 1952, makes all the medical school graduates seeking internships and residencies apply to a central clearinghouse and list in rank order their preferences for the programs they would like to join. The programs examine the applications and submit to the clearinghouse a list of candidates they would like to accept, also listed in rank order. Through a complicated algorithm, matches are made and are announced at 12:00 noon EST on "Match Day," the second Wednesday in March. They are binding on all the parties, including the schools and hospitals. (Two days before, "Black Monday," the students for whom no matches could be found are alerted to their plight, and the next day the "scramble" takes place in which their deans frantically call around and try to find them a place.)

Occupations, like crafts and professions, are sometimes described as horizontal in that the career path moves one across organizations, not necessarily advancing up a vertical hierarchy within an organization. The percentage of the U.S. workforce made up of professional/technical workers has more than doubled since 1950 and is now close to 18 percent. When craft workers are included, roughly 30 percent of the U.S. workforce can be counted in these "horizontal" careers.[2]

The lesson from both the craft and the professional models is that while it is clearly possible to solve the problems that market-based employment systems raise—acquiring skills, managing turnover, ensuring commitment—doing so with a craft-type model of employment requires a very substantial infrastructure that exists independent from the employers. No single employer can solve these problems alone. Doing so requires extraordinary cooperation at a minimum and the creation of powerful mechanisms for enforcing cooperative behavior. The experience of the construction trades in the United States in the past few decades illustrates the difficulty of maintaining these arrangements. As more employers avoided union organizing, the incentive for workers who received their training through union programs to stay in the union and keep paying dues declined. Union training programs have been shrinking, especially relative to the demand for skilled trades. Vocational schools and company-sponsored programs have stepped in to help fill the gap, but the problems of developing workforce skills and then identifying who has them remain.

Other examples of market-based employment systems discussed

here illustrate additional problems that must be managed if these arrangements are to succeed.

Pilots and Air Transport

An illustration of how the market creates different options for developing job-related skills can be seen in the familiar job of airline pilot. Again, the role of infrastructure is crucial. The Federal Aviation Administration (FAA) shapes the market for pilots by establishing the credentials that pilots must hold to obtain commercial licenses to fly various aircraft. With the appropriate licenses and certifications, a pilot can fly for any airline. How one goes about learning the material to pass those tests and getting the flight time to earn the credentials, however, is not part of the regulations. There are at present three distinct alternatives for earning a position as a pilot at a major carrier:

1. Do it on your own in the market. There are many paths for acquiring pilot credentials in the market. Most pilots begin by taking courses in one of the 1,700 private flight schools or, in some cases, through colleges and universities. While there is no requirement that students take any formal training whatsoever before taking the relevant exams, most do. After obtaining the minimum commercial licensing credentials, pilots typically join small airlines like commuter carriers to accumulate hours and then try to secure an entry-level position at a major carrier. There are also for-profit schools that provide training to move pilots more quickly into better jobs than they could do on their own.

2. Join the military, become a pilot (ideally a transport pilot rather than a fighter pilot), and, typically, after twenty years of service, retire and take a position at a major carrier.

3. Get hired by a carrier and have them provide your pilot's training, what is referred to in the industry as the *ab initio* approach.

The third method is typical for most carriers in the world, especially those in Western Europe, but is unheard of in the United States. Ironically, most *ab initio* training for these foreign carriers is actually conducted in the United States. Lufthansa, for example, has trained virtually all of its pilots since the 1950s in the American Southwest. These programs are apparently quite efficient. British Airway's program, for example, costs only about $80,000 from start to finish to produce qualified co-pilots for jet aircraft, as opposed to the several million dollar price tag for training by the U.S. military. Yet no U.S. carriers use this approach. In fact, U.S. carriers almost never pay for any of the costs of their pilots' commercial licenses. The reasons are instructive.

No carrier wants to pay for the expensive training of pilots, in part because of concerns that the enormous investment in those skills will simply go to a competitor who skims off trained workers by paying them a premium. European carriers like Lufthansa pay for it simply because they have no alternative. They have no sizeable pool of military pilots from which to draw, and there is no real private market for producing civilian pilots because the private, recreational market for aviation is very, very small. With pathways 1 and 2 above blocked, they pursue number 3. In addition to the fact that European carriers have no other alternative, the potential problem of their pilots moving on after training has been limited by the fact that they've had few places to go. Each country's air transport system has been dominated by a monopoly carrier—Air France, British Airways, Alitalia in Italy, Lufthansa in Germany. The loosening of regulations on competition have changed this situation somewhat.

In the United States, the carriers have not had to provide qualifying training because the presence of a market with suppliers able to provide these skills has made it possible to push the costs off onto the applicants. Pilots have to get those expensive skills and credentials before they even apply for jobs. For most of the early years of commercial aviation in the United States, the ranks of air transportation pilots were filled by a steady supply of ex-military pilots. The reason that this method dominated the private market for training is simple: the enormous costs of this very high-quality training were almost entirely underwritten by the government. There is no way that individuals could afford anything like that kind of training on the private market. The option of pursuing a rather lucrative career as a pilot at a major airline after a military career is an important attraction of military service. But there have never been enough military pilots leaving the service to meet the growing commercial demand for pilots. As a result, there is a queue: the major carriers offering better rates of pay and working conditions hired 93 percent of their pilots from military backgrounds, while the smaller turboprop carriers with lower wages got only 13 percent from the military.

In the early 1990s, when the industry was in something of a recession, the supply of qualified pilots for entry positions exceeded the demand. Airlines tightened their qualifications, and applicants had to secure more training on their own before applying to get a position. Toward the late 1990s, the situation reversed: a military drawdown reduced the number of military-trained pilots while commercial aviation expanded. The carriers now have to rely much more on the private market for pilots. For the carriers, here is the rub: they feel they are not getting enough high-quality applicants and have had to lower their standards. And there is not much they can do about it, because they do not see the applicants until after they are trained. Because the carriers wait for the market to provide them with pilots, they can control neither the recruitment of people into the field of aviation nor the development of their initial skills.

The problem for the airlines is that they are vitally dependent on the supply of skilled pilots, but they have essentially no control over that supply. They are like Will Durant's carriage company in pre-GM days, dependent on and vulnerable to autonomous suppliers. The supply of pilots comes from the private market, and the individual carriers simply pick and choose from the applicants they get. What if a carrier raised wages to attract better-quality applicants? An individual carrier could pull better-quality applicants away from competitors, but a wage increase would affect the quality of the overall supply of students entering the flight-training career path only if the wage structure of the entire profession increased—if all carriers, or at least most, agreed to raise their wages.

Individual carriers have tried to develop programs to improve the quality of applicants for their positions. But the problem is that there is nothing keeping the graduates from going to competitors elsewhere in the industry. The Federal Aviation Authority, for example, developed the Airway Science program for colleges, which involved constructing a model curriculum and offering those who complete it a fast track on an FAA career path. The graduates, however, ended up being hired by the carriers who paid more, and the FAA got little benefit from it. Northwest Airlines created a program with its commuter airline, Northwest AirLink, and the University of North Dakota to improve applicant quality. Students who completed the program would be hired into AirLink and, they hoped, eventually into Northwest itself. But the program failed in the student end because not enough signed up. The students had to bear the costs of the program, which were quite high, and Northwest could not guarantee that they would be hired.

A related problem with the market model, in contrast to either of the others, is that the opportunities for students to enter this path depend heavily on their own financial resources. Minority students in particular have less access to pilot careers because they have on average fewer resources, and the market path requires money up front.

Perhaps surprisingly, after pilots are hired into a major carrier, their company pays for all of their training, not only that required to keep their skills and certifications current (which the Fair Labor Standards Act may require them to pay) but also that needed to advance their credentials. Why will employers pay for further training when they will not pay for initial training? This situation results from the labor agreements between the carriers and the pilots, virtually all of whom are unionized. The agreements establish wage schedules that advance quite sharply with *company* seniority. Pilots who leave one carrier for another have to start at the bottom of the new carrier's seniority list and salary schedule. As a result, the pilots almost never leave the carrier that hires them initially. And, as a result, the carriers can make investments in their skills without fear that they will lose them.

As in the craft example, pilot unions (mainly the Airline Pilots Association) provide infrastructure that helps address problems of the market model. The turnover problem plaguing some other models of the employment relationship is essentially eliminated by steep, seniority-based contracts, and the issue of commitment is also handled in part because pilots have no other good employment options and therefore feel tied to their carrier. Professional norms as well as tight regulations control the performance of their tasks.

The general lessons to be learned from the employment system for airline pilots are that the presence of a private market for developing skills makes it possible for employers to push virtually all of the costs of entry-level skills off onto the applicants. In the process, however, the airlines have turned control of their supply of labor over to the market.

HIGHER EDUCATION

Most people believe that no sector of the economy is more insulated from change than higher education, no area where the pressures previously outlined are less relevant. After all, faculty have tenure, lifetime job security. In what way is their employment relationship in the market?

A quick review of contemporary practices in higher education suggests that now, even in higher education, long-term relationships between faculty and their employers are the exception rather than the rule. The dominant factor and the organizing principle in these relationships has for some time been the outside labor market. And in many ways, the employment practices of higher education may be a preview of where corporate America is heading.

True, most universities still have tenure for faculty, although many are reconsidering it, and some—like the University of Minnesota—are moving to abandon it altogether. Think for a moment about how tenure works. It is like making partner in a law firm. New faculty are hired into positions with contracts of fixed length, generally a maximum of seven years. Most colleges and universities have about half of their full-time faculty on these fixed-length contracts. A year or two before the contract expires, these untenured faculty are reviewed for promotion to tenured positions. The better the school, the worse the odds that promotion will occur. It is not unusual in some departments in better research universities to go decades without making a single tenure promotion. The "publish or perish" maxim highlights the fact that in most institutions the important part of a tenure judgment is based on scholarly work, which is directed at the academic community *outside* of one's own institution. The central mechanism of the tenure process, particularly at universities, is to ask senior faculty at other institutions about a candidate's work. Specifically, these outside referees are asked to evaluate a candidate in comparison with all of the other faculty in that field or discipline of a similar generation across the country or, in some cases, the world. For example, an English professor coming up for tenure at the University of Michigan would be reviewed by English professors at other leading universities, and they would be asked how this candidate compared with others in the labor market. When the reviews were completed, the University of Michigan committee would ask itself if this candidate was the best scholar available. Could it hire someone better from another university, from the labor market?

The more the tenure process relies on these labor market comparisons, the more the candidates themselves direct their work efforts away from their own institution and toward this outside research community. After all, if they are denied tenure, they have to find a job elsewhere. To do that, they need to focus on the work about which other employers will care. Getting junior faculty to invest time in efforts specific to their school, such as administrative work, is very difficult because they know that it will not enhance their reputation in the labor market. Most institutions understand that, and many explicitly protect junior faculty from such assignments because it takes time away from their pursuit of a tenured appointment.

Given the dominance of the labor market in this process, it is no surprise to find that the terms and conditions of employment get set by the market and become more or less standard within a field across institutions: Economics professors hired this year earn about the same amount with similar teaching loads and funds for research across similar institutions.[3] One consequence of the dominance of the labor market is that faculty hired in different years may have different employment contracts depending on the state of the market in any given year. The computer science professor hired this year at Penn State, when that job market is hot, could be paid more than senior colleagues in the same department who were hired several years ago.

But what about after tenure, what happens then? There is at least one other, similar review for promotion to full professor that operates in the same way. Some universities require additional reviews like these before they award other privileges, such as endowed chairs. The move toward posttenure reviews, already in place at schools like the University of Texas, means that these outside reviews will continue throughout one's career, determining pay and, in some cases, job security. The market discipline continues in other ways as well. All faculty know that the surest way to get the attention of your dean and colleagues and to secure extra benefits for yourself is to get an outside offer, an invitation to join the faculty at another college or university on better terms and conditions.[4]

What are the consequences of relying on the outside labor market to govern faculty careers? It focuses faculty activities on the kind of academic research that is valued by their peers in other institutions. It provides some protection for the hiring institution against the poor performance of junior faculty—if the outside audience does not like your work (or if you are not doing any), it is difficult to get promotions or other rewards within your own institution. Colleges and universities use this system to get an accurate and inexpensive evaluation of the quality of a professor's work even when they may have no competencies in that field themselves. A small college with only one criminologist with no other faculty knowledgeable about that field can nevertheless get a highly reliable evaluation of her work from the market. The system therefore provides a good method of motivating her performance.

On the other hand, this system makes it very difficult to get faculty to pay attention to issues that are not valued in the outside labor market, a fact that has hampered efforts to reform higher education. Getting faculty to make investments in teaching, in restructuring curricula, and in pursuing the educational mission of higher education is often like pulling teeth precisely because these efforts do not enhance their own reputation in the labor market, despite the fact that they are crucial for the success of an individual institution.

What if these institutions of higher learning were really opened up to the market, one might ask, certainly that would change things. In fact, the ancient British and European universities that we think of as being the most like ivory towers began their operations completely in the market, with tutors contracting individually with students for instruction. Even a hundred years ago in the United States, it was common for lecturers, especially in fields like medicine, to be paid for each lecture based on the number of students who attended. Much like the corporations earlier in the twentieth century, universities eliminated the individual contracting model and created permanent employment relationships with instructors. But they are returning to that market model with entrepreneurial programs like clinical practices in medical schools, executive education in business schools, or special fee-based teaching programs in the arts and sciences. What these programs have in common is that they operate in the market, where they are in competition with a range of providers in addition to other educational institutions.

The delivery of these programs is also governed by a market, the labor market. Executive education providers, for example, can use business school faculty to teach their programs. But they can also use faculty from other schools within their university. Or they can use consultants or freelance teachers, giving them an adjunct or temporary teaching appointment in the program. The teaching engagements are self-contained and short-term—sometimes lasting several weeks, other times a day or less. So the system operates like a spot market, with each match between program and instructor being unique. Because tenured professors are in competition with consultants and freelance teachers, they have to hit the same standards as these independent contractors to get work.

In this kind of employment relationship, information becomes crucial. The administrators putting programs together need to know who can pull off an acceptable presentation, and they can ill afford to alienate paying customers by making a mistake. Once they find someone who can manage a program well, they have no incentive to go looking for other presenters. Information as to who does presentations well gets around, and these successful presenters then get called by everyone. Practice makes perfect, and the more often these instructors do presentations, the better they get at it.

The natural outcome of this process is that the opportunities to teach get concentrated in a smaller and smaller group. The only thing that prevents this process from collapsing into a situation where all of the teaching is done by one instructor, the very best one, is the physical limits on that person's time and energy. As distance learning and other pedagogical devices increase the audience that one instructor can reach, many believe that teaching will increasingly be concentrated among a small group of "star" performers who have enormous bargaining power, just like an entertainer. ("Star" professors in medical schools have already begun sending their lawyers to negotiate compensation arrangements on their behalf with administrators.)

Another, more subtle consequence of this arrangement for the "employees" is that except for the very busiest instructors, they now have very little bargaining power and must work hard to keep their "customer" happy. Inside a regular organization, permanent employees had a monopoly on performing certain tasks. If you wanted a training session on teamwork skills, you had no choice but to ask Margy in the training department to do it. Teamwork was her beat. And if she was prickly to deal with, that was just part of the cost of doing business. But once the market is brought inside the firm and you have many options through the magic of outsourcing, the fact that Margy is difficult to deal with is more than enough reason to never call her again. And if Margy is paid in part by the assignment, she soon learns that it costs her money when she fails to be accommodating. The very best providers may be able to get away with traits that are not user friendly once they have established their reputation for performance. But they may never get the chance to develop that reputation if people find them difficult to deal with initially.

Institutes of higher education have also been adapting to a new competitive environment, primarily by developing a huge contingent workforce. A study by the U.S. Department of Education calculates that a substantial majority of college instructors—58 percent—are either part-time or temporary employees. The American Association of University Professors calculates that a third of the instructors at liberal arts colleges are part-time, as are 52 percent of those at two-year institutions. A well-known characteristic of life at large universities is that undergraduates often have a difficult time seeing a real professor. A study of the University of North Carolina concluded that two-thirds of the undergraduates were taught by nonstanding faculty, a situation that is common at other universities as well.[5] Although most institutions are loath to say so publicly, the system of contingent instructors is really driven by the constraints created by the tenure system. Contingent instructors are not only a much cheaper way of delivering courses, they also give the institutions a great deal of flexibility in terms of course offerings. Additional sections can be added on short notice to meet student demands and unpopular ones dropped. Some institutions are reasonably explicit about the use of contingent instructors to protect the standing faculty, and these are among the few real examples in the U.S. economy of the "core-periphery" of organizations and employment relationships described earlier.[6]

SILICON VALLEY

The phenomenal success of the electronics and hi-tech industry around California's Santa Clara County has focused attention on identifying the unique characteristics of Silicon Valley businesses that make them so successful. Perhaps the main conclusion is that the unique attributes of Silicon Valley enterprises seem not to reside so much within the individual firms themselves but outside them, in their relationships with each other and with the region's infrastructure. The most important of these attributes come from the labor market and are based on a very different employment relationship. Not only is the employment relationship much more horizontal, it is an important part of the region's distinctive competency. And it functions without the elaborate credentials, enforcement agreements, and other formal infrastructure of the professional and craft employment systems.

Economic geographer AnnaLee Saxenian describes the post–World War II competition in the electronics industry between the electronic firms around Boston's Route 128 and those in Silicon Valley.[7] While both had roots in university research communities (MIT in Boston and Stanford in Silicon Valley), the companies around Route 128 were organized on the dominant corporate model of the 1970s: highly integrated companies with internal employee development and long-term employment relationships. Start-up companies like Digital Equipment Corporation, Data General, and Wang tried to become as much like General Electric or IBM as quickly as they could.

The start-up companies in Silicon Valley took a different direction. The seminal event may have been the defection of seven founding executives from the Fairchild semiconductor company, one of the very first area hi-tech operations, to form their own companies. So many of the region's companies could trace their roots back to these seven executives and Fairchild that a poster was printed that outlines this corporate family tree. The precedent of quitting a company to form a new one was highly established, and the networks that were created in the process led to a much more casual employment relationship. Professor David Angel calculates that even in the 1970s, average turnover was 35 percent among Silicon Valley companies, most of which were growing, and almost 60 percent among smaller firms. Eighty percent of the electrical engineers who quit their jobs in the region went to work for Silicon Valley competitors, and their average tenure with a company was significantly shorter than with similar companies elsewhere.[8]

Data from Silicon Valley indicates that, compared with semiconductor companies elsewhere, they are much more likely to meet skill needs by hiring in experienced workers than by developing their own talent. That is, they "buy" rather than "make" the skills they need, particularly smaller firms. And they are much more likely to find those skills through networks of their current employees; 44 percent of vacancies were filled by referrals from current employees, compared with about 9 percent for comparable firms in other regions of the country.[9] Both the tradition of successful start-ups in the region and the density of companies made job-hopping from one to another easy. Saxenian quotes one executive who moved to Silicon Valley on its different norms: "Out here, it wasn't that big a catastrophe to quit your job on Friday and have another job on Monday, and this was just as true for company executives. You didn't even necessarily have to tell your wife. You just drove off in a different direction on Monday morning."[10]

The careers of the engineers and other employees in these companies were quite different from those in more traditional firms. While they changed employers quite frequently, they probably did not have to move their homes to do so, and they kept the same network of professional acquaintances in the region in the process. As with the academic model, the key credential for Silicon Valley employees was their reputation among their colleagues, outside their firm as well as inside. They also were quite likely to keep doing similar work as they changed companies. If they advanced within a company, it was commonly within their functional area. Even if they left to form a start-up, they would generally be brought in for their functional expertise. Their skills would be kept sharp either by going back to school or by learning on-the-job from new tasks and colleagues. And their big financial payoff might come anytime along their career from stock options when company performance exploded.

In more traditional firms, in contrast, they would have had a long-term career that would likely have moved them around the country and the globe, changing their functional occupations along the way as they advanced up a management hierarchy. They would have been exposed to a great deal of company training in the process, developed extensive networks within that company, and their big financial reward would come predictably at the end of their career with higher salaries and then retirement benefits.

One of the most important lessons Silicon Valley has to teach is how this more market-based employment relationship has helped shape other aspects of the way firms are organized and do business. Extensive evidence suggests that companies find it easier to start up where the skills already exist because they can hire in task-specific skills and industry experience. So having a pool of talent that can be hired away from competitors helps firms get started.[11]

Once in business, the ability to restructure the workforce and, in turn, their competencies is the key competitive advantage of Silicon

Valley companies. Saxenian describes the low point of the region's performance in the mid-1980s as being driven by efforts to go in the opposite direction, to integrate their operations and try to compete by lowering costs in established markets. Following the dismal performance that strategy produced, the region was revived in the 1990s by a new group of start-up firms that focused on innovation, product variety, and speed. They achieved these goals by moving sharply away from vertical integration and embracing suppliers and subcontractors. CEO Robert Graham of Novellus Systems, a semiconductor equipment company, offers his guide to company success: "Avoid vertical integration like the plague. Vertical integration forces a company to build in a high fixed cost, which assures loss of profitability when volume drops."[12] Instead, companies become very flat and specialize in a focused competency where they can more easily remain on the cutting edge. They purchase the other components they need from contractors who are also specializing. In a rapidly changing competitive environment, it is more than enough of a challenge for these companies to remain at the forefront in just one part of the market.

Companies rearrange their capabilities and develop new ones by hiring them from each other. The possibility of hiring in a state-of-the-art workforce for any given task also helps firms stay on the cutting edge of development. Even large firms based elsewhere find that they need to have operations in Silicon Valley to get access to the best ideas and talent. In fact, firms in the semiconductor industry across the country are bound together by a dense network of relationships in the labor market that is driven by hiring from each other.[13] Another adaptation is the widespread use of explicitly contingent workers. Temporary help employment in the region doubled in the first half of the 1990s.[14] Some observers calculate that as many as 40 percent of the jobs in Silicon Valley corporations are contingent, either part-time or temporary. Of course, given the short-term nature of so many of the employment relationships, the difference between a temporary worker and a permanent employee may not be much.

The model of casual employment relationships operating through networks is seen as driving the unique capability for innovation and flexibility of Silicon Valley firms. But surely there are drawbacks to it as well. And one of those comes with the practice of hiring away skilled workers. While this is a great way for firms to get the changing skills they need, it is a considerable burden on those firms whose employees are leaving. For example, Borland International, the software firm, is suing Microsoft for hiring away many of Borland's top software designers, hurting its ability to compete. Microsoft's reply, essentially, was, hey, welcome to the market: Microsoft "wants to hire smart people working on software problems, and if those people are at Borland, then the company wants to hire Borland people."[15]

With turnover rates as high as 60 percent in some segments of the region, it may seem impossible for companies to get anything done. One would think the continual disruption of losing employees and having to hire new ones would overwhelm efforts to get products out the door. Average turnover rates, of course, mask considerable variation within these organizations. The turnover of key employees, for example, is typically reduced through stock options and other techniques discussed in detail in Chapter 6. More important, the pace of change in the product market and the pressure to rearrange competencies inside the firm reduces the need for long-term relationships. During the two-year development and production life of a new disk drive, for example, it may be crucial to keep the company's design team together. After that drive is phased out, it may not be very important for them to stay with the company. In fact, if the replacement is a new design not based on the previous model, there may even be advantages on balance to bringing in an entirely new team to design it from a fresh perspective.

Another problem concerns employee development. If all firms want to hire experienced engineers, how does engineering talent ever get developed? Evidence suggests that even in Silicon Valley, the larger firms operating in more captive markets less subject to change hire engineering talent right from colleges and universities, sponsor more internal development for them, and have longer average tenure. Because these firms are more vertically integrated and have longer lead times for projects, they can afford the greater division of labor and career ladders that facilitate internal development. The more typical, fast-moving firms then poach these trained engineers.

A crucial mechanism for employee development, education and training, has been more thoroughly outsourced to the market in Silicon Valley than in virtually any other part of the country. Stanford's Honors Cooperative Program was a pioneering effort in providing part-time graduate degree training for area engineers. In the process, it also helped generate new networks for its graduates and, some argue, created a norm of information and idea sharing that cuts across companies. The region produces far and away more graduate engineering degrees than any other comparable region in the United States, most of them part-time, even though it is not a leader in producing undergraduate engineering degrees.[16] The opportunity for graduate training while one works is what reinforces the region's employment relationship. Bachelor degrees in engineering are generally earned before one starts work, and employees with those degrees are easily hired into the region from other areas.

The course offerings at area community colleges and proprietary schools have a particularly practical orientation, especially for technical skills, and duplicate the type of in-house training that is offered in larger companies. For example, Foothill College in Los Altos Hills began offering a two-year degree program several years ago in semiconductor processing, a highly specific skill in the semiconductor industry.[17] During the 1990s, while the total number of students in the region's post-secondary system remained about the same, the proportion in continuing education programs (extension programs, on-site courses) rose from about 25 to 30 percent of the total.[18]

Silicon Valley solves the problem of skill development, therefore, by outsourcing formal training to postsecondary institutions and by relying on larger, more traditionally oriented firms to provide initial work experience and training for at least some of the entry-level workers. It solves the turnover problem in part by making it relatively easy to hire replacement employees from the dense personal network of the current workforce. The system of work organization also addresses that issue. Because the typical firm is always innovating and often breaking from the paradigms represented by its previous products, it has less need for continuity in experience and employment. Work is organized around well-defined projects with fixed time lines, and during that period stock options or other compensation contingent on completing projects are used to retain workers.

The issue of commitment is addressed by the combination of this work organization arrangement and the tight network of relationships. Work experience is everything in finding better job opportunities. The other engineers and staff on a project have very good information about who pulled their weight on a project and know who they would want to work with again, who they would recommend to hire. Reputations, as a result, are very powerful, and they create strong incentives for employees to perform at a high level.

While there is no denying the extraordinary competitive attributes of the Silicon Valley system, it is important to remember the supporting conditions that this system requires. Among the necessary conditions are an adaptive and supportive postsecondary education system that offers the kind of training that firms elsewhere provide in-house. A related and more problematic requirement is that entry-level engineers need to have some initial experience, some work-based skills, before they are useful to a typical Silicon Valley firm. The fast-moving, entrepreneurial Valley firm is not organized in ways that provide such experience. And so the larger firms become the main source of those skills. A study of the computer disk drive industry, which is based in Silicon Valley, illustrates that virtually all of the talent that created it came from IBM. Virtually all of the key employees got their work-based skills from IBM before jumping ship to these small competitors.

A third requirement is a very high density of similar firms that makes for a large labor force in the region, even in highly defined occupations and specialties. Given that a particular industry has only so many firms worldwide, there are clear limits as to how many communities could support enough firms in a given industry to operate in the manner that Silicon Valley does. Communities like Austin, Texas, are striving to create an infrastructure that will allow them to operate like Silicon Valley. And in Taiwan, the massive Aspire Valley industrial community is an explicit attempt to mimic the Silicon Valley environment around information system companies. In the long run, it could be that the firms in many industries will be concentrated in dense communities like Silicon Valley.

Nor is the Silicon Valley an option for firms that don't fit the typical company profile. It seems to be the case that firms that need access to cutting-edge technology need to be located in Silicon Valley. Even firms that are located elsewhere, like IBM and Microsoft, need research outposts in the region to be part of the action. But firms with different needs can actually be ripped apart by trying to become part of that scene. For example, firms working on projects with very long-term horizons, where it is important to keep a research team together, need to be protected from the pressures of that competitive labor market. Even firms based in Silicon Valley have been known to move some operations outside, such as long-term development projects, to protect those operations from turnover. More generally, large firms that are vertically integrated only suffer damage from being in such an environment.

LESSONS LEARNED

It is no surprise that individual companies can succeed with arm's-length, market-based employment relationships that rely, for example, on poaching skilled workers from more traditionally oriented firms. It is more interesting to learn that entire industries can run successfully when the employment relationship is largely or even entirely governed by the market. These arrangements have some clear advantages for the firms. First, they allow employers to push the costs of training and development onto the employees themselves and then out into the market. Second, they make it possible for the employers to rearrange their own capabilities much more quickly, to bring in new skills and create new competencies very rapidly, as epitomized by the Silicon Valley firms. And they do so without increasing fixed operating costs.

These arrangements also come with their own constraints. As the earlier discussion of pilot training indicates, when training and development is pushed onto the market, employers lose control over the quality of the workforce they get. As the example of the employment relationship in higher education illustrates, it is very difficult to get employees to make investments in activities that are not valued by the outside labor market—in other words, to invest in skills that are truly unique to the organization. It also changes the way firms operate. Silicon Valley firms are wildly successful in markets driven by innovation and not very competitive in areas that require long, deep periods of development, such as perfecting products. In fact, firms trying to make the long-term investments necessary to compete in those markets would be pulled apart if they tried to operate in an environment like Silicon Valley.

Finally, all of these systems require infrastructure that is independent of the firms themselves to address the inherent problems created by market-driven employment relationships. Some of the infrastructure is government imposed, such as the regulations establishing and certifying pilot credentials; labor unions created equivalent standards for craft-based occupations. And some of it can spring up on its own. The outsourcing of training to entrepreneurial postsecondary institutions is perhaps the most obvious example. The most interesting point about the Silicon Valley example in this regard is how much of it seemed to develop spontaneously, such as the networks that provide information about the quality of different employees. As the business community there grows ever larger, however, it will be increasingly difficult to rely on that type of informal networking to get information.

CHAPTER 6

Adapting to the New Deal

THE EXAMPLES of industries and occupations in which mobility across firms is high, employee training and development take place in the market, and employees are unlikely to be committed to careers at individual firms illustrate not only that these alternative arrangements can work but also what it is that makes them work. Each of these models has infrastructure operating outside the firm that helps address the major problems created by the move to the market-driven new deal, the problems of employee development, retention, and commitment.

The Clinton Administration created a National Skills Standards Board with the goal of establishing the skill requirements for most jobs in the economy and, eventually, creating tests and credentials to certify the mastery of those skills. Efforts like these could in principle greatly facilitate the movement of employees across organizations. So far, however, these efforts have met so much resistance as to leave them essentially dead in the water. The prospects for extensive craft-based unionization of the economy or a substantial expansion of powerful professional associations that would standardize jobs and provide their own training are also slim. And for managers, the general progression toward broader job responsibilities and cross-functional orientations works against efforts to make even functional positions within management more like a profession (for instance, the human resource profession). More to the point, managers by definition are serving the unique goals of organizations as expressed by senior executives, not professional norms.

The Silicon Valley example is perhaps the most relevant in that it relates to more traditional, corporate jobs, and the infrastructure it requires is manageable—supportive education systems, plus information on employees and jobs managed through private networks. Because of such developments as the corporate search firm, which makes it easier to move employees across organizations, and the growing number of joint ventures that create networks of employees across firms, more and more firms may end up looking more like those in Silicon Valley, even if they don't physically reside in dense networks of similar firms. In that sense, the Silicon Valley example may be more a vision of the future for most firms than a practical guide for firms that currently are not in dense networks to emulate.

For most firms, the promising adaptations for addressing the problems created by the new deal at work lie not in infrastructure outside the firm but inside, with new practices designed to address the problems created by market-based employment relationships. The place to begin that discussion is with the perspective of the employer who is losing employees, the issue that drives the fundamental problems of employee retention, skill acquisition, and employee commitment.

THE POACHING PROBLEM

The arguments presented in earlier chapters suggest the reasons why employers are now more likely to look for the changing skills they need in the outside market as opposed to developing them internally. A survey of human resource executives and their company hiring practices shows a growing interest in hiring experienced employees since 1993. In particular, organizations that were themselves growing, where jobs had become broader based, more skilled, or more demanding, and where immediate performance was more important, all report increased hiring of experienced employees. In contrast, those employers that were expanding the proportion of inexperienced hires directly from college were doing so only because it was cheaper, a reaction to the rising prices of more experienced hires,[1] and apparently not because they preferred such applicants. Towers Perrin's Workforce 2000 Survey of more than three thousand employers found that about 40 percent said that lack of experience was a reason for them not to hire applicants for entry-level positions. A Wharton School study of performance in the financial services industry surveyed 70 of the leading life insurance companies and found their executives reporting that the most important source of new recruits for their firms is their competitors.

Anecdotes illustrate how widespread the poaching problem can be. St. Louis headhunter John R. Sibbald identified 150 up-and-coming executives, tracked them over time, and found that 80 percent had changed employers in fewer than two years. A. T. Kierney reports that the number of executive searches among its clients grew 15 percent over 1996, which was a record year. CEO searches in particular were up 28 percent.[2] Companies are increasingly suing each other over attempts to poach talent, as in the Borland International claim against Microsoft and similar lawsuits by Mays Department Stores against Bon-Ton Stores for hiring away its CEO.[3]

The poaching problem crosses national borders. When the information technologies market heated up in the United States, some U.S. companies headed to Canada, where the salaries were lower (and the temperatures colder), to poach staff. Manulife Financial notes that the exodus of its employees was particularly great from Saskatoon to firms in the warmer climates of the United States, with a great deal of the poaching taking place in the winter.

Nor is poaching limited to individual employees. In an example of team poaching, the head of Coopers and Lybrand's Madrid office took his entire team—ninety people, one third of C&L's Spain operation—to Ernst and Young.[4] Especially in hi-tech companies, where a project leader has assembled a team that works closely together, the entire team is likely to leave when the project leader gets an outside offer. The medical schools in the Philadelphia area have seen more than one occasion in which a complete research laboratory staff has followed a key researcher in moving from one school to another. When Allegheny Health Systems moved into the Philadelphia market, for example, it raided the cardiology and cardiac surgery departments of Presbyterian Medical Center to develop an instant presence in that specialty. Presbyterian then turned around and hired all but one of the cardiologists from Cooper Health Systems in nearby Camden. Cooper initiated talks with Allegheny, whose cardiac program is now booming, about a possible merger. It also filed a suit against Presbyterian for damaging its ability to compete.[5] (Allegheny subsequently filed for bankruptcy, and its medical school has essentially been "acquired" by another school, Drexel University.)

On a smaller scale, the proliferation of referral fees for recruiting, where employees receive a payment if someone they refer to the company is hired, has helped increase the flow of recruits across companies. Researchers who study social networks find that employees who leave are likely to pull others in their network out with them. Consider the case in which a key employee is hired from Company A to Company B. That person is told about vacancies in his area of the company and is given a financial incentive to recruit new workers. This person is quite likely to know workers in Company A with the requisite skills who would be good employees. So he contacts them about moving, and the poaching model advances. Such referrals work well for the hiring company but are a disaster for the losing employer. And some firms, like Microsoft, have included in their noncompete agreements provisions that prohibit employees who leave from trying to recruit away former coworkers.

Another manifestation of the growth of outside hiring has been the exploding market for job fairs, which have been transformed from mainly nonprofit, informal events run by third parties into for-profit events run by specialized companies that charge up to $5,000 per recruiting company. Particularly in the technology area, the attraction of the fairs is to find high-quality applicants who already have jobs but may be interested in moving. Recruiters also use them as a way to check out current salaries.[6]

Even small companies are willing and able to recruit senior executives from leading companies by throwing money at them. Alex J. Mandl, the heir apparent to head AT&T, was lured away to Associated Communications, L.L.C., a small operation that offered him a signing bonus of more than $20 million. A stream of AT&T executives have left for smaller companies when they were offered equity stakes with considerable upside potential.[7] A survey of clients of the Walker Group's human resource consulting practice found that one of these firms' biggest retention challenges was employee poaching by start-up firms that offered large equity stakes.

The use of outside hires to bring in new skills and competencies can in many cases substitute for more risky courses of action. Hiring outside executives, for example, has become a viable substitute for acquiring companies. AT&T wanted to enter the computer systems integration business but worried about whether it could integrate such a company acquired from the outside into the rest of AT&T's culture. Instead, AT&T turned to corporate recruiters and asked them to find the top fifty system integrators in the country. AT&T hired them and started its own operations, inside AT&T.

When companies decide that they want to change their business strategies or fine-tune some initiative, their first move is increasingly to bring in managers from other companies that are seen as leaders in those areas. For example, as the consumer electronics and computer industries move into each other's markets, they have begun to recruit each other's employees as a way to gain the other industry's expertise. "What you have is the NFL draft of electronics executives," says Bob Lee, head of Manpower in San Jose. The U.S. unit of Mitsubishi's consumer electronics group hired twenty engineers from computer companies to its research staff in one swoop, one-fifth of its total staff.[8]

A study of service companies that had decided to boost the responsibility and skill level of clerks found that most of these companies got the higher skills by hiring them in from the outside market rather than developing them internally.[9] When an oil company wants to expand the sales of products at its service stations, it hires managers from Pepsi and Frito-Lay with expertise in retailing to lead the challenge; when an airline wants to get better at customer relationships, it goes to Marriott to recruit executives with experience in how to please customers; when a power company prepares for deregulation, it hires from a phone company that has already gone through the transition. Instead of developing new business strategies and sweating through the details of an implementation plan internally, many companies instead shop for them by hunting for executives at companies that have already executed those strategies.

The most obvious effort to stem the poaching tide is simply to pay employees to stay. *Golden handcuffs* is the term used for compensation packages that pay employees for staying with the company. Typically these arrangements are options that can be redeemed only after so many years of service or pension plans that take time to vest. Companies like Emerson Electric are known for having such elaborate golden handcuffs that corporate recruiters avoid their executives. In that sense, these programs act much like burglar alarms do in reducing crime: just as alarms persuade criminals that it is easier to loot elsewhere, golden handcuffs stave off corporate recruiters.

Sometimes these golden handcuff programs do not work as expected. When Lou Gerstner arrived at IBM, he discovered that despite all the leveraged compensation and golden handcuffs in place for his key employees, they were being picked off by competitors right and left. The reason had to do with the decline in IBM's fortunes, and with that its stock price. As Gestner put it, "What I've got is an employee group with absolutely no incentive to stay here because every one of their options is under water."[10] And sometimes the effects of golden handcuffs can be downright perverse. Researchers in the semiconductor industry report that leveraged compensation in some situations actually seemed to reduce retention. They found that when large profit-sharing bonuses were distributed or a company's stock price was booming, and with it, the value of employee stock options, engineers often took that as an opportunity to cash in their profits and leave these larger companies for start-ups.[11] The payouts gave them the financial security to take bigger risks with their careers. Labor economists have long recognized a related consequence of such incentives: that when they pay out, the sharp increases in income they provide lead the average worker to work less, essentially "buying" more leisure by retiring early or shifting to an easier job with shorter hours. Companies like Microsoft, where 2,000 of its 17,000 employees are already millionaires,[12] has had to find techniques other than money to keep those people on board and motivated.

Once golden handcuffs become common across companies, they no longer keep recruiters at bay. They simply raise the size of the offers. Recruiting companies have responded to golden handcuff programs by essentially buying out the incentives. Some observers now call these payments "golden hellos." The enormous payment Alex Mandl received to leave AT&T was offered in part to offset the $10 million in AT&T stock options he forfeited on leaving. Such payments are spreading to middle management recruits now that the golden handcuffs are applied to these positions. One aspect of these buyouts is relocation payments, ostensibly to compensate for moving costs, which now average more than $500,000 for a newly acquired CEO, as opposed to about $45,000 for the average employee owning a home. Experts agree that these relocation expenses are mainly a tax-free method of compensating executives, one that also keeps their signing bonuses and other forms of compensation from looking even bigger.[13]

The recruiting companies have also gotten smarter about their efforts to buy out retention incentives. Signing bonuses like the one received by Mandl are paid out over a long period of time, five years in his case, to help retain new hires. When Continental Airlines hired Gordon Bethune from Boeing with a $1.5 million signing bonus, for example, the agreement was that he would pay back the entire amount if he left before the first year and 50 percent if he left before the second.[14] So the signing bonuses themselves essentially become incentives for employee retention.

And signing bonuses have become ubiquitous. A 1997 survey shows 40 percent of companies were offering hiring bonuses, even fast-food companies like Burger King that were known for high turnover and low wages. At many of these companies, including Burger King, the hiring bonuses are paid after the employees have been with the company for some time—three months at Burger King—in the form of a retention bonus. But the newly hired workers appear to be leaving after that.[15]

In this sense, golden handcuff operations and their counterstrategies are not really the answer to the problem of poaching. Under the right conditions, they *may* help individual companies retain employees by sending corporate recruiters to easier targets, much as burglar alarms redistribute crime to unprotected residences. But when labor markets get tight and more competitors adopt them, they simply drive labor costs up further. They become a nightmare for human resource managers who find themselves caught between the doomsday option of seeing the organization's talent and competency stream out the door and the almost-as-bad alternative of endless bidding wars that balloon compensation costs and disrupt internal reward systems. In the end, they become just another aspect of compensation: not introducing them will virtually assure that employees will be picked off, while doing so simply brings the relationship back to where it was. And once these financial incentives are exercised, they may well have the opposite effect, releasing employees from their ties to the company.

EMPLOYEE RETENTION

Poaching drives the retention problem, and turnover of employees is the driver of both the skills and the commitment problems. After all, if employers could be certain that they could retain employees, it would be possible to make and recoup investments in skills. And employees who saw their interests in being tied to the employer for some reasonably long period of time would be going a long way toward having a sense of commitment to that employer.

The first step in addressing the issue of employee retention is to recognize that it cannot be "solved" in the usual sense. There will be no silver bullet program or set of programs that will bind employees to the organization in the presence of attractive opportunities elsewhere. Employers can and should work hard to eliminate problems in the workplace that might drive their valued employees into the arms of competitors. But, as noted earlier, most people who quit do so to take jobs elsewhere, and dissatisfaction with current jobs drives turnover only when other positions are available. The "pull" of alternatives is the major driver of turnover, not just the "push" of problems in the current workplace. The growing need to find talent in the outside market will become the main driver of the retention problem, although employers exacerbate the problem by focusing employee attention on the labor market and giving them more information on other jobs, increasing the likelihood that they will leave.

Managing employee retention is much like managing the flow of a river system in which the goal is not to prevent water from flowing out but to control where it goes and at what rate. Despite the complaints about managers leaving, it is hard to imagine that many companies would really want lifetime employment relationships again even if they could make it happen. The speed at which markets change and companies restructure suggest that a company will at some point no longer have a need for certain skills and will lack the ability and inclination to retrain the employees whose value to the company had been based on those skills. Employers need new skills and a constant flow of new entrants. On the other hand, losing key employees before a project is completed can be even more devastating now than in the past, because now an organization's competencies are more embedded in individuals than they are in systems or bureaucracies.

The place to begin managing employee retention is with a brutally honest assessment of how long the organization would ideally like competent employees to stay with it. This is a very tough assignment to even contemplate in most organizations that still cling at least to the rhetoric of the lifetime employment model. In many cases, it can be relatively easy to estimate when it is crucial to keep workers and when to let them go. For jobs organized around projects, it is obviously crucial to keep work teams together until the project is completed. There may also be real advantages to carrying over some employees, and their learning, to the next project. Yet there also may come a time when the projects change enough that previous skills are outdated or when the goal of the project is a paradigm break requiring fresh faces. In stable organizations where the work really does not change, there may seem to be advantages to keeping the same employees forever. Here the issue is whether such a goal is realistic. As employees get more experience, their skills and interests change, and their expectations also rise. Keeping them in the same jobs may require paying them more than the job is worth or may risk boring them to the point where performance falls off.

While relatively few organizations try to manage commitment explicitly, the tools for doing so are relatively straightforward. And some organizations do manage it explicitly. The position of junior analyst in investment banking, for example, is a two-year appointment after which the young employees are expected to leave. Even though they are more skilled and useful after their stint, their tasks are simple enough that additional skills and experience are not that much more useful, and the next level of work in the firm requires further education.

As noted above, compensation can be an unpredictable mechanism for managing commitment. But it can play a role by manipulating when employees become "locked," or bound for some length of time, and "unlocked," or encouraged to leave. Consider, for example, consulting firms that have an interest in continually getting new blood into their organization not only to get new ideas but also to bring in new people with the stamina to put up with the grueling pace of work. Compensation in such firms rises rapidly through the partner promotions. After about fifteen years of service, many firms subtly encourage turnover by making opportunities for promotion and major salary increases come very slowly.

Managing employee retention is a competitive problem in that employers are competing with each other to retain workers. Programs that are easily copied by competitors, such as golden handcuffs or compensation, lead to no long-term improvements in retention. The better options are those which create unique ties to the organization that cannot be easily duplicated elsewhere.

SAS software has held its annual turnover to about 4 percent in an industry where the average is about six times higher. And SAS does it despite paying compensation that is noticeably below the industry average. The main retention device at SAS is to tie employees to the community by providing discounted prices for homesites as well as family friendly benefits such as child care. Some observers describe the SAS campus as akin to a giant plantation.[16] Harris Semiconductor is in a similar position with its facility in rural Pennsylvania. Turnover averages an amazingly low 2 percent, compared with more than 20 percent in the semiconductor industry. Certainly part of the explanation is that there are few other job alternatives in that region. If employees want to quit, they more or less have to move to find anything like an equivalent job.

The job opportunities issue is also the key to the low turnover rate among dual-career couples, who now account for more than 20 percent of all professional households. They resist relocating and turn down transfers more often because it's hard to find two new jobs. For that reason, they also prefer to locate in large cities because such locations offer more job choices.[17]

Carl Glaeser, general manager of INgage Solutions, a Phoenix-based division of AG Communications Systems, has held the turnover of software engineers to 7 percent, mainly by developing programs that create a social community in the workplace. Golf leagues, investment clubs, and softball teams all create social ties between workers and bind them to their current job. Leaving the company, even if you stay in the same region, means leaving your social network of company-sponsored activities. There are downsides to every program, of course, and arrangements that help to create community within an organization make the trauma of any potential restructuring enormous because it rips apart communities as well as corporations.

Similarly, companies that locate in rural areas find that while their employees stay put, it is hard to get them to locate there in the first place. Research labs in small communities, for example, find it difficult to attract experienced workers and are much more likely to hire new college grads as a result (43 percent of the hires as opposed to 6 percent in larger communities). This is because new graduates, as opposed to experienced hires, are already committed to moving somewhere because they are leaving school.[18]

Perhaps the most promising approaches to managing retention relate to how jobs and tasks can be organized—whether it is possible to structure the work process itself so that employees feel more tightly bound to the organization. Programs like quality circles lower turnover in several ways. They formalize and clarify goals, helping to achieve consensus in the work group. They also create a much stronger sense of team spirit and identification with the group, which helps retain employees. Work systems in which employees are not organized around groups are associated with higher turnover.[19] Similarly, firms that place more value on interpersonal issues, such as greater orientation toward teams and more respect for individuals, also have lower turnover; those which focus more attention on work tasks, concentrating on performance at the expense of relationships, have higher turnover rates.[20]

A benchmarking study of leading companies conducted by Arthur Andersen Business Consulting on reducing turnover in "hot" fields like finance and information systems found that most reported new efforts to bind employees to the organization through social relationships at the workplace. There is a greater use of teams, and employee roles and tasks are now more clearly defined in terms of their work group and other groups in the company.[21] Companies such as INgage Solutions try to build in attachment by involving employees in projects at the customer level, where they see the consequences of their work, and in the decision-making processes that shape the projects.

Other approaches redesign jobs to *accommodate* employee attrition rather than reduce it. The fast food industry, where employee turnover averages 300 percent, offers some classic examples. Customer service positions, with their irregular hours, have long been aimed at part-time workers like students, whose turnover rate is inevitably high. Burger-flipping jobs, with their high structure and remarkably low skill requirements, were designed so that new employees can easily transition into them.

Nevertheless, turnover can still be costly, and some fast food chains have worked hard to cut turnover. Chi-Chi's cut the rate to 120 percent for hourly workers and, most important, to less than 10 percent for managers. The company has arranged its systems so that turnover of the hourly staff can be accommodated relatively easily, in part because the managers have the tasks and organization-specific skills that are important to retain. They hold those key workers by changing the work design.[22] Cross-training and rotating workers makes it easier to adjust to losing workers unexpectedly; it also makes the jobs more interesting by creating more variety in them.[23] The semiconductor industry has responded to high turnover among operators in similar ways, by certifying operators on more machines, rotating them to new positions every three months.[24]

One might argue that United Parcel Service also adapted to the problem of high turnover with a strategy that expanded part-time positions to handle the demanding task of loading delivery trucks. Loading trucks is a simple task, but one with a high injury rate. In the past, it was handled by individual drivers, and it was thought to have been the least pleasant aspect of the driver's job. By unbundling it from the tasks of the driver, UPS reduced the turnover of drivers, who are more difficult to replace, while intensifying it among the new truck loading positions. Turnover in those jobs averages an amazing 400 percent per year. But with very high wages and low skill requirements, they are also easy to fill, typically with students who are unlikely to stay with a job for long in any case.[25]

Another alternative, particularly for less-skilled positions, is to address the problems outside the workplace that often force employees out of jobs. Problems with health care, child care, or housing, for example, contribute to poor performance and dismissals or force employees to quit. Marriott International has taken the lead in a more paternalistic approach, at first working one-on-one with individual employees. "Many managers spend 15 percent of their time doing social work," says Clifford J. Ehrlich, Marriott International's senior vice president of human resources. But managerial time is expensive, and efforts to trim managerial positions make that individual counseling expensive.

Instead, many companies have created programs that provide access to these kinds of services. Among its many programs, Marriott offers an Associate Resource Line, a toll-free referral service for social services, parenting classes, and 24-hour subsidized day care. Aramark offers English as a second language classes and conflict management training. ConAgra Refrigerated Foods Companies introduced child care and housing projects. Opryland Hotel created a company motel to house three hundred new hires at subsidized rates until they find housing. After finding that productivity was 20 percent higher for employees with more than one year of tenure, J. C. Penny introduced flexible work shifts to help retain more experienced workers. So great is the interest in these programs that the Families and Work Institute in New York has created a consortium of twenty-eight companies that share best practices for retaining low-wage workers.[26]

An alternative to retention is simply to get better at recruiting, finding workers who are more likely to stay (perhaps because they have fewer options), or to get better at replacing them if they leave. A study of hi-tech companies in Ireland found them working hard to find the best talent from universities but spending relatively little effort to retain them once hired. The companies were so successful at recruiting that they had little difficulty replacing those who left with new graduates. One-third of the technical staff was either in the process of leaving or planned to do so shortly. The faster-paced electronics firms in the study wanted even more turnover to get new skills, keep their costs down (paying new entrants less), and keep energy levels up.[27] Companies in the United Kingdom have responded to labor shortages by developing relationships with schools. Essentially, they've had the schools take over some of the screening and monitoring of candidates for entry-level jobs, helping the companies identify applicants who would be good fits with their operations.[28]

Improving recruiting efforts to address retention problems is particularly important in labor-intensive industries, where the great fear is that if employers raise entry-level wages, it will create pressure to increase pay for other jobs in the organization, raising wages across the board and making the firms uncompetitive. A great many companies are remarkably unsophisticated about hiring and use methods, such as unstructured interviews, that are worse than tossing a coin. In fact, a colleague and I found that the more intensive use of such selection techniques, even controlling for their cost, was actually associated with worse financial performance.[29] These companies could make enormous strides in improving their hiring practices with relatively little effort, and many of them are beginning to do so.

In the fast food industry, for example, where employee selection has historically been unsophisticated, companies like Longhorn Steaks have begun using interview guides with structured interview questions across all restaurants to get better at employee selection. The Price Chopper grocery chain has moved to computer-assisted interviewing that begins with telephone-based prescreening through a system of automated questions. When it comes to the actual interview, applicants spend forty-five minutes answering standardized questions on a computer monitor before moving on to a personal interview. The system not only cuts costs but creates real consistency across regions.[30] Temporary help agencies have also developed real competencies at recruiting and selection because they do so much of it, often directly for client companies. Temporary staffing companies like Uniforce encourage clients to try out temps for permanent jobs with programs like Smart Hire, through which Uniforce offers a ninety-day, no obligation trial. Client companies use the agencies to screen workers because it allows them to sidestep the restrictions of protective employment legislation. Thirty percent of temp agency workers find a full-time job through their temp assignments.

Other companies have attempted to improve their recruiting and find better workers by looking in applicant pools that other employers ignore. Burger King is pursuing nontraditional applicants like senior citizens more intensively.[31] Marriott's Pathways to Independence program is targeted at former welfare recipients, who might find it difficult to secure employment without the program. It teaches life skills (through self-esteem training, for instance) and basic academic and work skills in a six-week module, splitting the $5,500 cost with local social service agencies. So far the turnover rate of these employees has only been about 13 percent in jobs where turnover of 100 percent is common.[32]

Many employers are turning to groups like Goodwill Industries, which work with hard-to-employ groups, as a means of finding potential diamonds in the rough. Microboard Processing, a Connecticut-based assembler of electronics components, hires one-third of its new workers from high-risk applicants, including former drug addicts, welfare recipients, and those with criminal records. The company is careful at selection and often begins the new workers on simple landscaping jobs to see how they do before moving them inside to the assembly jobs. It also gives workers lots of slack during the first few months on the job, knowing that many of these employees are not used to the discipline of factory work. But the company says it is getting a hard-working pool of workers in return who are grateful and loyal to it for giving them a chance.[33]

Architectural Support Services, a computer-aided design company providing technical support for architects, illustrates another approach to improving recruiting. The company began life using textbook human resource practices, including hiring the best and brightest staff it could find. Yet it found its operations in shambles because of poor worker morale, which was driven by conflicts within the high-powered staff. The company thought hard about what it really needed in a workforce and realized that it did not need the best and the brightest in all of its staff positions. It went back into the labor market to hire, but this time shied away from pedigreed hiring, recruiting from community colleges instead of elite four-year institutions. It found a much more loyal and committed workforce that was a better match with its jobs.[34]

COOPERATION AMONG COMPETITORS

The sense that retention and recruitment are competitive exercises has kept most companies from seeking help from each other in these areas. But this was not always the case. One of the most interesting examples of companies cooperating to address skill needs and retention problems was in the aircraft industry. In the 1950s, companies like Lockheed, McDonnell-Douglas, and Northrop competed with each other fiercely for the government contracts that were their lifeblood. When a company won a new contract, it then faced the problem of hiring additional staff quickly to carry out that work. When a company lost a contract or simply finished a project, it then had the problem of excess staff to lay off.

An alternative arrangement that developed in southern California, where many of these firms had operations, was to "lend" teams of employees from one company to the other to meet these problems of peak demand. The company that lost a fighter contract, for example, would subcontract a team of employees with that expertise to the company that won the new contract for fighter aircraft. But the work teams remained employees of the first company. Lockheed reported that its program, known as Lending Employees for National Development (LEND), had a wide range of benefits. In addition to avoiding layoffs, the company also retained its investment in key employees, retained its capabilities to bid on future contracts, and broadened the experience of its leased employees.[35]

The aerospace industry saw another, very different type of cooperation between prime contractors and subcontractors. Complicated components for large projects would be created at a subcontractor, then moved to the prime contractor, where they would be assembled into a larger module and passed on to a final assembler, before being delivered to a client like NASA, all in a process that could take years. Some employees of the subcontractor could literally follow the component to the main contractors, becoming employees of those contractors and working alongside their staff.[36]

Some employers have also begun to cooperate in addressing issues of employee flows, even in hiring. Perhaps the most expansive example is the Talent Alliance, an organization that began at AT&T and has grown to include about thirty large companies. It began as a kind of sophisticated job bank during the era of downsizing and corporate unemployment. Companies that had to lay off skilled workers could essentially market them to other employers that might be looking for such skills. Similar programs operate regionally, like one in Milwaukee that brought area hospitals together essentially to internalize and rationalize the labor market for nurses, not within a single firm but within a network of firms. The Talent Alliance went a step further by providing standardized instruments for screening and evaluating employees and for matching them with jobs across member firms.

Other, more ad hoc collaborations are appearing among noncompeting companies. Cascade Engineering, a plastic parts manufacturer, and the local Burger King operations have sought economies by pooling their recruiting and selection efforts. Applicants who do not have the skill levels for Cascade's production positions but who otherwise seem like good workers are offered jobs at Burger King. And Burger King employees, who are otherwise expected to turn over quickly, are offered vocational counseling and the possibility of better positions at Cascade in the long run as both a short-term retention device and an incentive to take Burger King jobs in the first place.[37] This example illustrates the type of career development that individuals in the past would have experienced within a single company.

Selection mistakes are more likely as employers do more hiring, of course, and finding better ways to deal with those mistakes is another necessary adaptation. Cisco Systems, the Internet software company, has worked out new policies for addressing selection mistakes. It does a great deal of hiring not only because of the rapid turnover in that industry but also because the company is growing. Cisco has a three-month review for all new employees and a no-fault separation policy offering severance pay for employees who want out of the company.[38] Programs like these must be designed with care, of course, or they could encourage job hopping in a tight labor market. Employees with hot skills, for example, could stay the three months, collect the severance pay, and hop to another company.

Another inevitable approach to dealing with high rates of turnover is to make even more use of temporary help and contract employees. A benchmarking study conducted by the Corporate Leadership Council found that it took two days to staff a position through a temporary help firm versus about thirty days for external hires in the equivalent position.[39]

A final adaptation, one that is used in parallel with other approaches, is simply to adjust the organization and its work systems to avoid disruptions when employees leave more frequently. Organizing work around short-term projects with clear end points, for example, at least focuses the retention issue: It is crucial to keep employees until the project is completed. It matters far less after that. And keeping someone for a short, fixed period can be managed with compensation and other techniques. More teamwork and cross-functional systems that reduce the dependence on any one individual are other techniques for adjusting to turnover. As was demonstrated in the early days of industrialization, simplifying and standardizing jobs is a classic technique for dealing with turnover. Moving from legacy systems, even if they may suit the organization's needs, to more common, off-the-shelf systems is a way to ensure that the operating skills can be found in the market. The organization will not be devastated if current employees leave.

Information technology also helps employers cope by preserving some of the institutional memory that employees would otherwise take with them. Customer relationship software automates sales and gives clerks access to client histories, including prior sales and complaints, allowing them to sound familiar with accounts they know nothing about. Systems like Lotus Notes have been found to standardize interactions and keep records of decisions and crucial contextual information, providing something like an electronic record of employee knowledge.[40] Other programs, such as Livelink, allow all employees on an intranet to track and share documents in the system, while Lotus Development's Domino software allows individuals to search Notes databases to create documents. Pamela Hirshman, a project manager at Young & Rubicam, describes taking over a project in which all of the employees working on it had left. "The project file had a record of all the E-mails between the team and the client, and after reviewing about fifty of these, I was up to speed on the problems of the client and where the project was heading." New simulation software on team-based project management, such as "Project Challenge," allows new teams of workers to learn how to work together much more quickly than on-the-job experience would allow. Studies have found that information technology can be used to capture knowledge and transfer it across the organization, helping to protect against the loss of learning that occurs when employees leave.[41]

Perhaps the ultimate solution for turnover-prone jobs is simply to outsource them. A great many companies that outsource IT functions, for example, do so because they cannot retain the employees. Often their systems and projects are not sophisticated enough to hold the interest of employees who want to keep their skills sharp in a market where such skills can outdate themselves as quickly as milk in a grocery store.

EMPLOYEE TRAINING AND CAREER DEVELOPMENT

As the arguments presented earlier suggest, both the ability and the inclination of employers to train and develop employees internally has eroded. The interest in internal development is hampered by the fact that rapid changes in products, firm restructuring, and other uncertainties make it difficult to know what skills will be needed in the long run. And the problem of poaching dooms any efforts to finance such development, even when it makes sense to do in every other respect.

In some cases, the reduction in training creates a vicious circle of skill shortages that lead to even more outside hiring. Perhaps the best example of this is now occurring in multinational companies operating in developing companies like China, where the shortage of potential employees with managerial skills is acute. Companies with longer experience in China, like Xerox, IBM, and Bristol-Myers, find that as their competitors enter the market, they need staff with some experience in China. And they get them by poaching from other multinationals at an incredible rate. Not only has this bid up wages, but it has also sharply reduced the interest of these companies in developing their own talent because they fear—rightly—that they will lose their investments in new employees to a higher bidder who can pay more for a trained worker. As employee development declines, the labor shortage gets worse.

The problem of poaching has now eroded firms' ability to finance internal development even when they have the internal capabilities and long-term plans to make it worthwhile. Companies like Disney had near monopolies in their market niches for decades and developed their own talent because there was no option. But the rise of competitors in the theme park business has led to a great deal of poaching at Disney, whose park designers have become highly sought after by competitors. Kodak is another organization long known for internal development. It essentially recruited no one over the age of twenty-five before the early 1980s, instead developing all of its talent internally. All of that has changed as its business has become more volatile, especially the chemical business. Kodak now has an explicit goal to staff only about one-third of its core management with internally developed, long-service employees. In the film business, however, Kodak still develops virtually all of its talent internally. It can do that because there is no poaching; its main competitor, Fuji Film in Japan, so far has shown little interest in hiring Kodak employees. There are other exceptions as well. Insiders say that Pratt and Whitney's and General Electric's jet engine and turbine divisions, which together dominate the jet engine business, have had such an intense rivalry that it kept them from poaching each other's employees because they feared that outside hires would be disloyal, and made it both possible and necessary to develop employees internally.

Companies that have made big investments in employees are increasingly finding that those employees are systematically hired away by competitors after the training is completed. The German electronics company Siemens established a U.S. version of its vaunted apprenticeship programs with the opening of its new facility in Florida. The training program was terrific, and the graduates were highly qualified. What Siemens discovered, however, was that local companies were swooping in and hiring the apprentices, often before they completed their training. When Siemens complained to some of these companies that they were unfairly pirating its investment, the reply was, essentially, "Welcome to America." Just to show that the incentives for poaching cross borders, the U.S. competitors of the German automotive corporation Bosch suggest that Bosch's decision to open a research and development facility in the United States, rather than Germany, was driven by its interest in piggybacking on (or pirating, depending on your view) the knowledge of researchers from U.S. companies.

Researchers looking for employer programs that would help students make the transition to the workplace found very few that offered the kind of training and skills that transferred to other organizations. One of these companies, a metal-working contractor, explained the problem: "I've actually had competitors call me up and say I have an excellent school here. That's why we walked away from hiring vocational students: we get them up to speed, and they move over to competitors who don't want to spend the money to teach these guys anything."[42]

The difficulty that poaching creates for employer-financed training has led some to speculate that the solution may lie in public policy. But there has been little support for specific proposals, in part because substantial government administrative and regulations seem to be required to make them happen. The Clinton Administration's early efforts to put forward a small payroll tax for training that would be refunded to employers providing training equal to the value of the tax on their operations paralleled the French training tax but went nowhere. In Germany, employers that do not provide apprenticeship training pay fees to their local employer organizations, which are used to subsidize those employers that do provide training. In the United Kingdom, an Industrial Training Board program operated within industries to tax companies that provided little training and to transfer subsidies to those which did. But the program was abandoned in the 1980s, as were most youth apprenticeship programs, in favor of expansion of postsecondary education. One of the few simple proposals out there has been put forward by the Progressive Policy Institute and is intended to address the fact that employer expenditures are disproportionately targeted at executives. If training was viewed as an employer-funded benefit, much like pensions or health insurance, Internal Revenue Service regulations would require employers to offer it to all of their workers if they offered it to any (such as the executives). Otherwise, training would be viewed as taxable compensation.[43]

Anecdotal evidence suggests that while employers are interested in the idea of developing their employees, including those companies which have adopted the "employability" contract described earlier, they have not always made progress toward doing so. The Arthur Andersen benchmarking study of the practices of leading companies in hot job markets found these companies uniformly increasing their commitment to career development as a means of retaining employees. Exactly how they will do it is less clear, however, because traditional notions of internal development are no longer applicable.[44] Even in areas of low unemployment where firms were desperate for workers, employers felt that they had no responsibility to people who lack the basic skills to hold a job and were providing very little entry-level training. They were receptive to doing more, but only if it could be done cheaply.[45] I recently spoke to a group of insurance executives from about thirty-five different companies and asked them about the management training programs they went through when they entered the industry, generally fifteen to twenty years earlier. The typical program lasted about one year. Then I asked how long their programs were now. None of the companies had a program.

Perhaps the most straightforward of the attempts to make employer-provided training pay is to draw up a contract that binds employees to the company for some length of time after receiving the training. If employees want to leave before that period ends, they must pay back the employer some agreed upon amount that reflects the value of the training. Contracts like these are increasingly common in hi-tech companies such as Texas Instruments and EDS, but they are also occurring in other industries that require expensive, specialized training. An example is Nissan, which sends some employees on extended training programs to Japan. A similar arrangement was established for the Los Angeles Police Department to retain recent police academy graduates who were abandoning the city for jobs in the suburbs. The Los Angeles City Council passed a resolution stating that officers who left the LAPD within five years of graduating from the academy must pay the city back the costs of training—$56,000. The council is supporting state legislation that would require communities to reimburse city agencies when they hire away employees.[46]

It is not clear what impact such training contracts will have. In the case of the Los Angeles Police Department, for example, critics say the training contract may discourage applicants and that forcing officers who want to leave the department to stay would disrupt morale. In general, these contracts do support the ability of companies to finance training programs, although they may not improve retention. When employees break the contract, it is inevitably to take a job elsewhere, and in virtually every case their new employer pays the damages, just as they buy out golden handcuff retention incentives. This is the method described earlier that temporary help agencies use to finance their training—making their clients who hire away temps into permanent jobs pay a fee for doing so. Disputes over these contracts rarely go to court. One of my employment law colleagues offered an opinion on why: Employers know that they will likely be on both sides of these disputes at some point, and they have no interest in contributing to a body of complex case law that would only make these disputes more litigious in the future.

Other efforts in employee development take a more cost-effective approach. One involves turning the problem of churning in the workforce into an advantage by internalizing contingent work. AT&T developed its Resource Link program in 1991 to address some of the consequences of downsizing. Employees who were made redundant or surplus were placed in a pool available to what would otherwise be contingent jobs offered to outsiders. By now 40 percent of participants join the program voluntarily. They do so to expand their work experience, either to broaden their skills or to deepen them in some specific area. Half of these volunteers are in information systems or technical jobs where skills can quickly deteriorate unless they are continually updated. Resource Link reduces the need for these employees to move on to other organizations to keep their skills fresh. It also buffers these workers from business changes. The introduction of a new operating system, for example, no longer dooms the current programmers, who can move into the Resource Link pool.[47]

Arrangements like these obviously work only for very large firms whose portfolio of employee skills is wide enough to let them make good employee/position matches without going to the outside market. Such programs also require that barriers to movement within the company be reduced and that local operations make some accommodations for those employees who do have the precise skills needed in their contingent positions. This strategy is essentially similar to using the market, albeit internalizing it within a large firm, but it still represents a reasonably substantial investment in employee skills as compared with simply using the outside market.

The Talent Alliance described earlier also provides opportunities for swapping and sharing training programs across different organizations. A participating company like Johnson & Johnson may have excellent training on quality control that it makes available to the other companies in the alliance, possibly in return for access to their training programs. The Consortium for Supplier Training is a nonprofit group of about twenty major companies designed specifically to make training cheaper for the member companies. It standardized TQM coursework and created a common curriculum through a network of providers, including local colleges that are nominated by each company. The Bershire Plastics Network is yet another employer consortium, this one of competitors in the same region, who came together to address the problem of getting entry-level workers with adequate skills. They did so by providing common training for entry-level workers, making it much more affordable in the process.[48] In the union sector, the Hotel Employees and Restaurant Employees International Union, for example, bargained with twelve San Francisco hotels to fund a training program for new entrant workers. Those in the program now learn basic skills in the hospitality industry. The program also provides some credentialing arrangements that allow graduates to certify their skills and move more easily across employers in the region. One way to think of this arrangement is that it helps create something like a craft occupational labor market for these jobs and workers.[49]

The explosive growth of for-profit training providers and the establishment of a market for them is another example of the need to make training cheaper. Private providers can offer similar training programs to a number of employers, spreading the fixed costs across them. The rapid growth of business school executive education programs, for example, has been driven largely by employers who essentially outsource training to these providers. Even company-specific training is outsourced. In fact, the majority of the executive education programs at schools like Wharton are no longer open enrollment courses. They are programs designed specifically for individual companies.

The actual pedagogy of training delivery is also undergoing change. In the insurance industry, for example, agents are a key source of competitive advantage, but their rapid turnover has made the cost of traditional classroom-based training programs prohibitive. Innovative approaches for training agents create opportunities for trainees to make contributions while they are learning by combining training with work. For example, new agents become runners or apprentices to successful agents, performing tasks such as scheduling their appointments and learning skills such as the fine art of closing a deal. They also split commissions with the experienced agents, 70/30, which gives them a real incentive to perform.[50] This apprentice-like training avoids the fixed costs of classroom training, allows the trainees to contribute while they are learning, and puts trainees in a practical context that makes learning more likely to stick.

The information technology field has skill needs that change so fast that employees who are not learning may find themselves with obsolete skills in as short a period as a year if systems are changed. Most companies report that to hold onto sharp IT employees, they must keep their systems on the cutting edge. Even if they do not need new equipment or systems, they have to get them. As Gerry McCarthy, director of Wharton's Computing Services observes, IT people "want to play with the hot toys. That's what keeps them here." Companies like Unisys put their research tools on their intranet so employees can play with them, developing their skills.[51]

Traditional types of training are being offered more effectively. For example, Merrill Lynch has found a way to offer an incredible array of training for IT employees at its Princeton, New Jersey, training facilities, and has done it in a cost-effective manner by standardizing and modularizing the training. The company has turned training into a source of competitive advantage for recruiting and retaining employees. Other companies, like Davidson Plyforms, a furniture maker in Grand Rapids, have also modularized their training, making it possible to start unskilled workers learning very simple skills.[52] The Price-Chopper grocery store chain has moved to computer-based training for its hourly staff and cut its required training hours by 40 percent. Because the training can be delivered when workers are free (all that is required is a PC), the company is able to deliver a greater variety of training programs, forty new programs this year. It credits this more effective training with reducing turnover by 11 percent.[53] Internet providers are now offering complete arrays of training programs, from registering applicants to delivering the instruction, all over the Web.[54]

Another very important alternative for employers is to find ways to make employees share some of the costs of training. Employees certainly benefit from training, especially when it develops the kind of skills that trade on the open market and raise wages. They certainly have an incentive to help share in the costs of training if doing so would help them get more of it. In this regard, the framework of employment law in the United States represents a substantial constraint. The Fair Labor Standards Act, in particular, mandates that employers pay for all of the costs of required training and that they pay employees wages while they are receiving it. While it may be possible in effect to make employees share the costs of training by lowering their wages, employers cannot literally make them do so.

There are some creative ways around the legal prohibitions, however. The most straightforward is simply to require employees to attend certain training programs before they can be hired. At the state level, community college systems often facilitate these arrangements by setting up classes tailored to providing the skills that a particular employer needs. The employer then requires applicants to complete the community college courses on their own time (and on their own dollar) before they can be hired. The community colleges participate in these arrangements as a means of helping to support local businesses. Guilford Technical Community College in North Carolina has gone so far as to create simulated factory settings to train and then screen applicants for companies like Dow Corning and Banner Pharmacaps. The net effect is to push some of the costs of training new employees from the employer onto new workers and, in some cases, taxpayers.[55]

These efforts to push some of the costs of training onto applicants are not always successful, however. Companies that subsidize such programs may subject themselves to costly poaching. M&I Data Services, a Milwaukee data processing company, supports a six-month university computer programming training program for applicants, assigns them mentors and tutors to help them get through it, and offers to hire them if they graduate. Although the company is paying for the training, it does not have to pay wages to the applicants during the training as they are not yet employees. The advantage of the program for M&I is that it gives them access to a better crop of applicants. But interviews with those applicants suggest that M&I will not be able to hire them cheaply. They did not feel obligated to work for M&I and were willing to go to work for other firms if the price was right.[56]

Another method of encouraging employees to pay for the costs of their own development is employer-sponsored tuition reimbursement plans. Many companies offer these programs as a perk or benefit. In fact, they are typically administered out of benefit offices, not training budgets. Employers agree to pay some or all of the costs of postsecondary classes that their employees take. They rarely allow employees to take these classes on company time, however, and they sometimes require that the classes be relevant to the interests of the company before they will pay for them. Because employees are not paid while attending these classes (nor when doing the homework for them), it is a significantly cheaper method of employee development than an in-house program.

The Employee Scholar Program at Pratt and Whitney, a company long known for investing in its employees, is designed explicitly to help develop employee skills and is one of the most generous of its kind. It pays 100 percent of the tuition cost of any accredited degree program, gives employees paid time off for up to half of the class time, and gives the participants a hundred shares of company stock if they complete the program and graduate. Some arrangements for combining school and work are even more creative. Franklin University in Columbus, Ohio, partners with local employers like U.S. Health Corp. to recruit at high schools for a combination work-college program with part-time jobs at the company and tuition reimbursement for attending Franklin University.[57]

Employees are flocking to these programs. As mentioned earlier in the book, more than one-quarter of the students currently attending community colleges in the United States already have four-year bachelor's degrees. Most have full-time jobs. And the classes they are taking? Not English literature but classes on teamwork, TQM programs, information systems, and the like, the kinds of topics traditionally offered by in-house training programs.[58]

Interestingly, some employers who had invested heavily in education for their employees now wonder whether those degrees simply make it easier for employees to leave. Business schools like NYU, which runs a part-time MBA program in which employers foot most of the bill for students, find themselves embroiled in arguments about whether those students can use the school's job placement services. The employers who are paying the bills say no, but the students say yes. Japanese companies like Sony are rethinking their investments in sending employees to the United States for MBA programs because an increasing number of them do not return. The U.S. Naval Post Graduate Institute at Monterey offers a master's degree program in management that is virtually identical to an MBA program. In fact, insiders say that if the program offered only one more course in marketing, it could be accredited as an MBA program. But the institute has no interest in this. If the degree were an MBA, it would be more useful outside the military, giving enrollees an incentive to leave the service.

Employers can avoid paying for training if they don't require it but find a way to make it available to those employees who want it. Fifty-nine percent of temporary help agencies offer general skills training in computer use, for example. The employees of the agencies attend on their own time. It benefits the agencies by making the temps more employable, and most temps understand that it is in their interest to take these classes if they do not have the skills.[59]

The temporary help industry began with the D. J. Nugent Company in Milwaukee, which hired out its stevedores to a manufacturing plant in the 1920s when its own business declined. The modern version of temporary help for clerical positions was created a decade later by Samuel Workman, a calculator salesman who started a business in which he used those calculators to do inventory work for companies at night. He tapped a highly qualified and underused pool of labor to do that work: married women. Especially before World War II, many companies had "marriage bars" that forbade married women from being employed, presumably on the theory that the jobs were needed by men who had (or soon would have) families to support. Single women who got married were forced to quit. Workman hired these trained and competent women, and the stereotype of the temp as a young woman, the Kelley Girl, was born. No doubt many of them were sent back to work in their old companies, but under contract to Workman, just as in the 1980s and 1990s companies hired back their displaced workers as temps and contractors.

It is a surprise to discover how much training temp agencies today provide, especially because virtually all of that training is of a general variety, the kind that is obviously useful in other settings and can easily walk out the door. Companies like Manpower, the largest temporary staffing firm, invested heavily in computer-based training systems in the early 1980s. While estimates suggest that the average U.S. firm invests something less than the equivalent of 2 percent of its payroll budget on training, Manpower invests that much just on *research and development* for training.

Manpower offers its temps more than 150 self-paced, modular training programs, complete with performance benchmarks and work samples to assess proficiency. Each regional office surveys the employers in its area to learn what skills are needed and what training to support. Temporary staffing companies like Norell and Manpower have become so competent in training that they sell it successfully on the market, often adapting it to client needs. For example, Manpower reached a pathbreaking deal with IBM in the 1980s to design and deliver the training for IBM clients in the company's new computer systems. In return, Manpower also got first crack at understanding those new systems and designing the training for its own employees.

The important issue to understand is how these temporary staffing firms can provide entry-level training when ordinary firms can no longer do so. At least part of the answer lies in the structure of the financial incentives under which these firms operate. Most have contracts with their clients that not only govern the temporary help function but also acknowledge their role in screening employees for full-time positions. If a client company hires away a temporary worker from an agency, the client pays the agency a fee that is structured along the lines of what a headhunting firm would receive. Some temporary staffing firms have created alliances with recruiting firms to better perfect the placement aspect of their services. Manpower has gone a step further, creating an alliance with the outplacement firm Drake Beam Morin (DBM). Manpower offers DBM clients its training assistance in securing temporary positions that may well become permanent and in return gets access to a pool of workers that are already highly skilled and screened.[60]

So ubiquitous has the temporary help route to a full-time job become that it has even been incorporated into welfare reform efforts. America Works, a private, for-profit company, contracts with state welfare agencies to place recipients in full-time jobs. As with other temporary staffing firms, it has a real competency in testing, training, and then placing its employees (in this case, welfare recipients) in temporary jobs where employers are frequently trying them out for permanent positions. The client firm faces no cost barriers to make the position permanent because it pays no fee to America Works. The state welfare agencies have in essence already paid that fee.

But there are some legal complications even for employees seeking to gain skills on their own. For example, one way to get the kind of work-based skills that are in demand and that cannot be learned in the classroom is to take on volunteer work or internships. The complication is that the Fair Labor Standards Act prohibits volunteers or interns from doing work of value for a profit employer. In other words, to avoid violating the law, an unpaid intern cannot be doing anything that is useful from the perspective of the employer. The volunteer disk jockeys at radio station KTOZ, a small, struggling big band station, discovered this when the U.S. Department of Labor forced the station to start paying them at least the minimum wage and cough up thousands of dollars in back wages and penalties.[61] These restrictions greatly reduce an employer's interest in having interns around, as well as reducing the usefulness of the internships to interns.

Increasingly, employers get out of the picture altogether, and the provision of skills becomes a market transaction between employee and the training provider. The enormous boom in proprietary schools—for-profit trade schools—reflects this trend. Consider the strange but revealing case of the workers who design the circuitry on semiconductor chips, known as mask designers. Virtually all of the large semiconductor companies in Silicon Valley employ these workers, but none of them provide training in this area. To get these jobs, individuals attend private training schools such as the Institute for Business and Technology in Santa Clara. They pay about $5,000 in tuition, often out of their own pocket, for thirty weeks of evening classes. Many of the students, perhaps even a majority in a typical class, already work for semiconductor companies. When they graduate, they are swamped with job offers. If they end up back at their current employer, it is with a new job and a substantially higher salary.[62]

What is so interesting about this example is that it represents exactly the type of job and training that in the past would have been completely internalized. Employees interested in mask design would be sent to company training programs and then promoted to the new job. Now the process is completely externalized into the market. Employees interested in mask design leave the company and pay for their own training and then negotiate with their employer about reentering the company in a new position with a much higher salary. It may seem like madness, but it is easy to see why such arrangements would evolve when companies believe that any mask designer produced in-house would be poached away.

The tremendous interest that employees have in developing their skills and the constraints on doing so inside firms have created a market that is rapidly being filled by for-profit education and training companies such as the Institute for Business and Technology and Devry Inc., which operates the most extensive network of for-profit schools (see Figure 6-1).

These schools stay close to the needs of their customers, design user-friendly and convenient coursework, and invest heavily in student placement, because the ability to get their graduates a better job is what they are selling. The University of Phoenix is the largest for-profit provider of degree-based education. Seventy-two percent of its tuition revenues comes from employers paying for employee coursework, and the employers seem satisfied with it. Even traditional higher education offerings have been outsourced to these for-profit providers. UCLA and Berkeley, for example, offer students coursework in information technology that is in fact provided by CBT Systems and GartnerLearning.

One of the objections to for-profit education providers concerns whether they will maintain academic standards, whether they can be trusted to provide honest credentials for their students/customers. Will they fail paying customers? Because they are marketing their ability to place students in jobs, these schools may have an even stronger incentive not to pass students who cannot do the work. Not surprisingly, other for-profits have entered the market to provide objective evaluations of student performance. Standardized tests like the Graduate Management Admissions Test (GMAT) are now contracted out by the nonprofit Educational Testing Service to the for-profit testing division of Sylvan Learning, which administers the tests. Sylvan also produces a range of occupational proficiency tests that make it possible to separate the provison of education and training and the credible, objective assessment of that learning.[63]

More complicated than training is the issue of career development. For the reasons described earlier, companies are uncertain about what the career paths within their own organizations will look like in the future. And while the notion of helping employees build careers that will take them outside the company seemed like a reasonable component of an employment relationship when downsizing was the big prob-

Figure 6-1. Capital Raised by Selected Education Companies

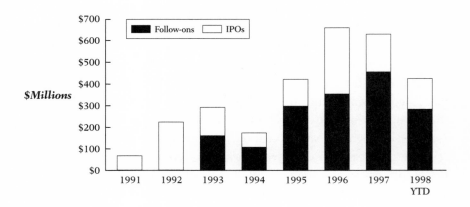

Source: NationsBanc Montgomery Securities LLC and Securities Data Corporation.

lem, it is problematic in tight labor markets, when retaining employees is the issue.

Developing managers internally not only requires up-front training dollars but also organizational resources and inclinations that may no longer exist. The organizational requirements of management development programs have almost by definition included slack resources because managers were placed in positions with the goal, at least in part, of developing their skills, not generating immediate, optimal performance on the job. Managers were also rotated around jobs and locations to help round out their experience, typically before they had mastered the position to the extent necessary to make real contributions to performance. The managers around them had to spend considerable time and effort helping the trainee or development candidate with various projects, especially when the goal was to develop cross-functional skills.

Jim Walker of the Walker Group consulting firm outlines the changes that have essentially eliminated the organizational resources required for such development efforts. First, lean staffing has reduced existing managers' time to do training. Companies like John Hancock report that the pressure to run lean has hurt employee development efforts. Second, the pressure to improve organizational performance in the short run has increased the pressure to get the best person in the job, not a trainee who will be passing through. Third, the "bumping" costs when managers are moved around, and the subsequent staff moves required to backfill the vacancies created, have increased, in part, because of the increasing resistance of employees to being moved. The biennial surveys of human resource executives by Runzheimer International find that internal company relocations of employees fell by about one-third between 1990 and 1994 and have been flat since, reflecting the increasing difficulty of developing employees internally and the greater interest in going to the outside market to fill vacancies.[64]

In an interesting irony, the difficulty of developing employees internally has both driven the interest in external hires and complicated the ability of search firms to find talent. Executive search firms report that they are taking on average twice as long to come up with suitable talent, even compared with just a few years ago, because the new flatter, leaner organizations do not generate talent as quickly. "Forty-five year olds are basically doing the same thing they were at thirty," says Roger I. Sekara, vice president of A. T. Kierney Executive Search. In turn,

junior executives are less likely to wait around with the same organization because they see fewer prospects for development.[65]

Even when limited career paths can be articulated, a number of
intractable problems stand in the way of their pursuit. One of the most
important parts of an employee's development has always been men-
toring-type relationships with superiors. The incentives for a manager
to develop employees have eroded because the need for internal development has declined. Most organizations have downplayed the importance of developing subordinates as part of a supervisor's appraisal,
especially relative to the all-important goal of improving performance.
Any employee development exercises that take time and energy from
the immediate tasks of the business create real dilemmas for supervisors. "This is where the rubber meets the road," says Brian Hackett of
the Conference Board, "when an employee says that they want to leave
the line for a few days of development activity, will the boss say, 'no
way'?"

Even if supervisors see the development of their employees as a
worthwhile goal, their ability to provide it themselves is also limited.
Wider spans of control mean that supervisors now have so many subordinates that it limits the time and energy they can devote to any one
individual. The nature of new work systems that stress teamwork and
empowerment reduces some of the day-to-day contact between supervisors and employees. The fact that employees and supervisors turn over
more quickly also means that the ability to develop mentoring relationships erodes.

Perhaps the most interesting reaction to the disappearance of
mentoring relationships inside firms is the decision of some workers to
look for them ouside the firm, in the market. The exploding field of
management coaches, or mentors for hire, is the most obvious manifestation. This approach is clearly something that only better-paid employees can pursue, typically executives. In addition to the fact that
mentoring may not be readily available inside the company, some employees may seek outside coaches for career development because they
don't trust what the company's experts tell them. Now that lifetime
relationships are a thing of the past, the interests of the employee and
the employer may not be closely aligned. The best prospects for career
advancement are likely to lie outside of one's current employer, and one's
current employer does not have an interest in pointing that out. The
executive coaching business has expanded to include agents—head-

hunters for the executive—who will go beyond giving advice on career management to fielding offers and negotiating employment contracts for clients.[66]

Efforts to address the need for career development within the company include programs that make career information easier to get, such as the intranet career center at Unisys. Unisys also offers employees development exercises outside the firm, such as executive education, as an explicit reward for good job performance.[67] As mentioned earlier in the book, career development efforts also include so-called Centers of Excellence, areas within a company where employees can turn for help. At companies like Bell Atlantic, these centers are organized around areas of functional expertise, such as marketing or accounting.

The fact that close relationships between supervisors and employees have eroded has led to other career management complications. Much of the art and science of motivating employees is typically directed at the supervisor-employee relationship, where deals are struck exchanging rewards for performance or employees are persuaded to buy into the goals or vision of the organization. As these relationships weaken, substitutes for leadership have to take their place, such as objective measures of performance and compensation.

Employers still face real problems in asking employees to make investments in company-specific capabilities because of the risk that those investments may not pay off for them. A recent survey found managers more reluctant to accept transfers for fear that if they lost their job after moving, they would no longer have a network of contacts in the region through which to find a new job. Fifty-four percent of the executives surveyed said that job insecurity will keep them from taking positions elsewhere. Paul Cappelli, president of the Ad Store in New York City (and no relation to me that I know of), turned down an offer to move to Chicago, saying, "If something should go wrong here, it would be easier to find another job. In Chicago, I'm a fish out of water."[68] A consequence of this fear is the growing competitive advantage enjoyed by employers based in regions with dense networks of competitors. Employees in hi-tech are willing to move to Silicon Valley and in finance to New York at least in part because the market is big enough that if (and when) their current job ends, they can find a new one without relocating.

The ultimate adaptation to the complications of trying to develop employees in a more mobile environment, and the one way to deal with employee reluctance to make firm-specific investments, is simply to turn the problem over to the market: Hire directly from the outside market rather than transfer. TransAmerica, for example, now makes it a practice to keep track of its executives who leave for positions elsewhere with the idea of eventually hiring them back. These executives already know the company, and if they acquire interesting skills on the outside, they may be more valuable to the company than if they had stayed.

Corporate recruiters have taken on some of the sophisticated record keeping of development, at least for executives. Spenser Stuart, one of the larger executive recruiting companies, retains an entire staff of researchers whose job it is to maintain a database on the careers and skills of 80,000 executives around the world. Employers looking to recruit thus have access to information on the skills and development experiences of potential candidates that may be at least as good as the records they maintain on their own internal employees, and the potential pool from which they can draw is huge. This increasing available information on candidates helps explain the extraordinary growth of the search industry (see Figure 6-2). Joint ventures and alliances are another means of going to the outside market to solve the development problem. One of the reasons that J. P. Morgan created the Pinnacle Alliance with IT contractors to manage its data centers was that it allowed Morgan access to skill sets that it found difficult to acquire. It also allowed Morgan to lock in those competencies during the contract period.[69]

There are companies that still make substantial investments in employee development. General Electric, for example, has the oldest management development program in the United States, dating from 1919. It continues to provide two years of general management training and work experience to college graduates in areas like finance, human resources, information systems, and engineering.

Other companies known for developing managers include Smith Klein, Pepsi, and Procter & Gamble. These large companies can offer diverse work experiences within the same corporate structure by means of their broad holdings and also by giving real responsibility early on. At the same time, corporate recruiters love to poach from these companies in large part because of the management development they offer. So why do the companies continue to offer it? One important reason is that it helps them with their own recruiting even if retention takes a hit down the road. Applicants know that going with a company like GE or Pepsi gives them a real opportunity for advancement—at other companies—precisely because recruiters will be interested in hiring them away. Fifty percent or more of the entering class of these management development programs are gone in five years, but it still may pay for the companies to have the programs because they make it possible to recruit better candidates and get a few years of productive work from them.

Employee Commitment

In the traditional employment relationship, where job security was exchanged for loyalty, companies needed loyalty to ensure good performance especially from their managers because the work they did was hard to monitor. Managers who lacked loyalty, or commitment, could easily shirk their responsibilities. Surely with the end of job security, that exchange-based motive for loyalty is gone. The broken psychologi-

Figure 6-2. Revenues of the Largest Retained Search Firms ($ millions)

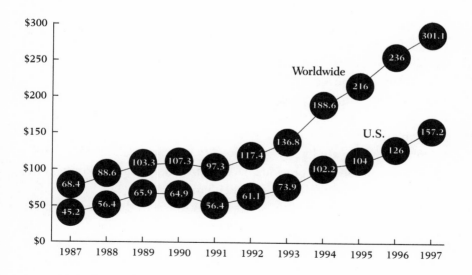

Source: © *Executive Recruiter News, published by Kennedy Information, LLC, Fitzwilliam, NH 03447, 800-531-0007. Reprinted with permission of the publisher.*

cal contracts (noted in Chapter 4) have often led to low morale and poor job attitudes. And at the same time, we have moved toward work systems that "empower" employees by removing bureaucratic rules, supervision, and other potential constraints on employee malfeasance. We have created an angry workforce and then given them greater opportunities to hit back at the organization.

There are other problems as well. Employees who see themselves moving on to other companies, or perhaps feel they will need to, are interested in building their resumes as quickly as they can. Individual employees compete with each other for choice assignments, wanting the public credit for successes and avoiding the blame for failures. These situations are particularly intense in professional organizations like law firms and investment banks, where employees on the same level must work together on discrete projects. *Fortune* editor Tom Stewart related a story about the dynamics on a movie set, now a jumble of contractors, as described earlier, where the assembled crew members are each trying to network their next job with a different subcontractor—a stagehand trying to hustle work with the special effects company, an aspiring writer looking for freelance work with the scriptwriter, someone else cozying up to the production company. These efforts at impression management may pull the overall project in different directions if the parties become more interested in their component of the project than the quality of the film as a whole.

As in addressing the other issues associated with the new deal at work, the place for managers to begin dealing with the problem of declining employee commitment is by asking the frank question, What is it about commitment that we really need? And how much of that commitment is important to have? GE chairman Jack Welch, whose company continues to pave the way in performance, has been quoted as saying that corporate loyalty is nonsense.[70] Many executives now use the phrase, "You want loyalty, get a dog," to indicate that the blind loyalty to corporations seen in previous decades produced the kind of dependency that inhibited performance and change.

Employers still need their employees to act in the interests of the organization—to work hard and effectively, to be good citizens, to put the interests of the organization on the front of their agenda. But at least some of the need for the kind of commitment associated with these behaviors has frankly been reduced by changes in organizations and in management practices.

The need for commitment in the past reflected in part the fact that it was very difficult to monitor how good a job someone was doing, especially those employees buried inside complex administrative structures. A variety of changes have made it possible to judge the performance of individual employees and managers more accurately. Decentralized operations that create profit-and-loss centers, equity carve-outs, and related aspects of restructuring bring smaller operating units right up against clear measures of market performance. More sophisticated systems of internal control, including the monitoring techniques of quality control programs, make it easier to judge the performance of operations that are removed from the market. For simple jobs, new information systems can more easily monitor and track employee performance on dimensions like calls answered per hour for call-center employees or clients contacted for sales agents. Other evaluation techniques, such as 360 feedback programs that assess the performance of subordinates, peers, and superiors, provide better indications of individual performance even when objective measures are hard to find. Once these measures are in place, it is conceptually simple to link performance to contingent compensation as a way to align the material goals of individual employees with those of the organization. In this sense, individuals are committed to the organization's goals out of self-interest. Loyalty is not required.

Commitment to the company as a whole, to the corporate entity, has also declined in importance. In the past, managerial employees in particular moved around the organization frequently, and their ultimate reward was a promotion somewhere, potentially anywhere, in the corporate structure. So it made sense for them to identify with the corporation as a whole and not with any particular part of it. Also, the staff jobs at corporate headquarters to which most managers aspired were responsible for directing and often reining in the divisions and local operations whose immediate goals could well be in conflict with those of the corporation as a whole. The demise of lifetime corporate careers and of corporate staff positions as ultimate career goals seem to have further undercut the need for loyalty to the corporation as a whole.

Of course, monitoring and financial incentives can never fully align the interests of employees and their organizations. And monitoring in particular can easily contribute to declines in what little remains of commitment as employees come to believe that their employer does not trust them. Even though its importance may be diminished, successful organizations still need employees to have some sense of commitment to the organization to ensure that jobs are carried out well. But the question remains, commitment to what? Commitment to the corporation is not required to ensure that employees perform their current jobs well, nor is commitment to the division or even to the plant. What is required is probably as simple as commitment to colleagues, to a work team, or to a project. Commitment is much easier to establish with other individuals than with an abstract entity such as a corporation. Contrast the following situations: An employee has a date with friends to spend the day at the lake but gets a message on her answering machine requesting her help with a last-minute proposal to a key client. She could easily pretend that she never got the message and go to the lake. In the first situation, the request comes from another division in the company, from managers that she does not know. In the second, it comes from her project team, with whom she works daily. It is much easier to believe that she will drop her plans and help out with the project in the second situation because of her identification with and commitment to the team members.

Many companies explicitly work to replace the decline in commitment to the organization as a whole with commitment to a team of individuals. Arrangements that increase the autonomy of teams and their accountability for performance help generate the peer pressure that drives individuals to sacrifice for the team. For example, the auto industry and other assembly-line operations in the past always maintained a pool of "relief" workers who were essentially substitutes when regular employees were absent. By making teams responsible for aspects of the line and then eliminating relief workers, management created a situation in which the team as a whole had to take on the extra work whenever one of its members was absent. The peer pressure on individuals to show up for work increased considerably, and peer pressure can substitute for commitment.[71] Team-based compensation and other incentives based on the performance of the group as a whole help to create the sense that the fate of the community relies on the performance of its individual members. Studies find, for example, that these gainsharing programs increase the extent of peer pressure—the monitoring of employee performance by the group.[72]

Not only can teamwork and the peer pressure for performance it generates help substitute for organizational commitment, but these efforts at building social relationships at work actually contribute to organizational commitment. Research shows, for example, that employees who have better relations with their coworkers are also more committed to the organization.[73] One of the reasons that employees in smaller organizations are more committed is probably because they have closer personal relations with a larger proportion of the organization's employees. Presumably, they come to think of the organization not as an abstract entity with which it is difficult to have an emotional relationship but as a collection of individuals with whom one already feels close ties.

A series of other practices and policies have also been found to raise the commitment of employees to the organization. They include the following:

- The more formalized the work activities are, including well-defined rules and policies, the greater is employee commitment. Such arrangements make it easier to see the goals of the organization and to associate them with one's interests.[74]

- Some of the most important factors that increase commitment have to do with the way work is organized. Employee participation increases the sense of commitment, as does working with greater autonomy.[75] The happy coincidence is that high-performance work systems that require greater commitment from employees also seem to generate it by giving greater participation in decision making and more autonomy, or control over their actions.

- Several studies show that workers are more committed when the organization indicates that it respects and appreciates their efforts. Some of the effect is based on the kind of reciprocity model described earlier. When employees believe that their employer is supportive of their well-being, they are more committed.[76] For example, if a company spokesperson explains why the company cannot make long-term promises about jobs (especially if the causes are outside the firm) and the company takes pains to protect its employees from downsizing as best it can, it may not see any reduction in commitment, even if it is forced to cut jobs.

- Employees who are made to feel that they are making an important contribution are also more committed to their employer. People want to be needed: the more valuable they are made to feel, the more they see themselves as attached to the organization.[77]

- Some of the arrangements for addressing the problem of attrition can also help improve commitment. As noted in Chapter 4, employees who believe that they have many options for jobs have been found to be less committed to the job they ultimately take, while those who believe that they have few good options are more committed to their ultimate choice.

Practices that can bind employees to an organization even temporarily, such as employment contracts or golden handcuffs, will cause them to be more committed to that organization by constraining their options. One way to reduce the decline in commitment is to stop advising employees that they should explore and develop career options elsewhere.

• Arrangements that address the problem of training and developing employee skills can help improve commitment as well. Research shows that training and other investments in employees raise worker commitment.[78] Again, the argument seems to be one of reciprocity, with workers providing increased commitment in return for the employer's investment in them.

The overall point for employers to remember about employee commitment to the organization under the new deal is that it is now driven much more by outside circumstances that are beyond the employer's control. As noted in Chapter 4, the same is also true for other aspects of job attitude and morale. Companies that work hard to maintain good morale will nevertheless find that the results of their climate surveys rise and fall with events outside the firm, such as the state of the labor market. As the labor market tightens and headhunting increases, expect employee commitment to decline, even in the face of all the programs to improve it. This is not a reason to avoid such efforts but simply a caveat on their likely effectiveness.

CHAPTER 7

Concluding Observations on the New, Market-Driven Employment Relationship

MOVING BACK toward the internalized system of employee development, returning to the protections of job security and long-term relationships, may not be possible if other employers are moving in the opposite direction, hiring increasingly from other employers. Nor is it clear that offering lifetime job security will enhance employee commitment by much in the current environment, given that opportunities elsewhere, in the market, are an important source of the erosion of commitment. These opportunities are outside the control of individual employers and are growing.

Many companies are now talking about reestablishing something like the old, long-term relationship with employees. Here are two examples. DuPont, the chemical giant, went through the same waves of restructuring that most large companies experienced but has begun to talk about the importance of re-creating lifetime career opportunities for employees. I heard a senior executive of the company describing the arrangements the company had in mind to provide long-term career opportunities, and he was asked by a member of the audience whether he thought the company would really be able to go through with it. In a moment of breathtaking candor, he replied that, no, he did not think this would actually come to pass, that the competitive environment could not support it. Then why was it being put forward? This model of lifetime careers was deeply imbedded in the values of the executives who ran the company, it was an important part of their experience with the company. It was being put forward again as a model because of its importance to their values and, quite possibly, because it is difficult to think about how to manage without it.

Lehman Brothers, one of the leading investment banking firms in the United States, operates in the middle of the fiercely competitive Wall Street investment community, where poaching has become a daily occurrence. I am told by insiders that it is not unusual now for junior analysts with one year of experience out of undergraduate school to be hired away by headhunters. Lehman Brothers saw an opportunity to go in a different direction, to seek a comparative advantage in human resources by developing talent internally rather than by hiring from outside. I was explaining my view of the changing employment relationship to a roomful of Wall Street executives when a representative from Lehman Brothers got up to explain how they were heading in the opposite direction, intending to develop their talent from within through greater investment in training. There was muffled laughter in the room, and afterward, I asked one of the snickerers to tell me what was so funny. "Guess where we'll be recruiting now," he said.

The managers and executives in U.S. industry at the turn of the last century could not imagine how their businesses could operate if their companies *internalized* the employment relationship, especially how they would be able to maintain discipline and motivation among the employees; many of them fought it for decades. It is not at all surprising, therefore, that many contemporary managers cannot imagine how their companies could operate with a return to market-based employment systems. The explanation in both cases relies on acknowledgment of how many other characteristics of the way companies operate are tied to the employment relationship. And it is difficult to think through all of the adaptations necessary, concerning not only employment practices but also more general issues associated with the way companies do business.

AREN'T THERE EXCEPTIONS?

Some observers believe that the costs associated with the erosion of these long-term relationships are so substantial that we should resist mightily any efforts to weaken them further. Frederick Reichheld's influential book *The Loyalty Effect* (1996) is an important source of support for this argument, pointing out the advantages of long-term relationships with customers and suppliers and also with employees.[1] Firms with these relationships may gain important advantages from them, but it is also worth asking whether characteristics unique to such firms allow them to have long-term relationships in the first place. A striking aspect of the examples he gives, which document the gains associated with long-term relationships in several areas, including employment, is that so many of the companies are privately held. The pressures from financial markets to maximize profits are less intense, and the pressures to pursue the restructuring strategies designed to squeeze out those profits are also reduced.

Certainly employee turnover is costly, and long-term relationships bring important advantages. But there can also be costs associated with the status quo, such as lost opportunities, that are difficult to measure. It is relatively easy to quantify the costs of turnover, of moving old managers out and bringing in new ones. It is far more difficult to quantify the costs of retaining managers with antiquated skills or the benefits of bringing in new ones who are a better fit with the changing needs of the organization. Keeping long-term employees does not necessarily mean that organizations cannot restructure and change their competencies, although it does vastly complicate the challenge of doing so.

A famous example over the years of the benefits of long-term employee relations is Lincoln Electric, the welding equipment producer with a no-layoff guarantee. It is often presented as an example of the benefits of preserving long-term relationships and protecting employees from the vagaries of the labor market. How it operates provides a good illustration of both the costs and benefits of these arrangements. Employees are protected from most but not all layoff risks (sharp declines in business can lead to layoffs). But voluntary turnover is quite high. And other aspects of its employment relationship have pushed more of the business risk onto employees, such as the fact that a sizeable share of compensation is variable. Individual workers are paid piecerates, and the large bonuses they receive are based on overall company profitability. While employment levels are not easily adjusted to changing company needs, labor costs do adjust because of the structure of compensation. And the 25 percent employee turnover in the first year of employment helps to adjust employment levels to company needs. Nor has Lincoln faced the need to reshuffle its capabilities or skill base as it has so far remained mainly in the same business, turning out roughly similar products with jobs that are more or less unchanged, at least compared with the situation in other companies.

Even with these adjustment mechanisms, critics point out that the no-layoff policy has hampered the company's ability to change, reducing incentives to develop new products that require less labor. Because expanding the workforce involves a potential lifetime commitment, Lincoln is also slower to hire and expand production in upturns.[2]

The companies that truly resist the move toward the market seem idiosyncratic in important ways, generally insulated from some of the pressures to restructure continually or able to achieve some the flexibility by other means. Examples of publicly held companies in reasonably dynamic markets that continue to make long-term investments in employees are rare. Still, they include companies like Exxon that have long-term business projects, such as the development of new oil fields. Like all companies, they need to have at least some key employees stay with them until a project is completed. It just happens that in their business, the projects may take twenty years or more to complete.

Companies do vary in their commitments to employees, sometimes within the same industry, and the differences seem best explained by the choices they have made in defining their competencies and strategies. My colleague Peter Sherer illustrated this principle in a study of the taxi cab business. Most taxi companies, it turns out, are really virtual organizations, either owner-operators who loosely band together around the infrastructure of a dispatcher or, even more virtual, driver-contractors who simply lease cabs on a daily basis. But some companies actually employ drivers directly. Such companies have regular clients with regular schedules—taking kids to piano lessons, bringing patients to doctors' appointments—where being punctual is the key asset. These (comparatively) long-term customers demand a more reliable network. Leased drivers who often do not drive on regular schedules or even owner-operators who are chasing down their own fares all over town cannot be relied on in the way that employees who are paid by the hour can.

The differences in the nature of products and strategies and the effect they have on choices about commitments to employees play themselves out in the corporate world as well. Coke and Pepsi, for example, have very different approaches toward employee management and development despite the fact that they seem to be in roughly the same business. Coke still hires mainly entry-level employees and develops them internally with the intention of keeping them with the company indefintely. Recently, Coke has been growing so fast that employees were not coming through the entry-level, internal development pipeline fast enough to meet demands, and it made headlines by hiring experienced talent aggressively from the outside. It still hired them into a management development track, however, which essentially duplicated Coke's traditional internal development track. The reason Coke takes this internal development/long-term relationship approach is that managing its brand name, the most recognized trademark in the world, is a skill that can only be developed internally. Projects at Coke are like oilfields at Exxon: they have very long timelines. Pepsi, on the other hand, brings in talent from all over and gives managers responsibility and new challenges early, and its employees have a reputation for moving on to opportunities at other companies. Pepsi has an entirely different business strategy, relying on innovation across a broad portfolio of changing products to sustain its business. It needs a continual supply of fresh ideas and energy to make that happen.

There have always been differences across employers in the nature of their commitments to employees, and some employers will continue to find it more useful to have longer-term relationships than others. The difference now is that the notion of "long-term" has shrunk. Explicit and implicit guarantees of job security are gone, the hiring of experienced employees from the outside is up, and internal development of entry-level hires is down. The employer's expectation of a long-term relationship with at least some of its key employees remains in some companies, but other aspects of the traditional model have already eroded even in these organizations.

Employees Adapt, Too

A fundamental reason why employers would find it difficult to return to the old, long-term relationship model of job security for the sake of employee loyalty, even if they wanted to, is that their employees are unlikely to go along with it. Some employees might want to return to the old model, but the new generation of employees hired into the company probably won't. They might be very willing to let the employer make an up-front investment in their skills, but whether they would stick around while other employers pursued better offers is a different matter entirely.

An intriguing model of how employees respond to change in the workplace suggests one reason why even current employees would have a hard time going back to the old model. The model argues that employees do not make decisions or judgments purely or even largely on the basis of a rational, cost-benefit model. Instead, they rely on "imaging," recalling the previous experiences in similar situations and basing their decisions on what happened then. An example of this kind of behavior can be seen in some people who experienced the hardships of the Great Depression. Often they continue to feel financially insecure, finding it difficult to take economic risks or to spend freely, even if they have become quite wealthy. Similarly, the generation of workers who "grew up" assuming their employer should be responsible for their careers are unlikely to forget the waves of downsizing and restructuring that violated what they believed to be an implicit contract with their employer. Their children, who are the next generation of workers, are also unlikely to forget. A recent national survey of employees found that 94 percent of those reporting saw themselves, not their employer, as responsible for their employability.[3] That perception is likely to endure for some time no matter what employers do. It is hard to see what could make employees give that control and responsibility back to the employer.

A similar kind of inertia may hamper adjustments in employee expectations as well. A revealing study of employees at a General Motors division during its restructuring and downsizing found that they quite accurately grasped the concept of a flattened organizational hierarchy and the reduction in promotion prospects associated with it. As a consequence of that flatter hierarchy, promotion rates after the restructuring were dramatically reduced for managerial employees, although they were relatively unchanged for low-level employees. While the managerial positions became broader, more interesting, and considerably more stable, the incumbents in those positions were hard-pressed to acknowledge those benefits and still defined their success in terms of career advancement up the narrower and less promising managerial hierarchy. The more they had advanced in their career up to that point, the more they held onto the belief that promotion was the critical indicator of their performance and success on the job.[4] A new deal that offers broader, more interesting jobs but less possibility of advancement does not appear to be enough to placate these workers.

Some employee expectations have been altered quickly, however, as they learn that a tighter job market provides better opportunities for job shopping. The *Wall Street Journal* noted that "With unemployment at nearly a quarter-century low, the seesaw of power is tilting from employer to employee." A recruiting manager observed that "Ten years ago, someone with three jobs was a 'job hopper.' Today, someone who is 30 and has had 10 years with one company, you ask if they are too conservative."[5] A cover story in *Fortune* advises employees to "surf" employers to maximize their chances for advancement: "These days, if you find yourself blocked, or no longer learning and growing, you may simply have to change jobs to give yourself a promotion."[6]

New entrants to the labor market always adjust more quickly to the changing realities of the workforce because they have had no prior experience with the old situation to shape their expectations. Survey evidence indicates that younger workers have more positive attitudes toward the workplace than "baby boomers," the first wave of whom are in their fifties now, because most of the younger workers weren't in on the restructuring wave.[7] There is ample evidence that the younger generation in the workforce both saw the new deal coming and have adjusted to its demands. I noticed a change among MBA students beginning in the late 1980s. Many of them saw their parents being downsized from corporations and their interests in being self-employed—becoming an entrepreneur or a marketable professional—increased sharply. Now the trend among MBAs is to begin shopping for career advancement with their first job.

A recent national survey of business school students finds them ranking job responsibilities and long-term career opportunities as the top two factors (out of a possible twelve, including salary) in determining their job choices.[8] Consulting firms are the top choice among students because they allow their new entrants to learn a lot, get wide experience, and to shop around—to see lots of possibilities for their next job. There is a clear parallel with the graduates of the previous generation, who looked for jobs with extensive management development trainee programs because these programs allowed them to shop around within the company. When graduates today get down to negotiating an offer, the key factor is increasingly the nature of the job experience they will be getting and whether it can be guaranteed. To put it bluntly, the graduates want to know what they will be able to put on their resume after a year or two should they have to leave. "Companies win over students by gearing the job—or at least the job description—to their needs," notes a recruiting consultant.[9]

Andrew Adams, the former director of Wharton's office of Career Development and Placement, observes that an increasing number of Wharton grads are not taking the job offer with the highest pay. And they are also passing on what have traditionally been the plum positions in investment banking and consulting firms in favor of jobs at small companies or start-up ventures. They are looking for a good match between their skills and interests and the opportunities of a job. And they are much more willing to take a risk to get a good match, passing up secure jobs at stable companies for the possibility of hitting it big with highly leveraged compensation and an entrepreneurial venture. In one of my MBA classes, I have students do a negotiations exercise in which they must make decisions about whether to take a risky job with the possibility of a big payoff or a secure one. Over time, I have seen them increasingly taking the risky choice, typically for compensation that on average, in terms of expected value, is only trivially more than in the secure job. Their willingness to roll the dice for a big reward has increased.

Andrew Adams notes that one reason for the greater willingness of MBAs to take more risk is that the downside is much less of a problem now. If the company fails or they are laid off, there is very little stigma attached to them. Potential employers are unlikely to view it as a failure at all and might actually be intrigued by what the applicant learned from the experience. Two other explanations also loom large. The first is that this new generation feels compelled to take more financial risk earlier because they do not believe there will be a pension waiting for them at the end of their career. They may also expect to deal with some periods of turmoil and perhaps job loss in their career when they will need financial reserves. They believe that they will have to earn their nest egg themselves and that they might as well take the risk to get it now, before they have families and other obligations. The second explanation resides in their understanding that the chances of advancement within a traditional corporation are greatly reduced compared with earlier periods. Taking a chance on a growing company where they can move up may be their best prospect for career advancement.

Other entry-level workers without the benefit of advanced degrees are also pursuing a strategy of skill and resume building, but with different tactics. For example, some use temporary appointments strategically to develop their skills and raise their salaries. Jason Elliott, a twenty-five-year-old temp in San Francisco, says, "The reason an agency is good is it gives you access to places you wouldn't otherwise have access to," where you can get experience and skills that are valuable elsewhere.[10]

DIFFERENT SKILLS PAY OFF NOW

Success in this new employment relationship demands not only different choices but also different skills. For someone comfortable with the old model of employment, in which the corporation cleared the career paths, few challenges will be as baffling as one that asks the person to take responsibility for his or her own career.

Once career planning starts encompassing movements across employers, most employees are completely at sea. Where can they turn for advice? At least inside their organization, human resource departments provide information and ideas about career advancement, even if employees wonder whether they can trust that advice. But who offers guidance or information about the labor market? Schools and universities offer some, but most career and placement offices are designed to help students find a first job. If you are a seasoned worker hoping for a career change that does not involve returning to school, they may have little expertise or even interest in your problems. Professional counselors such as vocational psychologists have traditionally been focused on helping people make a match between their interests and abilities and those of an occupation. While knowing which jobs are good matches with your interests is certainly an important step in the process of planning a career, it is only part of the solution. Understanding how to secure that job or how to advance in it is an entirely different issue, and advice about how to accomplish that is much harder to find.

The most important asset in managing a career across organizations is information, knowledge about where the opportunities are and how to access them. Because such information is specific to each organization, it is very difficult to obtain. Few institutions collect it. The power of corporate recruiters will continue to grow because they have

detailed knowledge about opportunities across organizations. The norms
of corporate life had suggested that recruiters be dealt with, if at all, at
arm's length. They were a necessary evil like a money lender. But the
new rules suggest that they be embraced and courted. A *Fortune* guide
to modern career management now advises readers to make time for
recruiters, to help them and secure their favors in return.[11]

The ability to both secure and present information to advance
one's career has become a skill that in many cases rivals in importance
the actual ability to perform the job in question. Learning about opportunities through networking and being able to market oneself are skills
that pay off handsomely now that individuals are required to make more
frequent matches in the labor market to get ahead.[12] Learning how to
pick the right employer becomes crucial in part because upward mobility becomes more a function of making the right moves across organizations—finding growing companies with a greater need to promote
from within. Being able to learn about companies and pick the right
ones is certainly a skill, albeit one that may be closer to stock picking
than traditional managerial competence. The older generation of managers, particularly men, schooled in the stoic work ethic of letting their
performance speak for themselves, find that this new approach puts
them at a severe disadvantage in the labor market. More than one
executive who found himself pushed out of his old job has confided that
while he was interested in positions elsewhere, he found it so difficult
to market himself that he simply stayed out of the fray.

An important part of self-marketing is picking one's projects carefully. Employees interested in moving on need visibility, and to get that,
they need success on highly visible projects. Some observers have suggested that employees in such situations might want to avoid teamwork
because their performance, and subsequent reputation, is likely to be
diffused within that of the team. With a more individualized project,
high performers may have a better chance of being noticed.

Jim Sicile was a cameraman for the ABC news show 20/20 until
the company decided to outsource that function to independent contractors. Suddenly he, too, became a contractor and noticed how his life
changed. Some of the changes were predictable. He had to become
more careful with money, to plan ahead and prepare for periods of
uncertainty, and to develop a network of contacts. But in some ways the
biggest challenges concerned the new social skills needed to handle
these new relationships. "You have to be nicer," he noticed, and ex-

plained that when cameramen were employees, the producers had to use them no matter how grumpy or difficult they were. "Now," he says, "they have a list of cameramen by their phone, and they just start calling. If you're difficult to deal with, they just go on to the next one." Another item on the *Fortune* quiz about prospects for movement across organizations is whether superiors and other important connections like you well enough to help advance your career.[13] A detailed study of the Hewlett-Packard company conducted in the midst of its continuing restructuring illustrates that the importance of social skills increasingly applies even within an organization, now that authority has become more ambiguous. Because managers in the company have less authoritative power, they've found that they must rely more on persuasion and negotiation to secure cooperation and resources from other autonomous divisions of the organization.[14]

Self-management and related personal skills also become more important in this new environment. The ability of individual employees to motivate themselves through techniques such as goal setting has been shown to increase employee performance, often dramatically. It is an increasingly important skill now that organizations are eliminating supervision and other aspects of management structures that monitor and motivate performance.[15] Other skills such as perseverance and resilience become more important determinants of success as individuals deal more frequently with the stresses of restructuring and downsizing and compete more frequently in the market for new positions. Whether employees will learn to adapt to the rough-and-tumble marketplace of the new employment relationship is an important question. Certainly they can learn to internalize the stresses and strains of constantly shopping for jobs, but learning how to suffer is not quite the same as finding techniques and mechanisms that solve these problems.[16] And it has important implications for the well-being of society.

This greater occupational orientation of employees complicates the job-searching process. As described in Chapter 4, employees appear to be changing employers more frequently but staying in the same occupations longer than in earlier decades. Ed McCabe, a long-time executive of Chemical Bank, which then merged with Chase Manhattan, describes the changing orientation succinctly: "I always thought of myself as a Chemical Bank manager who happened to be in human resources. The new generation of managers think of themselves as human resource managers who happen to be at Chemical." While turnover makes it more difficult for employers to provide training, the longer tenure of employees in the same occupation and field makes acquiring skills in that field even more valuable because they pay off longer and are the ticket to employability elsewhere.

As employees become more orientated to specific occupations, the turbulence problem gets worse as it becomes more necessary to churn skills and employees when companies restructure. The study of electronic firms in England described earlier found that the disciplinary orientation and narrowly defined skill base of the engineering talent in these companies made it difficult for the companies to redeploy them when they restructured. This increased the companies' reliance on hiring and firing to facilitate the restructuring.[17] And the engineers themselves, just like those in Silicon Valley, may believe that their best options for career advancement are to keep their functional skills on the cutting edge, as opposed to broadening those skills in response to the needs of a specific employer. In this sense, the behavior of the employers and the employees creates a vicious circle in which the actions of one party reinforce those of the other.

WHAT MAKES FOR FAIR PLAY?

Changes in the workplace inevitably create new winners and losers, and that is the case for the new employment relationship as well. The most obvious manifestations of this change are new compensation policies in which wages are based much more on prevailing levels in the outside labor market. Concerns about internal equity that dominate traditional compensation policies, such as greater pay linked to seniority, to more complex jobs, or to other criteria associated with job evaluation systems, go out the window. Steve Gross, director of the compensation practice for Mercer Consulting, observes that in most firms, the only real concern about pay now is whether they are paying the right amount to attract the talent they need. "And if you're complaining about internal equity issues, the response is, fine, go see what they're paying elsewhere."

Consider how this spot-market approach to compensation in a volatile field like computer programming overturns traditional employment relationships. With the exception of the "legacy" system, older skills in computer programming often have virtually no market value, and new programming skills that are in demand do not always build on old ones. Programmers may find that their wages are highest when they first enter the labor market because their programming skills are on the cutting edge. From that point on, however, their value and market compensation erodes, and they may well find themselves unemployable unless their skills are updated. Older, more experienced programmers may make much less than their younger counterparts. When a new operating system is introduced, the demand for old skills collapses, along with wages, while the demand for new skills and their accompanying wages skyrocket. Some companies that have grown tired of continually adjusting the wage structure for information system employees have simply created a "hot skill" premium that is temporarily attached to workers whose skills are in demand and is abruptly removed when those skills fall out of favor.

These equity issues are exacerbated by the greater use of contractors, consultants, and temps, each with different pay rates. Joint ventures and project work in which employees spend time working closely with employees in other organizations also create equity concerns. At issue is the fact that most individuals have a sense of what constitutes "fair" pay that may be independent from what the market generates. There is an extensive body of research suggesting that employees tend to operationalize the notion of fairness or equity through comparisons with others and that the most important or salient comparisons are with employees most similar to them; closest in terms of work performed, within the same organization, located physically nearby. They believe, for example, that individuals doing similar work should be paid similar wages, that more experienced workers should be paid more, that employees with more responsibility (further up the hierarchy) should be paid more.

The new employment relationship with its spot-market approach to compensation produces pay structures that are quite likely to be in conflict with these notions of equity. In essence, characteristics that are not valued in the outside labor market do not show up in the new pay structures. There are no premiums based on seniority or position in a hierarchy, for example. Compensation may well fall for an individual if his or her skills or performance declines. Contingent compensation tied to the performance of a group or an organization means that pay may vary even for similar workers doing the same job. The United Auto Workers common agreements on gainsharing with the Big Three auto companies, for example, led to much higher payouts for Ford workers than for GM workers because Ford outsourced more of its value chain and therefore had more profit per UAW member. Similar conflicts occur even within companies. Kodak, for example, had one foot in the old-line photography business and another in the Silicon Valley–based biotech and chemical industry, straddling two very different sets of employee relations with two separate sets of practices. The difficulty in managing these disparate relationships was one of the pressures pushing Kodak to consolidate its operations and move out of pharmaceuticals. Recent employee surveys show declines in perceptions of fairness and equity with respect to workplace pay and promotion issues, especially at the level of supervisors and the issues they address.[18]

The compensation practices associated with the new employment relationship may help explain the economic puzzle beginning in the late 1990s that coupled tight labor markets and low wage inflation. Part of the explanation concerns the reactions of employees to tight labor markets, while another part concerns the new ways in which employers are managing labor market problems without raising wages.

For employees, tight labor markets no longer imply job security. An October 1997 Roper Poll, taken during a period of considerable economic expansion, still found that 17 percent of U.S. workers thought they would be laid off in the next few years, while 53 percent thought they would change employers in the next five. The new management techniques that bring the market inside the firm reinforce the belief that employees are in competition to keep their jobs. Practices as innocuous as benchmarking convey information to employees about how their wages and costs stack up against those in other organizations, often including potential contractors that would be more than happy to have that function outsourced to them. Employees seem to have gotten the message rather clearly that they are responsible for their job security and that pushing up labor costs is not the way to get it.

Employers are relying on contingent compensation to keep key employees. For most employees, this compensation is contingent on productivity gains; for executives, it is paid out of shareholder value. Neither puts as much pressure on labor costs. As noted above, compensation structures that maintain pay differentials between areas and jobs by raising the entire wage structure when market wages drive some wages up are disappearing. In some companies, market-driven increases do not even spill over to other jobs in the same field, as the "hot skills" premiums described above illustrate. If the company changes operating systems or for other reasons no longer needs that skill, the premium goes away as well.

The other factor helping to reduce wage inflation pressures is simply that employer resistance is going up as new accounting techniques create profit-and-loss responsibilities at operating levels and punish employers for raising wages. Wage increases for new hires are especially resisted for fear that they will lead to demands for increases among current employees. In response, many companies have made investments in recruiting, seeking out nontraditional applicants such as welfare recipients or retirees and getting better at screening them to learn who will be a good fit. While these arrangements raise labor costs, they do not bid up wages in the market and may well be cheaper than raising wages to get better applicants.

Even though skill requirements seem to be rising, they are not putting much pressure on wages. Fifty-one percent of the employers in our 1997 National Employer Survey conducted with the Bureau of the Census report that the skills needed to adequately perform typical frontline jobs, such as sales clerks and production jobs, have gone up in the past three years; only 2 percent thought they had declined.[19] But most workers already have the skills needed to meet these rising demands because the demands are mainly associated with new work systems like TQM and teamwork, which push more responsibility and decision making onto employees.[20] Virtually every study indicates that employees like these new systems. One of my studies indicated that employees were even more satisfied with the level of their pay when these systems were present.[21] Another study indicates that while establishments with these arrangements pay higher wages, those wages are not associated with hiring more qualified applicants. The higher pay seems to be a premium used to encourage greater effort and attention on the part of the employees.[22]

Finally, the declining fear of union organizing on the part of employers, perhaps even more than the decline in union power at the bargaining table, has reduced wage pressures at unorganized companies where it had been routine policy to raise compensation at nonunion facilities to the level of union contracts to reduce employees' incentive to unionize. Nonunion employers report in private that they have pulled back the relative compensation and benefit levels at their nonunion facilities as a result.

Employers have found ways to manage in the face of tight labor markets without raising wages, and this may have played an important role in allowing the economy to operate with lower levels of unemployment than in the past without triggering inflation pressures. Current employees might prefer more wage pressure, although some are clearly benefiting from the tight labor markets, especially nontraditional employees who are better accommodated by the workplace. In the longer run, these more market-oriented pay and employment relationships make wage policies more sensitive to pressures from the outside market. In tight labor markets, such as computer programming, it might be that the new employment relationship is causing wages to escalate more quickly than in the past, at least for those occupations. The effect of these more market-driven pay arrangements is also to generate considerably greater inequality and no doubt contributes to rising inequality across and even within occupations.

A longer-term concern is that employers that have not been able to meet their hiring needs are simply letting vacancies stand empty rather than raise wages to fill them. During the early 1990s, employers in the United Kingdom had such severe problems filling vacancies that they were unable to respond to the economic expansion, and the country's economic recovery was choked off at least partially as a result.[23] Whether such shortages could occur in the much larger U.S. market is unclear, but the best medicine for reducing the risk is investments in education and training, a policy that should also help address more general issues of inequality in the labor market.

THE NEW DIVISION

In the traditional workplace, the most important division was between white-collar and blue-collar workers, supervisors and the management above them on one side and hourly frontline workers on the other. This division was reflected in labor law with the distinction between "nonexempt" workers who needed the protections of the Fair Labor Standards Act and "exempt" workers who did not because they were seen as inherently privileged, an intergral part of the organization. The restructuring of the workplace has made a mockery of that division. As illustrated in Chapter 4, managerial employees are now just as much at risk as their frontline counterparts. Especially where hourly employees are represented by unions, those workers often have more protections from layoffs and better support if they are downsized than do their managers.

The more important division in the workplace that has emerged in recent years is between the top executives and everyone else. This because of the perception that these senior executives have a deal that is fundamentally different from everyone else's. There is no doubt that the pressures on top managers are greater than in the past, and the chances of them being tossed out for failure to perform are arguably higher than for any other group of employees. It is also clear, however, that the financial rewards offered to them are extraordinary and are structured in ways that more than compensate for the greater pressures and risk of job loss. The highly leveraged compensation offered to CEOs and other top executives means that a single good year on the job can provide enough income to sustain them in style for the rest of their life; a really good year at a large company can ensure that their children and families never have to work. Virtually all top executives now have employment contracts that provide substantial compensation even if they are essentially fired. The thought of someone becoming a millionaire as a result of failing at a job rankles many people.

The most important driver of this new division is the fact that the interests of the executives and the rest of the organization are no longer clearly aligned. The compensation of the top executives at publicly held companies is heavily leveraged on the value of the company's stock, aligning their interests with those of the shareholders. Executives are clearly motivated to maximize company profits and to do whatever it takes to make that happen. Boards of directors are motivated the same way as a result of having their compensation increasingly loaded toward stock price and of successful shareholder lawsuits against boards that do not maximize shareholder value.

The rest of the employees in the organization do not have these incentives and arguably never could. Gainsharing plans may help align the interests of even hourly employees to the interests of shareholders, but most of these plans provide essentially symbolic financial incentives for employees compared with those available to executives. There are no plans, for example, in which a good year at a company will provide hourly workers with enough income to retire. There are no plans in which frontline workers can benefit on balance by eliminating their own jobs. None of the employees, except the top executive team, have enough at stake in the profits of the firm to truly think like shareholders. Their most important asset remains their labor.

This distinction becomes a practical problem because many of the actions that could maximize profits and shareholder value do not benefit employees. The decision to restructure an operation and lay off employees may well raise the company's stock price, but the affected employees will surely lose out on balance. An executive who decides to sell off a company division, putting herself out of a job in the process, will probably benefit financially from that decision because of the increased value of her stock options or "golden parachute" clauses in her employment contract that pay her when divisions are sold off; her employees will not benefit.

This new division between executives and the rest of the organization shows up strikingly in employee attitude data. The statement "I believe that management is looking out for my interests" showed the sharpest drop in national employee attitude data, with only about half as many agreeing in the late-1980s as in previous decades. The occupational group showing the sharpest declines in that question was middle managers. The attitude surveys of middle managers within one large company also showed the largest decline in their satisfaction with top management.[24] In 1995, only 19 percent of Americans had a great deal of confidence in the people running big business, and despite the economic success such companies were having, the numbers declined further to 12 percent in 1996. Eight-one percent believe that senior executives are benefiting but that most employees get no benefits from rising profits.[25] While job satisfaction rose 14 percentage points in one repeated survey from 1995 to 1997, the perception of how well employees thought their company was managed fell. In particular, 50 percent thought the company considered their interests in decisions affecting them in 1995, but only 41 percent thought so in 1997.[26]

These developments, not surprisingly, affect the amount of trust that employees say they have in the actions of top executives and, in turn, on the ability of those executives to lead. In 1988, for example, 33 percent of employees in an International Survey Research Corporation survey said that they often do not believe what management says. Despite increasing company success over the next few years, the percentage that did not believe management rose to 40 percent in 1996.[27] Other studies find that this lack of trust filters down the organization.

Respondents trust their own subordinates more than they trust their bosses, and the level of trust in one's boss declines as one moves down the organizational chart.[28]

The evidence in Chapter 1 suggested that declines in morale and attitude were not really affecting employers, that employee performance had not suffered. If concerns about inequities in pay or a lack of trust of management worsen, will it matter? The answer is yes because labor markets have tightened. When jobs are scarce and unemployment is high, employees cannot quit and are afraid to act out for fear of being dismissed. But when alternatives become more plentiful, the situation changes, and these attitudes once again have important effects on behavior. Recent surveys find that employee satisfaction has become "one of the key corporate priorities of the 1990s"[29] because of the understanding that tight labor markets make them relevant. Further, new studies of outcomes such as customer satisfaction, a crucial contingency in most organizations, are finding that employee attitudes are a central determinant of customer attitudes,[30] all of which are forcing companies to take employee attitudes more seriously. Some, like Kodak, are tying executive compensation to measures of employee attitudes.

Another implication of these developments is that the power and influence of the human resource function may rise rather dramatically. The traditional, long-term employment relationships that buffered employment from the outside market also buffered the organization and the human resource function from some of its problems. As noted earlier, managing employees was relatively simple over the past two decades when the combination of very slack labor markets, corporate downsizing, and the new employment relationship shifted all the power to the employer. The combination of the new employment relationship and tight labor markets is another story.

The power of a function within management is thought to be closely tied to the importance of the problem with which it is dealing. The more difficult and crucial the problem, the more important is the function designed to address it. The combination of tight labor markets and the new employment relationship creates fundamental problems for management and should raise the power of human resources signficantly. As Chapter 2 suggests, the influence and importance of human resources has seesawed over time, and these new developments will only exacerbate that tendency.

IMPLICATIONS FOR SOCIETY

The arguments presented as to how organizations can adapt to the new employment relationship, with its more individualistic, market-based orientation, do not imply that the adaptations will be easy or even that all organizations will be able to make them. In previous decades, the predominance of the traditional model of lifetime employment worked to the advantage of large, integrated companies with long planning horizons and hindered start-ups and other fast-moving companies. The new deal at work has the opposite effect, facilitating start-ups and companies that hire from the outside while dragging down those which try to maintain long-term employee relationships. The management techniques that have been described can help all organizations manage in this new environment. And many may find that they shift the way they do business and their operating strategies precisely because of the new deal at work. They may move away from longer-term projects and vertical integration precisely because they cannot retain or develop employees internally. But clearly those organizations that still need to take the long-term view have their work cut out for them.

The adaptations that help individual employers adjust to the new deal at work will not necessarily work for society as a whole, however. This is particularly so for the problem of developing employee skills. The difficulties that employers have in making investments in work-based training pay off come exactly at a time when most educators and observers of the workforce have come to believe that more work-based education and efforts that integrate school and work are exactly what is needed. The option of poaching workers from competitors may work for an individual employer, but it obviously cannot work for the economy as a whole. Yet that option will continue to be attractive. And the alternative of pushing the burden of skill development onto employees will prove inadequate to the need for skills in the economy. We will then face as a nation a shortage of employees with crucial work-based skills, even though academic skills may be plentiful. That shortage could affect the economy in various subtle ways, such as in the "dumbing down" of jobs or declining quality of products and services in addition to bidding wars for those who do have work-based skills.

One possible outcome is simply that employers will see no other option than to continue to invest in developing employees, new employees in particular, despite the diminishing incentives to do so. Some of the anecdotal evidence presented earlier suggests that because employees understand the need to keep their skills up-to-date, workplace training and development may be an employee benefit that helps with recruiting and retention. Some employers may continue to see it as the right thing to do in terms of social responsibility, traditionally the most important factor pushing employers to work with young employees and schools in particular. There is some evidence that these investments have been going up, with a virtual explosion in the past few years in efforts by employers to work with schools in developing their students. After decades of remarkably little employer involvement, 26 percent of employers now report that they have some involvement with schools in helping assist students to make the transition from school to work. The explanation for this explosion of interest clearly seems to be the perceived labor shortage and the sense that these investments may help give employers first pick in recruiting the best students.[31]

Another outcome of the new deal at work is the increased pressure on schools to better prepare students to enter the workforce. In higher education, the pressure has created a frenzy as parents and students gauge potential colleges based on ratings that report the salaries of graduates, the opinions of corporate recruiters, and especially the acceptance rates at elite professional schools. Most of the pressure to reform public schools has arguably come from the employers in each community who have applied political pressure and in some cases provided the resources to help schools restructure. Like the newer programs that pull nontraditional workers into the labor force and help them succeed, the efforts of these organizations represent some of the enormous social benefits associated with tighter labor markets.

The new employee relationship makes some considerable demands on infrastructure. Both a high level of information and a series of contracts to enforce training agreements are needed to make the new employment arrangements function effectively. Meaningful credentials are needed to communicate skill levels to employers and to serve as goals for employees. Potential employees need to be able to judge the quality of a training experience, just as employers need to judge the quality of a potential employee. Internalized systems of employment offered employers detailed and accurate information about the abilities of their employees that will be difficult to duplicate in the outside labor market. One consequence, then, is that there may be more "slippage" with these new arrangements—that is, employees with the necessary abilities and talent may be passed over because they lack the necessary credentials.

All markets demand infrastructure to operate honestly and efficiently. The need for information about jobs and workers, guidelines and enforcement of contracts, and other aspects of infrastructure will rise as the new relationship takes hold. Some industries have developed mechanisms for providing aspects of this infrastructure, such as the various skill standards and credentials in the automotive repair industry maintained by the Society of Automotive Engineers. But at present the government is the only player in a position to deliver the credential systems, remedial training programs, protection for the displaced, and other arrangements on a national scale that could truly make the new system operate effectively.

As the labor market becomes more important, it suggests that there will be more hiring and firing, more contracts, and more concern about how to enforce them. The labor law governing such actions will continue to get a workout that will make even more obvious how far its New Deal beginnings, based on the model of industrial employment, are out of step with the contemporary scene. Both employers and employees will need strong incentives not to cheat in these transactions; mechanisms will be required to prevent reneging on training contracts. And once the parties start turning to the courts to adjudicate their disputes, experience suggests that there will be no way back out. The external hiring of executives has already become a litigious and therefore expensive and time-consuming exercise. The legal costs of hiring and firing might seem capable of swamping the benefits of hiring from the outside, except for the fact that internal promotions and transfers have also become highly litigated in an era where the social contract in the workplace no longer governs behavior.

An aspect of the new employment relationship that many may find even more troubling is the extent to which it contributes to inequality in outcomes. Employees with good skills, superior information about opportunities, and an overall high level of "marketability" will find that their job prospects are enhanced under the new market-oriented system; those who lack skills and information and are less marketable may find their prospects deteriorating. Further, over the course of their working life, all employees are likely to see much greater volatility in their prospects because employment is more subject to the conse-quences of changes in the supply and demand for various skills. Employees like those in the information technology area, for example, already find that their prospects can change from "the sky's the limit" to essentially unemployable, even in the same company.

This volatility, combined with the declining ability of employers to develop employees internally, dramatically increases the need for individuals to get skills on their own. Getting those skills requires assets— money, in particular—that are not distributed equally in society. Those who already have assets are likely to do even better in the more individualized workplace, while those who do not will do worse.

Much of contemporary American society has been built around stable employment relationships, with predictable career advancement and steady growth in wages. This work environment has made possible long-term individual investments in home ownership and college educations for children, community ties and the stability they bring, and a quality life outside work that is enhanced by reducing risk and uncertainty on the job. There is already at least anecdotal evidence that younger employees are more worried about getting a nest egg for financial security sooner and may be willing to take more risk to get it. If employees are forced to take on more of the risks of doing business, managing their own careers along the lines of entrepreneurs, how will the stresses and demands of these additional responsibilities affect them? Surely it will spill over to their life outside of work, to their families, as it clearly has during the period of restructuring. How society will adapt to these developments is an open question.

The final question that lingers in the minds of many observers after a long discussion of the implications of the new deal at work is simply whether, on balance, this change is a good thing. Behind this question are inevitably a series of assumptions about how one defines "good." Some observers are inclined to view these developments as driven essentially by executive fiat: the top executives had discretion as to whether to keep the old system or move to the new deal at work, and they chose the latter essentially to line their own pockets. For these observers, the change is clearly bad because the motives were selfish. If, on the other hand, one accepts that there is an array of powerful pressures forcing executives and their organizations in the direction of the new deal and that their discretion was severely limited, attribution of motives becomes much more difficult to sustain.

There is no doubt that the break with the traditional, internal employment relationship was a fundamental violation of psychological and social contracts for the workers affected, and there is also no doubt that those employees bore that violation with relatively little recompense. There is no doubt about the winners and losers here: The change was good for most employers and bad for a great many employees. There is also no doubt that those employers who tried to minimize the costs to employees are commendable while those that did little for them are not.

When we think about the market-driven new deal in action, however, it is much more difficult to sustain a discussion framed around questions of "good" and "bad." Markets are very good at efficiency. They are disconnected entirely from the issue of fairness. They generate quite astonishing levels of inequality based on shifts in supply and demand. Over time, bargaining power and benefits, more broadly defined, will shift back and forth from employers to employees, as they have from the 1980s to the 1990s, based on the tightness of the labor market. The new deal and the labor market behind it will continue to undo the internal compensation systems that were designed in part to accommodate employee notions of fairness that are based on factors other than market power. The new deal generates new and exciting opportunities for employees in demand, especially for those who were stifled inside the bureaucracies of the traditional employment relationship, and arguably worse alternatives for those not in demand. In that sense, a summary answer to whether the new deal is a good thing is simply that it is good for efficiency and opportunity and bad for traditional notions of fairness based on concepts of equity.

Perhaps the final recommendation to make concerning the new deal at work is to take the long view and note that this, too, will surely pass. Changes in markets, production techniques, corporate governance, and other factors will change the employment relationship again, perhaps even quicker than in the past. It may cycle back between the poles of internal development and the outside labor market, generating critiques the next time about the challenges of adapting to lifetime employment relationships.

Notes

Preface

1. Peter Cappelli, et al., *Change at Work* (New York: Oxford University Press, 1997).

2. Jeremy Rifkin, *The End of Work: The Decline of the Global Labor Force and the Dawn of the Post-Modern Era* (New York: Putnam, 1996).

3. William Bridges, *Job Shift: How to Prosper in a Workplace Without Jobs* (Reading, MA: Addison Wesley, 1994).

4. Michael B. Arthur and Denise M. Rousseau, *The Boundaryless Career: A New Employment Principle for a New Organizational Era* (New York: Oxford University Press, 1996).

5. Cliff Hakim, *We Are All Self-Employed* (San Francisco: Berrett-Koehler, 1994).

6. Charles Heckscher, *White-Collar Blues* (New York: Basic Books, 1995).

7. Ibid.

Chapter 1

1. James Rosenbaum, "Tournament Mobility: Career Patterns in a Corporation," *Administrative Science Quarterly* 24, no. 2 (1979): 220.

2. See Alvin W. Gouldner, "The Norm of Reciprocity: A Preliminary Statement," *American Sociological Review* 25 (1960): 161–178.

3. Donald T. Regan, "Effects of a Favor and Liking on Compliance," *Journal of Experimental Social Psychology* 7 (1971): 627–639.

4. See Sandra L. Robinson, Matthew S. Kraatz, and Denise M. Rousseau, "Changing Obligations and the Psychological Contract: A Longitudinal Study," *Academy of Management Journal* 37 (1994): 137–152.

5. Denise M. Rousseau and R. J. Anton, "Fairness and Obligations in Termination Decisions: The Role of Contributions, Promises, and Performance," *Journal of Organizational Behavior* 12 (1991): 287–299.

6. Denise M. Rousseau, *Psychological Contracts in Organizations* (Thousand Oaks, Calif.: Sage Publications, 1995).

7. Providing, of course, that the dismissals did not violate any of the employment protection legislation by adversely affecting protected groups, such as women and minorities. See F. S. Forbes and I. M. Jones, "A Comparative, Attitudinal, and Analytic Study of the Dismissal of At-Will Employees without Cause," *Labor Law Journal* 37 (1986): 157–166.

8. To be fair, the situation was somewhat different in nonunion establishments where management was more interested in securing commitment from its employees. Here the goal was generally to prevent them from joining unions, a goal that is significantly less challenging and inclusive than identifying with the goals of the organization.

9. Some large part of the 27 percent who report that they never offered the old deal in the first place are simply rationalizing. (I have, for example, heard human resource managers of large corporations say with a straight face that they never had a deal offering job security for loyalty because nothing like that was ever in their written employment policies.)

10. Personal communication, May 1997.

11. *HR Executive Review: Implementing the New Employment Contract* 4, no. 4 (1997).

12. This statement was from the pen of the CEO to his employees, which may account for its bluntness. It is recounted in Patricia A. Milligan, "Regaining Commitment," in *The New Deal in Employment Relationships: A Council Report,* Report No. 1162-96-CR Conference Board, New York (1996).

13. From an internal company publication.

14. Apple's deal predates the most recent wave of new deals in the workplace. It is summarized in Barbara Ettorre, "The Contingency Workforce Moves Mainstream," *Management Review* 83 (February 1994): 10–16.

15. Thomas D. Sugalski, Louis S. Manzo, and Jim L. Meadows, "Resource Link: Reestablishing the Employment Relationship in an Era of Downsizing," *Human Resource Management* 34, no. 3 (Fall 1995): 391.

16. Ibid.

17. Mary Anne Walk, "Building a New Deal around a Concept," in *The New Deal in Employment Relationships*, Report No. 1162-96-CR, Conference Board, New York (1996): 27.

18. Sugalski et al., "Resource Link," 389–403.

19. "The New Social Contract: Redefining GTE's Employment Relationship" (GTE Corporation, Stamford, Conn.), August 1996.

20. Robert Kuttner, "Talking Marriage and Thinking One-Night Stand," *Business Week,* October 18, 1993, 16.

21. In brief, the quid pro quos that unions secured in return for making concessions on labor costs were on issues that did not raise current labor costs. They included stock options for union members, agreements on capital investments and other ways of securing future employment, and deals about future compensation.

22. "Redefining GTE's Employment Relationship."

23. It is important to recognize, of course, that surveys of current employees include the survivors of previous restructurings as well as new employees who never experienced the old deal. Their responses are not necessarily an accurate indicator of how employees respond to a new deal. Many of those who had trouble with it have been pushed out, and some of those who remained have rationalized their new situation and come to accept it.

24. *HR Executive Review: Implementing the New Employment Contract,* 12.

25. Towers Perrin, *1997 Towers Perrin Workplace Index* (New York, 1997).

26. Milligan, "Regaining Commitment."

27. Towers Perrin. See also Stephen M. Bookbinder, "The Employee Perspective," in *The New Deal in Employment Relationships.*

28. See Jeffrey Pfeffer and John Lawler, "Effects of Job Alternatives, Extrinsic Rewards, and Behavioral Commitment on Attitudes toward the Organization: A Field Test of the Insufficient Justification Paradigm," *Administrative Science Quarterly* 25 (1980): 38–56.

29. Peter Cappelli and Peter D. Sherer, "Satisfaction, Market Wages, and Labor Relations: An Airline Study," *Industrial Relations* 27, no. 1 (Winter 1988): 56–74.

30. Charles Hulin and M. R. Blood, "Job Enlargement, Individual Differences, and Worker Responses," *Psychological Bulletin* 69 (1968): 41–55.

31. T. S. Bateman and S. Strasser, "A Longitudinal Analysis of the Antecedents of Organizational Commitment," *Academy of Management Journal* 27 (1984): 95–112.

32. Charles O'Reilly, III, and Jennifer Chatman, "Organizational Commitment and Psychological Attachment: The Effects of Compliance Identification and Internalization on Prosocial Behavior," *Journal of Applied Psychology* 71, no. 3 (1986): 492–499.

33. John P. Meyer, Natalie J. Allen, and Ian R. Gellatly, "Affective and Continuance Commitment to the Organization: Evaluation of Measures and Analysis of Current and Time-Lagged Relations," *Journal of Applied Psychology* 75, no. 6 (December 1990): 710–720.

34. Arne L. Kalleberg and Torger Reve, "Contracts and Commitment: Economic and Sociological Perspectives on Employment Relations," *Human Relations* 45, no. 9 (1992): 1103–1132.

35. J. E. Mathieu and D. M. Zajac, "A Review and Meta-analysis of the Antecedents, Correlates, and Consequences of Organizational Commitment," *Psychological Bulletin* 108 (1990): 171–194.

36. Stephen R. Barley, "The Turn toward a Horizontal Division of Labor: On the Occupationalization of Firms and the Technization of Work," working paper, Cornell University School of Industrial and Labor Relations, Ithaca, NY, 1992.

37. George A. Ackerlof, Andrew K. Rose, and Janet L. Yellen, "Job Switching and Job Satisfaction in the U.S. Labor Market," *Brookings Papers on Economic Activity,* no. 2 (1988): 495–582.

38. James L. Price, *The Study of Turnover* (Ames: Iowa State University Press, 1977).

39. J. Paul Leigh, "The Effects of Unemployment and the Business Cycle on Absenteeism," *Journal of Economics and Business* 37 (May 1985): 159–170.

40. Peter Cappelli and Keith Chauvin, "A Test of an Efficiency Model of Grievance Activity," *Industrial and Labor Relations Review* 45, no. 1 (October 1991): 3–14.

41. Paul R. Jackson, Elizabeth M. Stafford, Michael H. Banks, and Peter Warr, "Un-

employment and Psychological Stress in Young People: The Moderating Role of Employment Commitment," *Journal of Applied Psychology* 68 (1983): 525–535.

42. I am indebted to Karl Price of the Walker Group for this example.

43. Ganesan Shankar and Barton A. Weitz, "The Impact of Staffing Policies on Retail Buyer Job Attitudes and Behaviors," *Journal of Retailing* 72, no.1 (Spring 1996): 31–56.

44. Brian S. Moskal, "Company Loyalty Dies, a Victim of Neglect," *Industry Week* 242, no. 5 (1 March 1993): 11–12.

45. Commitment was followed closely in their ranking by "trust," which many would see as a related concept. See *HR Executive Review: Implementing the New Employment Contract,* 10.

46. Thomas A. DeCotiis and Timothy P. Summers, "A Path Analysis of a Model of the Antecedents and Consequences of Organizational Commitment," *Human Relations* 40, no. 7 (1987): 445–470.

47. J. E. Mathieu and D. M. Zajac, "A Review and Meta-analysis of the Antecedents, Correlates, and Consequences of Organizational Commitment," *Psychological Bulletin* 108 (1990): 171–194.

48. O'Reilly and Chatman, "Organizational Commitment and Psychological Attachment."

49. Gary S. Becker, "Investments in Human Capital: A Theoretical Analysis," *Journal of Political Economy* 71 (1962): 9–49.

50. "Report on Employer Provided Training," U.S. Bureau of Labor Statistics press release, 19 July 1996.

Chapter 2

1. William Bridges, "The End of the Job," *Fortune,* 19 September 1994, 62–74, and "Rethinking Work," *Business Week,* 17 October 1994, were among the more prominent cover stories on this topic.

2. This example is described in Alfred D. Chandler, Jr., *Strategy and Structure: Chapters in the History of the American Industrial Enterprise* (Cambridge, Mass.: MIT Press, 1962), 116.

3. Alfred D. Chandler, Jr., *The Visible Hand: The Managerial Revolution in American Business* (Cambridge, Mass.: Belknap Press, 1977), 3.

4. See David Landes, *The Unbound Prometheus* (Cambridge: Cambridge University Press, 1969).

5. See S. H. R. Jones, "The Origin of Work: A Historical Dimension," *Journal of Economic Behavior and Organization* 3 (1982): 117–137.

6. A good description of the problems of the putting-out system is in Dan Clawson, *Bureaucracy and the Labor Process: The Transformation of U.S. Industry, 1860–1920* (New York: Monthly Review Press, 1980), 44–49.

7. E. L. Trist and K. W. Bamforth, "Some Social and Psychological Consequences of the Long Wall Method of Coal-Getting," *Human Relations* 4, no. 1 (1951): 6.

8. I am indebted to Sid Winter for this observation.

9. See Katharine Stone, "The Origins of Job Structures in the Steel Industry," *Review of Radical Political Economics* 6, no. 2 (Summer 1974): 113–173.

10. See David Montgomery, "Workers' Control of Machine Production in the Nineteenth Century," *Labor History* (Fall 1976): 488.

11. See John Buttrick, "The Inside Contracting System," *Journal of Economic History* 12, no. 3 (Summer 1952): 205.

12. These examples come from Clawson, *Bureaucracy and the Labor Process*, 81–89.

13. See Clawson, *Bureaucracy and the Labor Process*, 81.

14. Buttrick, "Inside the Contracting System," 205.

15. Clawson calculates that "the average contractor made more than three times as much as the average employee," so a foreman could receive some premium over the average worker and still cost about one-third of the contractor's earnings (*Bureaucracy and the Labor Process*, 101).

16. Daniel Nelson, *Managers and Workers: Origins of the New Factory System in the United States, 1880–1920* (Madison: University of Wisconsin Press, 1975), 35.

17. Buttrick, "Inside the Contracting System," 220.

18. Nelson, *Managers and Workers*, 43.

19. Sumner H. Slichter, *The Turnover of Factory Labor* (New York, 1919), 375. The quote is cited in Nelson, *Managers and Workers*.

20. Sanford M. Jacoby, *Employing Bureaucracy: Managers, Unions, and the Transformation of Work in American Industry, 1900–1945* (New York: Columbia University Press, 1985), 21.

21. Nelson, *Managers and Workers*, 79.

22. See Chandler, *The Visible Hand*, 272–277, for a description.

23. For an account, see Stephen Meyer, *The Five Dollar Day: Labor Management and Social Control in the Ford Motor Company* (Albany: State University of New York Press, 1981).

24. Hugh G. J. Aitken, *Taylorism at Watertown Arsenal: Scientific Management in Action, 1908–1915* (Cambridge, Mass.: Harvard University Press, 1960), 88.

25. Louis D. Brandeis, *Other People's Money, and How Bankers Use It* (New York: Harper and Row, 1967).

26. Alfred D. Chandler, Jr., "The United States: Seedbed of Managerial Capitalism," in *Managerial Hierarchies: Comparative Perspectives on the Rise of the Modern Industrial Enterprise*, ed. Chandler and Herman Daems (Cambridge, Mass.: Harvard University Press, 1980), 9–40.

27. See Daniel M. G. Raff and Lawrence H. Summers, "Did Henry Ford Pay Efficiency Wages?" *Journal of Labor Economics* 5, no. 4, pt. 2 (1987): S57–S86.

28. Jacoby, *Employing Bureaucracy*, 279.

29. In *Employing Bureaucracy*, 133–136, Jacoby provides evidence of the employee response to tighter labor markets.

30. See Thomas A. Kochan and Peter Cappelli, "The Transformation of the Industrial Relations and Human Resources Functions," in *Internal Labor Markets*, ed. Paul Osterman (New York: Oxford University Press, 1984); James Baron et al., "War and Peace: The Evolution of Modern Personnel Administration in U.S. Industry,"

American Journal of Sociology 92 (1986): 350–383; and Jacoby, *Employing Bureaucracy.*

31. Jacoby, *Employing Bureaucracy,* 162–179.

32. Sumner H. Slichter, *The Challenge of Industrial Relations* (Ithaca: Cornell University Press, 1947), 35.

33. An encyclopedic guide to employment practices during this period, especially for nonexempt workers, can be found in Sumner H. Slichter, James J. Healy, and E. Robert Livernash, *The Impact of Collective Bargaining on Management* (Washington, D.C.: Brookings Institute, 1960). More detailed information on practices targeted at management is available in Fred Foulkes, *Personnel Practices of Large, Non-Union Companies* (Englewood Cliffs, N.J.: Prentice-Hall, 1980). Virtually every human resource practices textbook has normative descriptions similar to these.

34. The theory of "implicit contracts" asserts that firms are better able to absorb risk than are individuals, and employees basically pay a premium (by accepting lower wages) to have the employer absorb the risk of product market variations on compensation.

35. Foulkes, *Personnel Practices.*

36. D. Quinn Mills, "Seniority versus Ability in Promotion Decisions," *Industrial and Labor Relations Review* 38 (1985): 421–427.

37. F. S. Roethlisberger and William J. Dickson, *Management and the Worker* (Cambridge, Mass.: Harvard University Press, 1927).

38. C. Wright Mills, *The American Middle Class* (New York: Oxford University Press, 1953).

39. William H. Whyte, *The Organization Man* (New York: Simon and Schuster, 1956).

40. Ibid.

41. Mills, *The American Middle Class,* 186.

42. Ibid., 109–120.

43. See David R. Roberts, "The Determinants and Effects of Executive Compensation" (Graduate School of Business Administration, Carnegie Institute of Technology, 1954).

44. Whyte, *The Organization Man,* 163.

45. There was some evidence for this view. See Arthur R. Cohen, "Upward Communications in Experimentally Created Hierarchies," *Human Relations* 11 (1958): 41–53.

46. Rosabeth Moss Kanter, *Men and Women of the Corporation* (New York: Basic Books, 1977), 130.

47. Ibid., 55.

48. Ibid., 38.

49. Daniel Yankelovich, "The Meaning of Work," in *The Worker and the Job,* ed. Jerome M. Rosow (Englewood Cliffs, N.J.: Prentice-Hall, 1974), 19–47.

50. Robert S. Smith, "Comparable Worth: Limited Coverage and the Exacerbation of Inequality," *Industrial and Labor Relations Review* 41 (1988): 227–239.

51. Walter Y. Oi, "The Fixed Employment Costs of Specialized Labor," in *The Measure of Labor Cost,* Jack Triplett (Chicago: University of Chicago Press, 1983).

52. See, for example, William G. Ouchi, *Theory Z* (Reading, Mass.: Addison-Wesley, 1984), and J. C. Abegglen and G. Stalk, Jr., *Kaisha: The Japanese Corporation* (New York: Basic Books, 1985).

53. David Sedgwick, "Proving Ground: Brazil Offers Makers and Suppliers a Place for Beta Testing Manufacturing Ideas," *Automotive News*, 4 August 1997.

Chapter 3

1. Every year over the Labor Day weekend, when its Armonk training facility in Westchester County was otherwise vacant, IBM would bring in twenty or so management professors from leading business schools to tell them about IBM's people management practices. A good part of this discussion comes from what I learned at those meetings.

2. Mills, "Seniority versus Ability in Promotion Decisions,"421–427.

3. D. Quinn Mills, *The IBM Lesson: The Profitable Art of Full Employment* (New York: Times Books, 1988).

4. Ibid., 202.

5. A good description of the community reaction can be found in John Hoerr, "Big Blues for Laid-Off IBM Workforce," *Business and Society Review*, 22 March 1994, 35.

6. Ira Sager, "The Few, the True, the Blue," *Business Week*, 30 May 1994, 124.

7. David Kilpatrick, "Lou Gerstner's First 30 Days," *Fortune*, 31 May 1993, 57.

8. Ibid.

9. Dean Minderman, "Big Blues," *Credit Union Management*, February 1995, 15–17.

10. Shirley Barnes, "In the Out Door: Restructuring at IBM Has Meant Hiring for Specific Skills," *Chicago Tribune*, 7 July 1996, 2.

11. A. A. Berle and Gardener Means, *The Modern Corporation* (New York: Macmillan, 1932).

12. *Economic Report of the President, 1995*, Washington, D.C.

13. United Nations, *World Investment Report: Transnational Corporations and Integrated International Production* (New York, 1993), 243, 248.

14. I am indebted to Michael Useem for this analysis.

15. McKinsey & Company, *Manufacturing Productivity* (McKinsey Global Institute, Washington, D.C., 1993).

16. Louis S. Richman, "How Jobs Die—And Are Born," *Fortune* 128, no. 2, 26 July 1993, 26.

17. See, for example, Constantinos Markides, "Diversification, Restructuring, and Economic Performance," Working paper, London Business School, London, UK, 1993, and Jaideep Anand and Harbir Singh, "Asset Redeployment, Acquisitions and Corporate Strategy in Declining Industries," *Strategic Management Journal*, July 1997, 99–118.

18. Edward H. Bowman, Harbir Singh, Michael Useem, and Raja Hadury, "When

Does Restructuring Work?" working paper, Reginald Jones Center, Wharton School, Philadelphia, Penn., 1996.

19. Michael C. Jensen, "The Eclipse of the Public Corporation," *Harvard Business Review,* September–October 1989, 61–74.

20. Andrei Schleifer and Lawrence H. Summers, "Breach of Trust in Hostile Takeovers," working paper 2342, National Bureau of Economic Research, Cambridge, Mass., 1987.

21. S. Bhagat, A. Schliefer, and R. Vishny, "Hostile Takeovers in the 1980s: The Return to Corporate Specialization," *Brookings Papers on Economic Activity* (1990).

22. Steven Kaplan, "The Effects of Management Buyouts on Operating Performance and Value," *Journal of Financial Economics* 11 (1989): 5–50.

23. Frank R. Lichtenberg and Donald Siegel, "Productivity and Changes of Ownership of Manufacturing Plants," *Brookings Papers on Economic Activity* (1987).

24. Jagadeesh Gokhale, Erica L. Groshen, and David Neumark, "Do Hostile Takeovers Reduce Extramarginal Wage Payments?" *Review of Economics and Statistics* 77 (1995): 470–485.

25. D. L. Worrell, W. N. Davidson III, and V. M. Sharma, "Layoff Announcements and Stockholder Wealth," *Academy of Management Journal* 34 (1991): 662–678.

26. Wayne E. Cascio, Clifford E. Young, and James R. Morris, "Financial Consequences of Employment-Change Decisions in Major U.S. Corporations," *Academy of Management Journal* 40, no. 5 (1997): 1175–1189.

27. John Holusha, "A Profitable Xerox Plans to Cut Staff by 10,000," *New York Times,* 9 December 1993, D1, D5; Laurie Hays and Gautam Naik, "Xerox to Cut 10,000 Jobs, Shut Facilities, *Wall Street Journal,* 9 December 1993, A2, A4.

28. Riverside Economic Research, *Brancato Report: Equity Turnover and Investment Strategies* (Fairfax, VA: Victoria Group, 1994).

29. Michael Useem, "Corporate Restructuring and the Restructured World of Senior Management," in *Broken Ladders: Changes in the Mangerial Career Path,* ed. Paul Osterman (New York: Oxford University Press, 1997).

30. Jennifer E. Bethel and Julia Liebeskind, "The Effects of Ownership Structure on Corporate Restructuring," *Strategic Management Journal* 14 (1993): 15–31.

31. Laurie Hays, "IBM's Finance Chief, Ax in Hand, Scours Empire for Costs to Cut," *Wall Street Journal,* 26 January 1994, A1, A6.

32. See "The Real Key to Creating Wealth," *Fortune,* 20 September 1993, 83.

33. "Office Workers Rub Elbows as More Workplaces Shrink," *Wall Street Journal,* 7 May 1977, B1.

34. Mary Kane, "Accounting Firm Leading Evolution of Corporate Office," *Newark Star Ledger,* 19 June 1994, 5.

35. "Pinnacle Alliance Delivers Benefits to J. P. Morgan during First Year of Operation," *M2 Presswire,* 16 July 1997.

36. Richard A. Lambert, David F. Larker, and Robert Verrecchia, "Portfolio Considerations in Valuing Executive Compensation," *Journal of Accounting Research* 29 (1991): 129–149.

37. Wendy Bounds, "Kodak Gives Fisher Options to Purchase 750,000 of Its Shares," *New York Times,* 20 December 1993, B2.

38. Jonathan Auerbach, "Director's Cut: The Trend toward Stock-Based Pay Has Spread to Board Members," *Wall Street Journal*, 11 April 1994.

39. "Ming the Merciless," *Financial World*, 21 June 1994.

40. Glenn Collins, "Tough Leader Wields the Ax at Scott," *New York Times*, 15 August 1994, D1.

41. John A. Byrne, "The Shredder," *Business Week*, 15 January 1996, 56.

42. Ibid.

43. Ibid.

44. Tony Jackson, "Scott's Clean Sheet," *Financial Times*, 27 October 1994, 18.

45. Byrne, "The Shredder."

46. Margaret M. Plunkett, "Scott Refocuses on Tissues; Sells Subsidiary for $1.6 Billion," *Associated Press*, 11 October 1994.

47. Margaret M. Plunkett, "County Grants Scott $280,000 in Jobs Incentives," *Palm Beach Post*, 4 October 1995, 4b.

48. Byrne, "The Shredder," 56.

49. Jackson, "Scott's Clean Sheet."

50. Mary Kane, "Downsizing: Profit vs Pain," *Atlanta Journal and Constitution*, 14 January 1996.

51. Joseph Weber, "Scott Rolls Out a Risky Strategy," *Business Week*, 22 May 1995, 48.

52. This example comes from our study of performance in the insurance industry at the Wharton School.

53. In many insurance companies, however, the agents are not employees of the company at all but are independent contractors who deal with several insurance companies. The dilemma for the companies is how to monitor and control the actions of these agents over whom they have no direct supervisory control. One way is through the MIS system, which the agents use. This system not only provides the agents with information, structuring their decisions, it also keeps track of the decisions made by the agents and reports them back to the company.

54. See also Michael Hammer and James Champy, *Reengineering the Corporation: A Manifesto for Business Revolution* (New York: Harper Business, 1993); Gene Hall, Jim Rosenthal, and Judy Wade, "How to Make Reengineering *Really* Work," *Harvard Business Review*, November–December 1993.

55. Descriptions of many of these features can be found in John A. Byrne, "The Horizontal Corporation," *Business Week*, 20 December 1993, 76–81.; Gordon Donaldson, *Corporate Restructuring: Managing the Change Process from Within* (Boston: Harvard Business School Press, 1994); Stephen J. Garone, *Building a High-Performance Organization* (New York: Conference Board, 1993); David A. Nadler, Marc S. Gerstein, Robert B. Shaw, and Associates, *Organizational Architecture: Designs for Changing Organizations* (San Francisco: Jossey-Bass, 1992); and Michael Useem, "Management Commitment and Company Policies on Education and Training," *Human Resource Management*, 32 (1993): 411–434.

56. Peter Cappelli and K. C. O'Shaughnessey, "Skill and Wage Changes in Corporate Headquarters, 1986–1992" (Philadelphia: National Center on the Educational Quality of the Workforce, 1995).

57. In fairness, these movies were more along the lines of a television series episode than a modern feature film. For the early years of the industry, see B. Hampton,

History of the American Film Industry: From Its Beginnings to 1931 (New York: Dover Press, 1970).

58. See Michael Storper, "The Transition to Flexible Specialization in the U.S. Film Industry: External Economies, the Division of Labor, and the Crossing of Industrial Divides," *Cambridge Journal of Economics* (United Kingdom) 13 (1989): 273–305.

59. See Al Haas, "Carmakers Look to the Niche Markets to Bolster Sales," *Philadelphia Inquirer,* 25 May 1997, G35.

60. Stanley F. Slater, "Competing in High Velocity Markets," *Industrial Marketing Management* 22 (1993): 255–263.

61. Pahkaj Ghemawat, "Sustainable Advantage," *Harvard Business Review,* May–June 1986, 69–70.

62. George Stalk, Jr., "Time—The Next Source of Competitive Advantage," *Harvard Business Review,* July–August 1988, 41–51.

63. James Womack, Daniel Jones, and Daniel Roos, *The Machine That Changed the World* (New York: Rawson-Macmillan, 1991).

64. Abbie Griffin, "Metrics for Measuring Product Development Cycle Time," *Journal of Production Innovation and Management* 10 (1993): 112–125.

65. Sunder Kekre and Kannan Srinivasan, "Broader Product Line: A Necessity to Achieve Success?" *Management Science* 30 (1990): 12–16.

66. Ken Auletta, "The Microsoft Provocateur," *The New Yorker,* 12 May 1997, 70.

67. Charles E. Morris, "Why New Products?" *Chilton's Food Engineering* 6 (1993): 130, and Stalk, "Time—The Next Source of Competitive Advantage."

68. Milton D. Rosenau, "From Experience: Faster New Product Development," *Journal of Production Innovation and Management* 5 (1988): 150–153.

69. G. Causer and C. Jones, "Responding to 'Skill Shortages': Recruitment and Retention in a High Technology Labor Market," *Human Resource Management Journal* 3, no. 3 (1993): 202–221.

70. "When You Have to Move for Work," *Detroit News,* 2 March 1998, A4.

71. C. K. and G. Hamel, "The Core Competence of the Corporation," *Harvard Business Review,* May–June 1990, 79–91.

72. Edward E. Lawler, Susan Mohrman, and Gerald Ledford, *Employee Involvement and Total Quality Management: Practices and Results in Fortune 500 Companies* (San Francisco: Jossey-Bass Publishers, 1987); Gerald F. Davis and Suzanne K. Stout, "Organization Theory and the Market Corporate Control: A Dynamic Analysis of the Characteristics of Large Takeover Targets, 1980–90," *Administrative Science Quarterly* 37 (1992): 605–633; Peter Doeringer et al., *Turbulence in the American Workplace* (New York: Oxford University Press, 1991).

73. Sara L. Beckman, "Evolution of Management Roles in a Networked Organization: An Insider's View of the Hewlett-Packard Company," in *Broken Ladders: Managerial Careers in the New Economy,* ed. Paul Osterman (New York: Oxford University Press, 1996).

74. Steve Kaufman, "Couple Operate a 'Virtual Winery,'" *Philadelphia Inquirer,* 11 May 1996, D1.

75. Information technology also makes markets more efficient by making the information necessary for them to operate easier and cheaper to use. Electronic brokerage is perhaps the most obvious illustration. Producers that find it inefficient to compete for small orders can learn about other, similar orders and combine them into

an efficient size. Even proprietary information systems have a way of eventually leading to markets. United Airline's Apollo System, the first of the on-line reservation systems, originally booked only United flights. Then American Airlines countered with its Sabre, which listed the flights of competitors as well, capturing more attention from travel agents. Apollo then had to open its system, too. Other competitors, such as Rosenbluth Travel, repackage the information from these reservation systems to eliminate proprietary aspects (such as listing United flights first on the Apollo system), further enhancing the market information. My colleague Eric Clemons describes how Bloomberg made its fixed-income securities trading system available to other dealers and created an electronic market for those securities in the process.

76. Steve Lohr, "I.B.M. May Quit Hilltop Headquarters," *New York Times,* 13 January 1994, A1, D3.

77. Vijay Gurbaxani and Seungjin Whang, "The Impact of Information Systems on Organizations and Markets," *Communications of the ACM* 34, no.1 (1991): 59–73.

78. See H. Russell Johnston and Michael R. Vitale, "Creating Competitive Advantage with Interorganizational Information Systems," *MIS Quarterly,* June 1988, 153–165.

79. E. Brynjolfsson, T. Malone, J. Gurbaxani, and A. Kambil, "Does Information Technology Lead to Smaller Firms?" *Management Science* 40, no. 12 (1994).

80. David Sedgwick, "Proving Ground: Brazil Offers Makers and Suppliers a Place for Beta Testing Manufacturing Ideas," *Automotive News,* 4 August 1997.

81. Paul Osterman, "How Common Is Workplace Transformation and How Can We Explain Who Adopts It?" *Industrial and Labor Relations Review* 47 (1994): 173–188.

82. Johnston and Vitale, "Creating Competitive Advantage."

83. Barry A. Macy and Hiroaki Izumi, "Organizational Change, Design, and Work Innovation: A Meta-analysis of 131 North American Field Studies—1961–1991," in *Research in Organizational Change and Development,* ed. Richard W. Woodman and William A. Pasmore (Greenwich, Conn.: JAI Press, forthcoming).

84. Hall, Rosenthal, and Wade, "How to Make Reengineering *Really* Work," 191.

85. NLRB *v.* Bell Aerospace, 416 U.S. 267, 1974.

86. Not all of the requirements of labor law are so easily eliminated with contract workers. Safety and health legislation applies equally to contract workers, for example. Although the requirements for coverage differ from act to act, in general, contractors are required to comply where they directly supervise other contract workers. See H. Lane Dennard and Herbert R. Northrup, "Leased Employment: Character, Numbers, and Labor Problems," *Georgia Law Review* 23 (1994): 683–728.

87. See Holusha, "A Profitable Xerox," and Hays and Naik, "Xerox to Cut 10,000 Jobs."

88. Edward Potter and Judith Youngman, *Keeping America Competitive: Employment Policy for the 21st Century* (Lakeland, CO: Glenbridge Publishers, 1994).

Chapter 4

1. See, for example, "The Upsizing of America," *Wall Street Journal,* 20 September 1996.

2. See William Wiatrowski, "Small Businesses and Their Employees," *Monthly Labor Review,* October 1994, 29–35.

3. Robert S. Smith, "Comparable Worth: Limited Coverage and the Exacerbation of Inequality," *Industrial and Labor Relations Review* 41 (1988): 227–239.

4. Walter Y. Oi, "The Fixed Employment Costs of Specialized Labor," in *The Measurement of Employment Cost,* ed. Jack Triplett (Chicago: University of Chicago Press, 1983).

5. Robert Levring and Milton Moskowitz, *The 100 Best Companies to Work for in America* (New York: Doubleday, 1993).

6. Corporate Leadership Council, *Perfecting Labor Markets: Redefining the Social Contract at the World's High-Performance Corporations.* Report (Washington, D.C.: Advisory Board, 1995).

7. See Richard Belous, "How Human Resource Systems Adjust to the Shift toward Contingent Workers," *Monthly Labor Review,* March 1989, 7–12.

8. Harriet Gorlin, *Issues in Human Resource Management* (New York: Conference Board, 1985).

9. Arlene A. Johnson and Fabian Linden, *Availability of a Quality Work Force* (New York: Conference Board, 1992).

10. Al Ehrbar, "Price of Progress: Reengineering Gives Firms New Efficiency, Workers the Pink Slip," *Wall Street Journal,* 16 March 1993, A1.

11. Ibid.

12. A national probability sample by Louis Harris in 1991 found that roughly 50 percent of firms had laid off "substantial" numbers of employees in the previous five years; a survey of over 500 large employers in 1993 found that 72 percent had layoffs in the previous three years (Wyatt's 1993 Survey of Corporate Restructuring). In the Family and Work Survey, a national probability survey of employees conducted in 1993, 42 percent reported that their employer had downsized in that year alone.

13. American Management Association, *1994 AMA Survey on Downsizing: Summary of Key Findings* (New York: American Management Association, 1994), 2.

14. Karen Pennar, "Economic Anxiety," *Business Week,* 11 March 1996, 50.

15. Joseph Nocerra, "Living with Layoffs," *Fortune,* 1 April 1996, 69.

16. American Management Association, *1996 AMA Survey on Downsizing, Job Elimination, and Job Creation* (New York: American Management Association, 1996).

17. Henry S. Farber, "The Changing Face of Job Loss in the United States, 1981–1995," working paper 360, Industrial Relations Section, Princeton University, 1996.

18. *1994 AMA Survey on Downsizing.*

19. Peter Cappelli, "Examining Managerial Displacement," *Academy of Management Journal* 35 (1992): 203–217.

20. Farber, "The Changing Face of Job Loss."

21. "Beyond Downsizing: Staffing and Workforce Management for the Millennium" (Woodcliff Lake, N.J.: Lee Hecht Harrison, 1997).

22. Alan Gustman et al., "Retirement Research in the Health and Retirement Survey," *Journal of Human Resources,* 30 *Health & Retirement Study Supplement* (1995), 557–583.

23. Farber, "The Changing Face of Job Loss."

24. James Medoff, *Middle-Aged and Out of Work: Growing Unemployment Due to Job Loss among Middle-Aged Americans* (Washington, D.C.: National Study Center, 1993).

25. Johanne Boisjoly, Greg J. Duncan, and Timothy Smeeding, "Have Highly Skilled Workers Fallen from Grace? The Shifting Burdens of Involuntary Job Losses from 1968 to 1992" (unpublished manuscript, University of Quebec, Rimouski, Quebec, Canada, 1994).

26. Chris Lee, "Trust Me," *Training,* January 1997, 28–37.

27. Julie Amparano Lopez, "Many New Executives Are Being Discharged with Stunning Speed," *Wall Street Journal,* 4 March 1994, 1.

28. Thomas Nardone et al., "1992: Job Market Doldrums," *Monthly Labor Review,* February 1993.

29. Jennifer M. Gardner, "Recession Swells Count of Displaced Workers," *Monthly Labor Review,* June 1993, 14–23. See also Robert G. Valletta, "Has Job Security in the U.S. Declined?" *Federal Reserve Bank of San Francisco Weekly Letter,* No. 96-07, 16 February 1996. Valletta finds that employers have become more likely to dismiss workers permanently in downturns than in previous decades, when temporary layoffs were more common.

30. Respondents were asked how secure jobs were in their company, with 1=very satisfied with job security and 5=very dissatisfied. In 1985, the average score was 2.13, rising to 2.7 in 1996. This material was prepared for the National Research Council's report of occupational classifications.

31. These are unpublished, proprietary surveys made available to the author. I thank Steve Stannard, president of SRA in Chicago, and Steve Gross, managing partner at Hay Associates in Philadelphia, for making them available.

32. "Employee Loyalty Takes Hit: Workplace Stress Weakens Job Commitment; Salaries Easily Lure Workers," New York: Reuters, 6 July 1998.

33. "Give 'Em That Old Time Ambition," *Training,* February 1992, 74.

34. Brian O'Reilly, "The New Deal: What Companies and Employees Owe One Another," *Fortune,* 13 June 1994, 44.

35. "Measuring Change in the Attitudes of the American Workforce," in *Wyatt Work USA* (New York: Wyatt Company, 1995).

36. U.S. Department of Labor, *A Guide to Responsible Restructuring* (Washington, D.C.: GPO, 1995).

37. Interestingly, all of these effects abated with time. One year later, only 36 percent of these firms reported that morale still suffered (*1996 AMA Survey on Downsizing*).

38. Lee, "Trust Me," 28–37.

39. Jerald Greenberg, "Equity and Workplace Status: A Field Experiment, *Journal of Applied Psychology* 23 (1998): 606–613.

40. Interestingly, those workers who were overcompensated, in terms of receiving much nicer offices than their performance had merited, worked much harder, at least initially, to prove that they deserved the better accommodations.

41. Robinson et al., "Changing Obligations and the Psychological Contract."

42. See, for example, Sandra L. Robinson, "Trust and the Breach of the Psychological Contract," *Administrative Science Quarterly* 41 (1996): 574–599.

43. Wyatt, "Measuring Change in Attitudes."

44. Joel Brockner, Steven Grover, Michael N. O'Malley, Thomas F. Reed, and Mary Ann Glynn, "Threat of Future Layoffs: Self-Esteem and Survivor's Reactions: Evidence from the Laboratory and the Field," *Strategic Management Journal* 14 (1993): 153–166, and Joel Brockner, Steven Grover, Thomas F. Reed, and Rocki Lee DeWitt, "Layoffs, Job Insecurity, and Survivors' Work Effort: Evidence of an Inverted-U Relationship," *Academy of Management Journal* 35 (1992): 413–425.

45. Anne H. Reilly, Jeane M. Brett, and Linda K. Stroh, "The Impact of Corporate Turbulence on Managers' Attitudes," *Strategic Management Journal* 14 (1993): 167–179.

46. Raoul V. Mowatt, Dean Takahashi, and Brandon Bailey, "The Big High-Tech Thieves: Employees," *Philadelphia Inquirer*, 30 May 1996, F3.

47. Reilly et al., "The Impact of Corporate Turbulence on Managers' Attitudes."

48. There is a sharp division in the perceptions of executives and lower-level employees on these restructuring issues that is illustrated in the results of another survey of executives and front-line workers in the same organizations conducted by Kepner-Tregoe. The company found that while 70 percent of executives reported that restructuring efforts met their expectations for the company, only 40 percent of workers so reported; similar figures concerning attitudes on downsizing were 73 percent and 45 percent, respectively. Executives estimated that morale was worse for 27 percent of their workers as the result of restructuring initiatives, while 51 percent of workers reported that it was worse. See *House Divided: Views on Change from Top Management and Their Employees* (Princeton: Kepner-Tregoe, 1995).

49. *1994 AMA Survey on Downsizing*.

50. *Wyatt's 1993 Survey of Restructuring—Best Practices in Corporate Restructuring* (New York: Wyatt Company, 1993).

51. The bias in surveys like these tends to be in the other direction, indicating that downsizing causes poor performance even when there is no necessary relationship. Some of the firms that are downsizing are doing so because they are already having financial troubles and are trying to cut costs to survive. In such cases, the poor performance is actually driving the downsizing. See the *1996 AMA Survey on Downsizing*.

52. Louis Harris and Associates, *Laborforce 2000 Survey* (New York: Louis Harris, 1991).

53. Rob Briner, "Feeling for the Facts: The Relationship between Employee Stress and Performance," *People Management*, 9 January 1997, 73.

54. *Availability of a Quality Workforce* (New York: Conference Board, 1992). Report #1010.

55. I am indebted to Robert McKersie for this observation.

56. D. Kahneman, J. L. Knetch, and R. H. Thaler, "Fairness as a Constraint of Profit Seeking Entitlements in the Market," *American Economic Review* 76 (1986): 727–782.

57. For a survey, see Joel Brockner, "The Effects of Work Layoffs on Survivors: Research, Theory, and Practice," in *Research in Organizational Behavior* 10 (1990): 212–255.

58. Rosabeth Moss Kanter, "Transcending Business Boundaries: 12,000 World Managers View Change," *Harvard Business Review*, May–June 1991, 151–162.

59. Matthew Shank, Gail Paulson, and Thomas Werner, "Perceptual Gaps in the

American Workforce," *Journal for Quality and Participation* 19, no.6 (October–November 1966): 60–64.

60. *Wyatt's 1993 Survey of Corporate Restructuring.*

61. Useem, "Management Commitment and Company Policies on Education and Training."

62. Peter T. Kilborn, "The Workplace, After the Deluge," *New York Times,* 5 September 1993, Business Section, 3–4.

63. Rosemary Batt, "From Bureaucracy to Enterprise? The Changing Jobs and Careers of Managers in Telecommunications Service," in *Broken Ladders,* ed. Osterman.

64. Peter Cappelli and Keith Chauvin, "An Inter-plant Test of the Efficiency Wage Hypothesis," *Quarterly Journal of Economics* 106, no. 3 (August 1991): 769–787.

65. Robert Hoppock, *Job Satisfaction* (New York: Harper and Row, 1935).

66. Jeanne M. Carsten and Paul E. Spector, "Unemployment, Job Satisfaction, and Employee Turnover: A Meta-analytic Test of the Muchinsky Model," *Journal of Applied Psychology* 72 (1987): 372–381.

67. For the first of these studies, see Jone L. Pearce, "Toward an Organizational Behavior of Contract Laborers: Psychological Involvement and Effects on Employee Co-Workers," *Academy of Management Journal* 36, no. 3 (1993): 1082–1092.

68. Peter Cappelli and Peter D. Sherer, "Assessing Employee Attitudes under Two-Tier Pay Plans," *Industrial and Labor Relations Review* 43, no. 2 (January 1990): 225–244.

69. Sharon Cohany, "Workers in Alternate Employment Arrangements," *Monthly Labor Review* 119, no. 10 (October 1996): 31–45.

70. Among the recent empirical work, Swinnerton and Wial (1995) find a substantial overall reduction in job tenure in the United States over the past twenty years. Using similar data from the Current Population Survey and arguably better techniques, both Diebold, Neumark, and Polsky (1995) and Farber (1995) find that overall rates of job tenure have been remarkably constant over the same period. Using longitudinal data from the Panel Study on Income Dynamics (PSID) and a question that is less prone to error (explicit job change as opposed to months of tenure in a current job), Gottschalk and Moffitt (1994), Marcotte (1995), and Rose (1995) find a substantial increase in job changes for men in the 1980s compared with the 1970s. The data from the PSID indicates that both employer separations and quits increased over this period. Jaeger and Stevens (1988) are able to reconcile the two data sources and find modest changes overall—some increase for older men in the mid-1980s and for less educated men and women of all ages. (See the Bibliography for complete information on the sources cited in this note.)

71. A report by the Bureau of National Affairs found that turnover in 1997 was at an eight-year high. See Sue Shellenbarger, "Employers Are Finding It Doesn't Cost Much to Make a Staff Happy," *Wall Street Journal,* 19 November 1997, B1.

72. Allison J. Wellington, "Changes in the Male/Female Wage Gap," *Journal of Human Resources* 28, no. 2 (1993): 383–411.

73. See, for example, Henry S. Farber, "Are Life-time Jobs Disappearing? Job Duration in the United States: 1973–1993," working paper #341, Industrial Relations Section, Princeton University, 1995.

74. Anette Bernhardt, Martina Morris, Mark Handcock, and Marc Scott, "Job Instability and Wage Inequality: Preliminary Results from Two NLS Cohorts," working paper, Columbia University, February 1997.

75. Christopher J. Ruhm, "Secular Changes in the Work and Retirement Patterns of Older Men," *Journal of Human Resources* 30, no. 2 (1995): 362–385.

76. See, for instance, David Neumark, Daniel Polsky, and Daniel Hansen, "Has Job Stability Declined Yet? New Evidence for the 1990's" (paper presented at the Conference on Labor Market Inequality, University of Wisconsin, revised October 1998).

77. Henry S. Farber, "Trends in Long-Term Employment in the United States, 1979–1996," working paper 384, Industrial Relations Section, Princeton University, July 1997.

78. See, e.g., Robert G. Valletta, "Has Job Security in the U.S. Declined?" Federal Reserve Bank of San Francisco, February 1996.

79. Ibid.

80. See Daniel Polsky, "Changes in the Consequences of Job Separations in the U.S. Economy," working paper, University of Pennsylvania, October 1996. Henry Farber, in "The Incidence and Costs of Job Loss: 1982–91," uses repeated cross-sectional data (as opposed to Polsky's longitudinal data) and concludes that the displacement rate for workers with more tenure has not increased (*Brookings Papers on Economic Activity: Microeconomics,* no. 1 [1993]: 73–119).

81. See, for example, Stephen Rose, *The Decline of Employment Stability in the 1980s* (Washington, D.C.: National Commission on Employment Policy, 1995), and John Bishop, *The Incidence of and Payoff to Employer Training: A Review of the Literature with Recommendations for Policy* (Philadelphia: National Center on the Educational Quality of the Workforce [EQW], 1994).

82. Gillian Flynn, "Contingent Staffing Requires Serious Strategy," *Personnel Journal,* April 1995, 50.

83. Michael Barier, "Now You Hire Them, Now You Don't," *Nation's Business,* January 1994, 30–32.

84. Louis Uchitelle, "More Downsized Workers Are Returning as Rentals," *New York Times,* 8 December 1996, 1.

85. Flynn, "Contingent Staffing," 50.

86. Jaclyn Fierman, "The Contingency Work Force," *Fortune,* 24 January 1994, 33.

87. "Interim Managers: Tempers and Temporaries," *Director* 47, no. 2 (September 1993): 69–70.

88. "Temporary R&D Employees in Unique Roles at DuPont and Henkel," *Chemical and Engineering News* 72, no. 9 (28 February 1994): 26–27.

89. Richard S. Belous, *The Contingent Economy* (Washington, D.C.: National Planning Association, 1989).

90. This estimate, and all of the statistics below on temporary workforce, come from Lewis M. Segal and Daniel G. Sullivan, "The Growth of Temporary Services Work," *Journal of Economic Perspectives* 11, no. 2 (Spring 1997): 117–136.

91. Susan N. Houseman, *Temporary, Part-Time, and Contract Employment in the United States: New Evidence from an Employer Survey* (Kalamazoo, Mich.: W. E. Upjohn Institute for Employment Research, 1997), and *The EQW National Employer Survey: First Findings* (Philadelphia: EQW, 1995).

92. Aaron Bernstein, "At UPS, Part-Time Work Is a Full-Time Issue," *Business Week,* 16 June 1997, 88–90.

93. Houseman, *Temporary, Part-Time, and Contract Employment in the United States.*

94. These figures are from the Current Employment Statistics Survey for SIC Code 7363 "Help Supply Services."

95. Katharine G. Abraham, "Restructuring the Employment Relationship: The Growth of Market-Mediated Work Arrangements," in *New Developments in the Labor Market,* ed. Katharine Abraham and Robert McKersie (Cambridge, Mass.: MIT Press, 1990), 85–118.

96. L. Goldin and E. Applebaum, "What Was Driving the 1982–1988 Boom in Temporary Employment? Preferences of Workers or Decisions and Power of Employers?" *Journal of Economy and Society* 51 (1992).

97. Lawrence Mishel and Jared Bernstein, *The State of Working America, 1994–1995* (Washington, D.C.: Economic Policy Institute, 1995).

98. Laura Leete and Juliet B. Schor, "Assessing the Time Squeeze Hypothesis: Hours Worked in the United States, 1969–1989," *Industrial Relations* 33, no. 1 (January 1994): 25–43.

99. Nardone et al., "1992: Job Market Doldrums."

100. Organization for Economic Cooperation and Development, *Employment Outlook* (Paris: 1993), 10.

101. National Association of Temporary and Staffing Services, *Temporary Help Services Continue to Create Employment Opportunities Despite Millions of Job Casualties* (Alexandria, Va.: NATSS, 1996).

102. G. Magnum et al., "The Temporary Help Industry: A Response to the Dual Internal Labor Market," *Industrial and Labor Relations Review* 38 (1985): 599–611.

103. Alison Davis-Blake and Brian Uzzi, "Determinants of Employment Externalization: A Study of Temporary Workers and Independent Contractors," *Administrative Science Quarterly* 38, no. 2 (June 1993): 195–223.

104. National Association of Temporary and Staffing Services (NATSS), *Profile of the Temporary Workforce* (Alexandria, Va.: NATSS, 1994).

105. Paul Klebnikov, "Focus, Focus," *Forbes,* 11 September 1995, 42–44.

106. Jan Szymankiewicz, "Contracting Out or Selling Out? Survey into the Current Issues Concerning the Outsourcing of Distribution," *Logistics Information Management* 7, no. 1 (1994): 28–35.

107. Katharine G. Abraham and Susan K. Taylor, "Firms' Use of Outside Contractors: Theory and Evidence," working paper No. 4468, National Bureau of Economic Research, Cambridge, Mass., September 1994.

108. Bureau of National Affairs, "The Changing Workplace: New Directions in Staffing and Scheduling," Washington, D.C.: Bureau of National Affairs, 1986 (BNA Special Report).

109. Mishel and Bernstein, *The State of Working America,* 229.

110. Angela Clinton, "Flexible Labor: Restructuring the American Work Force," *Monthly Labor Review,* August 1997, 3–17.

111. See "DuPont Turns over Its Computer Work to Two Contractors," *Philadelphia Inquirer,* 3 June 1997, C1.

112. National Association of Temporary and Staffing Services (NATSS), *Temporary Help/Staffing Service Industry Continues to Create Employment Opportunities* (Alexandria, Va.: NATSS, 1994).

113. Farber, "The Changing Face of Job Loss."

114. Michael Beer and R. O. Von Werssowetz, *Human Resources at Hewlett-Packard* (Boston: Harvard Business School Press, 1981).

115. Lee Dyer et al., "Contemporary Employment Stabilization Practices," in *Human Resource Management and Industrialization: Text, Readings, and Cases,* ed. Thomas A. Kochan and Thomas A. Barocci (Boston: Little, Brown, 1985), 203–214.

116. Catharine Hakim reported in 1990 that the percentage of workers who were not in full-time employment rose from 30 to 36 percent from 1981 to 1988 ("Core and Periphery in Employers' Workforce Strategies: Evidence from the 1987 E.L.U.S. Survey," *Work, Employment, and Society* 4 [1990]: 157–188). More recent figures put the number as high as 40 percent ("The Flexible Workforce and Patterns of Working Hours in the U.K.," in *Employment Gazette* [London: Department of Employment, 1994]), with twice as many sixteen-to-twenty-four year olds in temporary as in permanent jobs. A survey by the Confederation of British Industries (CBI) (in *Flexible Labor Markets: Who Pays for Training?* [London: CBI, 1994]), found that more than 80 percent of firms reported an increase in their employment flexibility, broadly defined (temporary help, contracting out, flextime, etc.). In another study, 60 percent of firms predicted that one-quarter of their workforce would be "complementary" or other than full-time employees within the next four years (*Survey of Long-Term Employment Strategies* [London: Institute of Management and Manpower, Plc., 1994]).

117. Laurie Hunter et al., "The 'Flexible Firm': Strategy and Segmentation," *British Journal of Industrial Relations* 31 (1993): 383–407.

118. "Finding the Time—A Survey of Managers' Attitudes to Using and Managing Time," *Management Services* 39, no. 6 (June 1995): 3–6.

119. Part-time work doubled between 1969 and 1991 to 22.5 percent of the workforce (William G. Harley, "The Politics of Flexibility: An Empirical and Theoretical Investigation of the Implications of 'Labor Flexibility' for Workers and Trade Unions in Australia," University of Queensland, Department of Government, unpublished Ph.D. thesis, 1994), and casual work has risen, mainly in the growing service sector, from 13 to 20 percent of the workforce from 1982 to 1989 (P. Dawkins and K. Norris, "Casual Employment in Australia," *Australian Bulletin of Labor* 16 [1990]: 156–173). With respect to work organization, there is evidence of sharp increases in total quality management efforts that are associated with increased employee autonomy, from 15 percent of establishments in 1988 to 24 percent by 1991 (Australian Bureau of Statistics, *Manufacturing Technology Statistics* [Canberra: AGPS, 1993]). And narrow job descriptions appear to be giving way to broader arrangements (R. Green and D. MacDonald, "The Australian Flexibility Paradox," *Journal of Industrial Relations* 35 [1991]: 142–156).

120. Harley ("The Politics of Flexibility") uses the 1989–90 Australian Workplace Industrial Relations Survey to examine the level of flexibility reported by employers and concludes that only the ability to adjust employment levels—"would you vary employment in response to demand"—ranks high among flexibility measures (flexibility in pay, in deploying workers, in work schedules, in product market decisions, etc., are not given strong preference by employers).

121. Gordon Anderson et al., "Flexibility, Casualization, and Externalization in the New Zealand Workforce," *Journal of Industrial Relations* 36 (1994): 491–518.

122. Abraham, "Restructuring the Employment Relationship."

123. Commission on the Skills of the American Workforce, *America's Choice: High Skills or Low Wages* (Rochester: National Center on Education and the Economy, 1989).

124. Edward Lawler et al., *Employee Involvement and Total Quality Management: Practices and Results in Fortune 1000 Companies* (San Francisco: Jossey-Bass, 1992).

125. Osterman, "How Common Is Workplace Transformation?"

126. *The EQW National Employer Survey: First Findings* (Philadelphia: EQW, 1995).

127. Harry C. Katz, *Shifting Gears: Changing Labor Relations in the U.S. Automobile Industry* (Cambridge, Mass.: MIT Press, 1985).

128. Peter Cappelli, "Are Skill Requirements Rising? Evidence for Production and Clerical Workers," *Industrial and Labor Relations Review* 46, no. 3 (April 1993): 515–530.

129. Peter Cappelli and K. C. O'Shaughnessey, *Changes in Skill and Wage Structures in Corporate Headquarters, 1986–1992* (Philadelphia: EQW, 1995).

130. Stephen Rose, *The Decline of Employment Stability in the 1980s* (Washington, D.C.: National Commission on Employment Policy, 1995).

131. Marianne Bertrand, "From the Invisible Hand to the Invisible Handshake? How Product Market Competition Changes the Employment Relationship," Harvard University Department of Economics manuscript, November 1997.

132. Steffanie L. Wilk and Elizabeth A. Craig, "Should I Stay or Should I Go? Occupational Matching and Internal and External Mobility," working paper, Department of Management, Wharton School, 1998.

133. Mishel and Bernstein, *The State of Working America*, 145.

134. Ibid.

135. Katharine Abraham and James E. Medoff, "Experience, Performance, and Earnings," *Quarterly Journal of Economics* 95 (1980): 703–736.

136. Clair Brown, ed., "The Competitive Semiconductor Manufacturing Human Resources Project" (The Competitive Semiconductor Manufacturing Program at U.C. Berkeley, July 1997). One of the complications of this study is that it does not have data on total compensation. If noncash compensation was becoming more prominent for more senior employees, it could create the spurious appearance that returns to experience were declining.

137. Keith Chauvin, "Firm-Specific Wage Growth and Changes in the Labor Market for Managers," *Management and Decision Economics* 15 (1994): 21–37.

138. Dave Marcotte, "Evidence of a Fall in the Wage Premium for Job Security" (Northern Illinois University: Center for Governmental Studies, 1994).

139. Polsky, "Changes in the Consequences of Job Separations."

140. Peter Gottschalk and Robert Moffitt, "The Growth of Earnings Instability in the U.S. Labor Market," *Brookings Papers on Economic Activity*, no. 2 (1994): 217–272.

141. I thank Steve Gross, then of Hay Associates in Philadelphia, for providing me with these unpublished figures.

142. Sandra O'Neal, Towers Perrin, "Recent Trends in Compensation Practices (presentation to the Board of Governors of the Federal Reserve System, 23 October 1997).

143. U.S. Bureau of Labor Statistics Employee Benefits Surveys, 1989 to 1997, calculations presented by the Federal Reserve Board of Governors, 23 October 1997.

144. Richard A. Ippolito, "Toward Explaining the Growth of Defined Contribution Plans," *Industrial Relations* 34 (1995): 1–20.

145. Robert Clark and Ann McDermed, *The Choice of Pension Plans in a Changing Economy* (Washington, D.C.: American Enterprise Institute, 1990).

146. For reviews of these studies, see Laurie J. Bassi, Anne L. Gallagher, and Ed Schroer, *The ASTD Training Data Book* (Alexandria, Va.: American Society for Training and Development, 1996), 3.

147. Bassi et al., *ASTD Training Data Book,* 45.

148. Jill M. Constantine and David Neumark, *Training and the Growth of Wage Inequality* (Philadelphia: EQW, 1994).

149. Norman Bowers and Paul Swaim, *Probing (Some of) the Issues of Employment Related Training: Evidence from the CPS* (Washington, D.C.: U.S. Department of Agriculture, Economic Research Service, 1992).

150. See, for instance, Kiyoshi Mori, "Industrial Sea Change: How Changes in Keiretsu Are Opening the Japanese Market," *Brookings Review* 12, no.4 (1994): 20.

151. For an account of this process, see Kevin Sullivan, Linda Chan, Don Shapiro, and Chris Pomery, "Wage Spiral Makes Bosses' Heads Spin," *Asian Business* 48, no. 8 (August 1988): 59–60.

152. See Shintaro Hori, "Fixing Japan's White Collar Economy: A Personal View," *Harvard Business Review,* November–December 1993, 157–172.

153. There may well be "double counting" in these figures, as some part-time workers may also be counted as temps. See Susan Houseman and Machiko Osawa, "Part-Time and Temporary Employment in Japan," *Monthly Labor Review,* October 1995, 10–41. The more recent figure of 20 percent part-time was calculated by the Japanese Management and Coordination Agency, reported in Emily Thorton, "More Cracks in the Social Contract," *Business Week,* 27 October 1997, 70E20.

154. Akira Ikeya, "Companies Relying on More Part-Time Workers," *Nikkei Weekly,* 2 October 1995, 3.

155. Joann S. Lubin, "Japanese Are Doing More Job Hopping," *Wall Street Journal,* 18 November 1991, 1.

156. Japan Association of Corporate Executives (Keizai Doyukai), "Management Focused on the Efficient Use of Capital," Tokyo, 1998.

157. See Merril Goozner, "A Musical of Japan's 'Salarymen,'" *Philadelphia Inquirer,* 28 December 1994.

158. Ann P. Bartel, "Training, Wage Growth and Job Performance," *Journal of Labor Economics,* 13, no. 3, (July 1995) finds, for example, that training is higher (lower) where unemployment rates are low (high), suggesting that employers help provide skills through training where labor markets are tight but are less likely to do so/more likely to buy them on the outside market when labor markets are slack. This is similar to Cappelli's result that the upskilling of jobs occurs where unemployment is falling and outside labor markets are tightening ("Are Skill Requirements Rising? Evidence for Production and Clerical Workers," *Industrial and Labor Relations Review,* March 1993). Paul Osterman also finds that establishments that give more attention to skills in making hiring decisions are less likely to provide training, an example of the "make-or-buy" trade-off ("Skills, Training, and Work Organization in American Establishments," *Industrial Relations,* April 1995, 125–146). Finally, Bishop, in *The Incidence of and Payoff to Employer Training,* concludes that while more educated workers tend to take jobs that offer more training, schooling and training are substitutes for improving job performance if one controls for job choice. So schools and external providers of training can be at least partial substi-

tutes for employer-provided training, helping to inject the market into training decisions.

159. Osterman, "Skills, Training, and Work Organization in American Establishments."

160. Bishop, "The Incidence of and Payoffs to Employer Training."

Chapter 5

1. In more recent times, the funds for training came mainly from employers through collective bargaining contracts. But the union and its monopoly position remained the mechanism for organizing both the funds and the training.

2. Barley, "The Turn toward a Horizontal Division of Labor."

3. One of the more interesting rumors about the academic economics market is that universities in the past routinely engaged in illegal price fixing to set entry-level wages. The "chairman's breakfast" at the annual meeting of the American Economics Association was allegedly the scene of the crime. Threats of legal action are said to have discouraged the practice.

4. These market mechanisms are obviously oriented to research and therefore are not useful for institutions that focus only on teaching. Because these outside reviews mainly determine rewards for faculty who already have tenure, faculty who are willing to forgo these rewards are essentially immune to them, hence the interest in these posttenure reviews that can be used to dismiss recalcitrant faculty.

5. See, for example, Roger G. Baldwin and Jay L. Chronister, "Full-Time Non-Tenure-Track Faculty," *NEA Higher Education Research Center Update* 2, no. 5 (1996) or, for a topical discussion, see Ron Grossman and Charles Leroux, "Part-Timers Are the Cheap Labor of U.S. Colleges," *Chicago Tribune*, 20 August 1993, 1.

6. For a description of some of these core-periphery arrangements, see Richard Chait and Cathy A. Trower, *Where Tenure Does Not Reign: Colleges with Contract Systems* (Washington, D.C.: American Association for Higher Education, 1997).

7. AnnaLee Saxenian, *Regional Advantage: Culture and Competition in Silicon Valley and Route 128* (Cambridge, Mass.: Harvard University Press, 1994).

8. See David P. Angel, "The Labor Market for Engineers in the U.S. Semiconductor Industry," *Economic Geography* 65, no. 2 (April 1989): 99–112.

9. David P. Angel, "High-Technology Agglomeration and the Labor Market: The Case of Silicon Valley," *Environment and Planning* 23 (1991): 1501–1516.

10. Saxenian, *Regional Advantage,* 35.

11. N. Dorfman, "Route 128: The Development of a Regional High–Technology Economy," *Research Policy* 12 (1983): 299–316.

12. Saxenian, *Regional Advantage,* 125.

13. For evidence, see E. Rogers and J. Larsen, *Silicon Valley Fever,* New York: Basic Books, 1984.

14. See Silicon Valley Joint Venture, *Joint Venture's Index of Silicon Valley: Measuring Progress Toward a 21st Century Community* (San Jose, CA, 1997), 7.

15. "Borland Says Microsoft Raided," *USA Today,* 8 May 1997, 6b.

16. *Joint Venture,* 16.

17. A survey of these offerings is provided in Elizabeth Useem, *Low Tech Education in a High Tech World: Corporations and Classrooms in the New Information Society* (New York: Free Press, 1986).

18. *Joint Venture,* 15.

Chapter 6

1. Sara L. Rynes, Marc O. Orlitzky, and Robert D. Bretz, Jr., "Experienced Hiring versus College Recruiting: Practices and Emerging Trends," *Personnel Psychology* 50, no. 2 (1997): 309–339.

2. Timothy D. Schellhardt, "Talent Pool Is Shallow as Corporations Seek Executives for Top Jobs," *Wall Street Journal,* 26 June 1997, 1.

3. Ibid.

4. Richard Donkin, "Careers on and off the Rails," *Financial Times,* 20 December 1995, 11.

5. See Andrea Gerlin, "Presbyterian Raids Cooper Cardiologists," *Philadelphia Inquirer,* 27 September 1997, 1.

6. Claudia H. Deutsch, "High-Technology Job Fair Is Now an Industry in Itself," *New York Times,* 29 September 1997, 4.

7. Dennis Kneale, Gautam Naik, and Bart Ziegler, "Dialing for Dollars: AT&T's Heir Apparent Jumps to a Tiny Firm that Offers Huge Pay," *Wall Street Journal,* 20 August 1996.

8. David E. Kalish, "The Competition that Spawns Bidding War for High-Tech Talent," *Philadelphia Inquirer,* 22 May 1997, F4.

9. Thomas R. Bailey and Annette D. Bernhardt, "In Search of the High Road in a Low-Wage Industry," *Politics and Society* 25, no. 2 (June 1997): 179–201.

10. David Kilpatrick, "Lou Gerstner's First 30 Days," *Fortune,* 31 May 1993, 57.

11. Clair Brown, ed., "The Competitive Semiconductor Manufacturing Human Resources Project." (The Competitive Semiconductor Manufacturing Program at U.C. Berkeley, July 1997.)

12. Barbara Ettorre, "How Are Companies Keeping the Employees They Want?" *Management Review* 86, no. 5 (May 1997): 49.

13. Joann S. Lubin and Joseph B. White, "More Companies Relocate CEO's in Style," *Wall Street Journal,* 7 April 1997, 1.

14. Alex Markels, "Signing Bonuses Rise to Counter Rich Pay Plans," *Wall Street Journal,* 21 August 1996, 1.

15. Joann S. Lubin, "Now Butchers, Engineers Get Signing Bonuses," *Wall Street Journal,* 2 June 1997, B1.

16. Randall Lane, "Pampering the Customers, Pampering the Employees," *Forbes,* 14 October 1996, 74–80.

17. Susan L. Bradbury, "Dual Career Couples in R&D Labs," *Research and Technology Management* 31, no. 1 (January–February 1994): 45–47.

18. Ibid.

19. Kimberly Buch, "Quality Circles and Employee Withdrawal Behaviors: A Cross-

Organizational Study," *Journal of Applied Behavioral Science* 28, no. 1 (March 1992): 62–73.

20. John E. Sheridan, "Organizational Culture and Employee Retention," *Academy of Management Journal* 35, no. 5 (1992): 1036–1056.

21. "Career Development and Employee Orientation Practices Aim to Increase Retention and Productivity," *Business Wire,* 29 May 1997, 7.

22. Jeff Weinstein, "Personnel Success," *Restaurants and Institutions* 102, no. 29 (9 December 1992): 92–113.

23. Ibid.

24. Clair Brown, ed., "The Competitive Semiconductor Manufacturing Human Resources Project."

25. Some of the details about the UPS approach to part-time work can be found in Bernstein, "At UPS, Part-Time Work Is a Full-Time Issue." Interestingly, the idea of targeting students for these part-time jobs is credited to Jimmy Hoffa, the late Teamsters president, who is said to have argued that no one would be upset that these jobs were only part-time if they appeared to be creating jobs for students. (That is, until the Teamster strike of 1997 aimed in part at issues associated with these jobs.)

26. "Low Wage Lessons," *Business Week,* 11 November 1996, 108–116.

27. Patrick McGovern, "To Retain or Not to Retain?" *Human Resource Management Journal* (United Kingdom) 5, no. 4 (Summer 1995).

28. D. Winstanley, "Recruitment Strategies and Managerial Control of Technological Staff," in *White Collar Work: The Non-Manual Labor Process,* ed. C. Smith, D. Knight, and H. Willmott (London: Macmillan, 1991).

29. Peter Cappelli and Stephanie Wilk, "The Determinants and Consequences of Selection Decisions" (working paper, Department of Management, Wharton School, Philadelphia, 1997).

30. Deena Amato-McCoy, "Price Chopper CBT Slashes Training Time for Cashiers," *Supermarket News,* 19 May 1997, 69.

31. Carolyn Walkup, "Companies Vie for Workers as Labor Pool Evaporates," *Nation's Restaurant News,* 20 February 1995, 1.

32. "Low Wage Lessons."

33. Jeffrey A. Tannenbaum, "Making Risky Hires into Valued Workers," *Wall Street Journal,* 19 June 1997, B1.

34. Thomas Petzinger, Jr., "A Creative Staff Finds New Strength in Its Differences," *Wall Street Journal,* 11 April 1997, B1.

35. This description is taken from Herbert R. Northrup and Margot E. Malin, *Personnel Policies for Engineers and Scientists: An Analysis of Major Corporate Practice (Philadelphia: Industrial Research Unit of the Wharton School, 1985),* 220–222.

36. I am indebted to Richard Beaumont, president of Organizational Resource Counselors, for this description.

37. David Wessel, "Up the Ladder: Low Unemployment Brings Lasting Gains to Town in Michigan," *Wall Street Journal,* 24 June 1997, A1.

38. Dominic Bencivenga, "Employers and Workers Come to Terms," *HR Magazine,* 20 June 1997, 1–6.

39. Corporate Leadership Council, *Perfecting Labor Markets.*

40. See, for instance, Judith S. Olson et al., "Computer-Supported Cooperative Work: Research Issues for the 1990s," *Behavior and Information Technology* 12, no. 2 (1993): 115–129.

41. Dennis Epple, Linda Argote, and Kenneth Murphy, "An Empirical Investigation of the Micro Structure of Knowledge Acquisition and Transfer through Learning by Doing," *Operations Research* 44, no. 1 (January–February 1996): 77–86.

42. Judith Combes Taylor, *Learning at Work in a Work-Based Welfare System: Opportunities and Obstacles—Lessons from the School-to-Work Experience* (Boston: Jobs for the Future, April 1997).

43. Michael Kramer, "Job Training Has to Be Reworked," *Time,* 20 January 1997, 20.

44. "Career Development and Employee Orientation Practices Aim to Increase Retention and Productivity," *Business Wire,* 29 May 1997, 7.

45. Taylor, *Learning at Work in a Work-Based Welfare System.*

46. "Lawmakers Vote to Require Early-Departing LAPD Recruits to Pay for Training," *Metropolitan News Company,* 17 January 1996, 14.

47. Sugalski, "Resource Link."

48. Details of these and other networks of companies engaged in similar efforts are provided in *Manufacturing Networks: A Report from the Partnership for a Smarter Workforce* (Washington, D.C.: Partnership for a Smarter Workforce, 1996).

49. "Low Wage Lessons."

50. Carole King, "'Mentoring' May Be Remedy for Retention's Blues," *National Underwriter,* 28 June 1993, 11.

51. Bencivenga, "Employers and Workers Come to Terms."

52. David Wessel, "Up the Ladder: Low Unemployment Brings Lasting Gains to Town in Michigan," *Wall Street Journal,* 24 June 1997, A1.

53. Amato-McCoy, "Price Chopper CBT Slashes Training Time for Cashiers," 69.

54. See, for example, "Productivity Point International Announces Enterprise-Wide Training Solutions via the World Wide Web," *Business Wire, Inc.,* 11 November 1996.

55. See Fred R. Bleakley, "To Bolster Economies, Some States Rely More on Two-Year Colleges," *Wall Street Journal,* 26 November 1996, 1.

56. Joann S. Lubin and Joseph B. White, "Dilbert's Revenge: Throwing Off Angst, Workers Are Feeling in Control of Careers," *Wall Street Journal,* 11 September 1997, A1.

57. Troy May, "Going to School on the Company Tab," *Business First—Columbus,* 28 February 1997, 17.

58. I am indebted to James McKinney, president of the American Association of Community Colleges, for this statistic.

59. See Alan Krueger, "How Computers Have Changed the Wage Structure: Evidence from Micro Data, 1984–1989," *Quarterly Journal of Economics,* February 1993, 33–60.

60. This arrangement is described in the *1997 Update to the Jobs for the Future Report on Manpower.*

61. "On the Air, but Not on the Payroll," *Philadelphia Inquirer,* 3 August 1995, E6.

62. Dean Takahashi, "Trade School Grads Wooed by Flurry of Job Offers," *Philadelphia Inquirer,* 27 June 1995, G1.

63. I am indebted to Michael Moe of Montgomery Securities in San Francisco for this information about the for-profit education industry.

64. Roy Furchgott, "Earning It: Job Uncertainty Makes Offers Easier to Refuse," *New York Times,* 20 October 1996, 9.

65. Schellhardt, "Talent Pool Is Shallow."

66. Hal Lancaster, "Managing Your Career: If Your Career Needs More Attention, Maybe You Should Get an Agent," *Wall Street Journal,* 20 October 1998, B1.

67. Bencivenga, "Employers and Workers Come to Terms."

68. Furchgott, "Earning It: Job Uncertainty Makes Offers Easier to Refuse."

69. "Pinnacle Alliance Delivers Benefits to J. P. Morgan during First Year of Operation," *M2 Presswire,* 16 July 1997.

70. Gary D. Kissler, "The New Employment Contract," *Human Resource Management* 33, no. 3 (Fall 1994): 335–352.

71. Denise M. Rousseau, "Organizational Behavior in the New Organizational Era," *Annual Review of Psychology,* 1 January 1997, 9.

72. T. M. Welbourne, D. B. Balkin, and L. R. Gomez-Mejia, "Gainsharing and Mutual Monitoring: A Combined Agency-Organizational Justice Interpretation," *Academy of Management Journal* 38 (1995): 881–899.

73. T. Rotondi, "Organizational Identification and Group Involvement," *Academy of Management Journal* 18 (1975): 892–897.

74. R. E. Michaels, W. L. Cron, A. J. Dubinsky, and E. A. Joachimsthaler, "The Influence of Formalization on the Organizational Commitment and Work Alienation of Salespeople and Industrial Buyers," *Journal of Marketing Research,* 25 November 1988, 376–383.

75. J. E. Mathieu and D. M. Zajac, "A Review and Meta-analysis of the Antecedents, Correlates, and Consequences of Organizational Commitment," *Psychological Bulletin* 108 (1990): 171–194.

76. See Robert Eisenberger, Peter Faolo, and Valerie David-LaMastro, "Perceived Organizational Support and Employee Diligence, Commitment, and Innovation," *Journal of Applied Psychology* 75, no. 1 (February 1990): 51–59.

77. R. M. Steers, "Antecedents and Outcomes of Organizational Commitment," *Administrative Science Quarterly* 22 (1972): 76–84, and Eisenberg et al., "Perceived Organizational Support."

78. Arne L. Kalleberg and Torger Reve, "Contracts and Commitment: Economic and Sociological Perspectives on Employment Relations," *Human Relations* 45, no. 9 (1992): 1103–1132.

Chapter 7

1. Frederick F. Reichheld, *The Loyalty Effect: The Hidden Force behind Growth, Profits, and Lasting Value* (Boston: Harvard Business School Press, 1996).

2. See Barnaby J. Feder, "Recasting a Model Incentive Strategy," *New York Times,* 5 September 1994, 33.

3. *1997 Towers Perrin Workplace Index* (New York: Towers Perrin, 1997).

4. Crysta J. Metcalf and Elizabeth K. Briody, "Reconciling Perceptions of Career

Advancement with Organizational Change: A Case from General Motors," *Human Organization* 54, no. 4 (Winter 1995): 417–428.

5. Joann S. Lubin and Joseph B. White, "Dilbert's Revenge: Throwing Off Angst, Workers are Feeling in Control of Careers," *Wall Street Journal*, 11 September 1997, A1.

6. Justin Martin, "Job Surfing: Move On to Move Up," *Fortune*, 13 January 1997.

7. Michael Reinemer, "Work Happy," *American Demographics* 17, no. 7 (July 1995): 26–30.

8. Dan Nagy, Fuqua School of Business, Duke University, 1996 (unpublished paper).

9. Shelly Branch, "MBAs Are Hot Again—And They Know It," *Fortune*, 14 April 1997, 155–157.

10. Laurie J. Flynn, "For Some, Steady Job Isn't the End of the Road," *New York Times*, 20 May 1996, D8.

11. Martin, "Job Surfing."

12. For an exposition on these points, see R. J. DeFillipi and M. B. Arthur, "The Boundaryless Career: A Competency-Based Perspective," *Journal of Organizational Behavior* 15 (1994): 307–324.

13. Martin, "Job Surfing."

14. Beckman, "Evolution of Management Roles in a Networked Organization."

15. For an elaboration of this argument, see Denise M. Rousseau, "Organizational Behavior in the New Organizational Era," *Annual Review of Psychology* 48 (1997): 515–546.

16. For a discussion, see Karl E. Weick, "Enactment and the Boundaryless Career: Organizing as We Work," in *The Boundaryless Career: A New Employment Principle for a New Organizational Era*, ed. Michael Arthur and Denise M. Rousseau (New York: Oxford University Press, 1996).

17. Causer and Jones, "Responding to 'Skill Shortages.'"

18. "Towers Perrin 1997 Workplace Index Reveals Growing Concerns in Employer Delivery on 'The New Deal' Contract," 15 September 1997 (Towers Perrin press release).

19. These are unpublished figures from the National Employer Survey, August 1997, conducted for the National Center on the Educational Quality of the Workforce by the Bureau of the Census. They can be obtained through the National Center on the Educational Quality of the Workforce.

20. An interesting discussion of companies that have pursued "high-performance" work systems that make greater demands of front-line workers finds that they have not in general been associated with higher wages for the employees. See Bailey and Bernhardt, "In Search of the High Road in a Low-Wage Industry."

21. Cappelli and Sherer, "Satisfaction, Market Wages, and Labor Relations: An Airline Study."

22. Peter Cappelli, "Technology, Work Organization, and the Structure of Wages" (working paper, Wharton School, Philadelphia, September 1997).

23. See Jonathan Haskel and Christopher Martin, "Do Skill Shortages Reduce Productivity? Theory and Evidence from the United Kingdom," *Economic Journal* 105 (March 1993): 386–394.

24. Batt, "From Bureaucracy to Enterprise?"

25. Keith H. Hammonds et al., "Writing a New Social Contract," *Business Week*, 11 March 1996, 60.

26. Towers Perrin 1997 "Workplace Index" press release.

27. Lee, "Trust Me."

28. Brian Moskal, "Hide This Report Card!" *Industry Week* 243, no. 17 (19 September 1994): 27–29.

29. See Robert Taylor, "Europe's Unhappy World of Work," *Financial Times*, 14 May 1997, 18.

30. Anthony J. Rucci, Steven P. Kirn, and Richard T. Quinn, "The Employee-Customer Profit Chain at Sears," *Harvard Business Review* 76, no. 1 (January–February 1998): 83–97.

31. See Peter Cappelli and Daniel Shapiro, *Employer Participation in School-to-Work Programs: Results from the National Employer Survey* (Philadelphia: National Center on Post-Secondary Improvement, 1997).

Bibliography

Abegglen, J. C., and G. Stalk, Jr. *Kaisha: The Japanese Corporation*. New York: Basic Books, 1985.

Abraham, Katharine G. "Restructuring the Employment Relationship: The Growth of Market-Mediated Work Arrangements." In *New Developments in the Labor Market*, edited by Katharine Abraham and Robert McKersie, 85–118. Cambridge, Mass.: MIT Press, 1990.

Abraham, Katharine G., and James E. Medoff. "Experience, Performance, and Earnings." *Quarterly Journal of Economics* 95 (1980): 703–736.

Abraham, Katharine G., and Susan K. Taylor. "Firms' Use of Outside Contractors: Theory and Evidence." Working Paper No. 4468. National Bureau of Economic Research, Cambridge, Mass. September 1994.

Ackerlof, George A., Andrew K. Rose, and Janet L. Yellen. "Job Switching and Job Satisfaction in the U.S. Labor Market." *Brookings Papers on Economic Activity,* no. 2 (1988): 495–584.

Aitken, Hugh G. J. *Taylorism at Watertown Arsenal: Scientific Management in Action, 1908–1915*. Cambridge, Mass.: Harvard University Press, 1960.

Amato-McCoy, Deena. "Price Chopper CBT Slashes Training Time for Cashiers." *Supermarket News*, 19 May 1997, 69.

American Management Association. *Annual Survey on Downsizing and Worker Assistance*. New York, 1990.

———. *1994 AMA Survey on Downsizing: Summary of Key Findings*. New York: American Management Association, 1994.

———. *1996 AMA Survey on Downsizing, Job Elimination, and Job Creation*. New York: American Management Association, 1996.

Anand, Jaideep, and Harbir Singh. "Asset Redeployment, Acquisitions, and Corporate Strategy in Declining Industries." *Strategic Management Journal,* July 1997, 99–118.

Anderson, Gordon, Peter Brosnan, and Pat Walsh. "Flexibility, Casualization, and Externalization in the New Zealand Workforce." *Journal of Industrial Relations* 36 (1994): 491–518.

Angel, David P. "High-Technology Agglomeration and the Labor Market: The Case of Silicon Valley." *Environment and Planning* 23 (1991): 1501–1516.

———. "The Labor Market for Engineers in the U.S. Semiconductor Industry." *Economic Geography* 65 (1989): 99–112.

Applebaum, Eileen, and Rose Batt. *Transforming Work Systems in the United States.* Ithaca, N.Y.: ILR Press, 1994.

Arthur, Michael B., and Denise M. Rousseau. *The Boundaryless Career: A New Employment Principle for a New Organizational Era.* New York: Oxford University Press, 1996.

Atkinson, J. "Manpower Strategies for Flexible Organizations." *Personnel Management,* 16 August 1984, 28–31.

———, and N. Meager. "Is Flexibility Just a Flash in the Pan?" *Personnel Management,* 18 September 1986, 26–29.

Auerbach, James A., and Jerome T. Barrett, eds. *The Future of Labor-Management Innovation in the United States.* Washington, D.C.: National Planning Association, 1993.

Auerbach, Jonathan. "Director's Cut: The Trend toward Stock-Based Pay Has Spread to Board Members." *Wall Street Journal,* 11 April 1994.

Australian Bureau of Statistics (ABS). *Manufacturing Technology Statistics.* Canberra: AGPS, 1993.

Bailey, Thomas R., and Annette D. Bernhardt. "In Search of the High Road in a Low-Wage Industry." *Politics and Society* 25, no. 2 June (1997): 179–201.

Baldwin, Roger G., and Jay L. Chronister. "Full-Time Non-Tenure-Track Faculty." NEA Higher Education Research Center, update 2, no. 5, 1996.

Barier, Michael. "Now You Hire Them, Now You Don't." *Nation's Business,* January 1994, 30–32.

Barley, Stephen R. *The Turn toward a Horizontal Division of Labor: On the Occupationalization of Firms and the Technization of Craft.* Working Paper, Cornell University School of Industrial and Labor Relations, Ithaca, NY, 1992.

Barnes, Shirley. "In the Out Door: Restructuring at IBM Has Meant Hiring for Specific Skills." *Chicago Tribune,* 7 July 1996.

Barnevik, Percy. "The Logic of Global Business." *Harvard Business Review,* March 1991.

Baron, James N., Frank R. Dobbins, and P. D. Jennings. "War and Peace: The Evolution of Modern Personnel Administration in U.S. Industry." *American Journal of Sociology* 92 (1986): 350–383.

Bartel, Ann P. "Training, Wage Growth, and Job Performance." *Journal of Labor Economics* 13, no. 3 (July 1995).

Bassi, Laurie J., Anne L. Gallagher, and Ed Schroer. *The ASTD Training Data Book.* Alexandria, Va.: American Society for Training and Development, 1996.

Bateman, T. S. and S. Strasser. "A Longitudinal Analysis of the Antecedents of Organizational Commitment." *Academy of Management Journal* 27 (1984): 95–112.

Batt, Rosemary. "From Bureaucracy to Enterprise? The Changing Jobs and Careers of

Managers in Telecommunications Services." In *Broken Ladders: Managerial Careers in Transition,* edited by Paul Osterman. New York: Oxford University Press, 1996.

———. "Management Labor Markets in Telecommunications." In *White Collar Internal Labor Markets,* edited by Paul Osterman. New York: Oxford University Press, forthcoming.

Becker, Gary S. "Investments in Human Capital: A Theoretical Analysis." *Journal of Political Economy* 70 (1962): 9–49.

Beckman, Sara L. "The Evolution of a Networked Organization: An Insider's View of the Hewlett-Packard Company." In *Management Employment Systems,* edited by Paul Osterman. New York: Oxford University Press, 1996.

Beer, Michael, and R. O. Von Werssowetz. *Human Resources at Hewlett-Packard.* Boston: Harvard Business School Press, 1981.

Belous, Richard S. *The Contingent Economy.* Washington, D.C.: National Planning Association, 1989.

———. "How Human Resource Systems Adjust to the Shift toward Contingent Workers." *Monthly Labor Review,* March (1989): 7–12.

Bencivenga, Dominic. "Employers and Workers Come to Terms." *HR Magazine,* 20 June 1997, 1–6.

Berger, Joseph. "The Pain of Layoffs for Ex-Senior I.B.M. Workers." *New York Times,* 22 December 1993, B1, B5.

Berger, Lance A., and Martin J. Sikora, eds. *The Change Management Handbook.* New York: Irwin Professional Publishing, 1994.

Berle, A. A., and Gardiner Means. *The Modern Corporation.* New York: Macmillan, 1932.

Bernhardt, Annette, Martina Morris, Mark Handcock, and Marc Scott. "Job Instability and Wage Inequality: Preliminary Results from Two NLS Cohorts." Working paper, Columbia University, New York, NY, February 1997.

Bernstein, Aaron. "At UPS, Part-Time Work Is a Full-Time Issue." *Business Week,* 16 June 1997, 88–90.

Bertrand, Marianne. "From the Invisible Hand to the Invisible Handshake? How Product Market Competition Changes the Employment Relationship." Harvard University Department of Economics manuscript, November 1997.

Bethel, Jennifer E., and Julia Liebeskind. "The Effects of Ownership Structure on Corporate Restructuring." *Strategic Management Journal* 14 (1993): 15–31.

"Beyond Downsizing: Staffing and Workforce Management for the Millenium." Woodcliff Lake, N.J.: Lee Hecht Harrison, 1997.

Bhagat, S., A. Schleifer, and R. Vishny. "Hostile Takeovers in the 1980s: The Return to Corporate Specialization." *Brookings Papers on Economic Activity,* no. 1 (1990).

Bishop, John. *The Incidence of and Payoff to Employer Training: A Review of the Literature with Recommendations for Policy.* Philadelphia: National Center on the Educational Quality of the Workforce (EQW), 1994.

Blackburn, McKinley L., David E. Bloom, and Richard B. Freeman. "The Declining Economic Position of Less–Skilled American Men." In *A Future of Lousy Jobs? The Changing Structure of U.S. Wages,* edited by Gary Burtless. Washington, D.C.: Brookings Institution, 1990.

Blair, Margaret M., and Martha A. Schary. "Industry–Level Pressures to Restructure." In *The Deal Decade,* edited by Margaret M. Blair. Washington, D.C.: Brookings Institution, 1993.

Bleakley, Fred R. "To Bolster Economies, Some States Rely More on Two–Year Colleges." *Wall Street Journal,* 26 November 1996, A1.

Boisjoly, Johanne, Greg J. Duncan, and Timothy Smeeding. "Have Highly Skilled Workers Fallen from Grace? The Shifting Burdens of Involuntary Job Losses from 1968 to 1992." Unpublished manuscript. University of Quebec (Rimouski), 1994.

Bookbinder, Stephen M. "The Employee Perspective." In *The New Deal in Employment Relationships: A Council Report.* Report No. 1162–96–CR. New York: Conference Board, 1996.

"Borland Says Microsoft Raided." *USA Today.* 8 May 1997, 6b.

Bounds, Wendy. "Kodak Gives Fisher Options to Purchase 750,000 of Its Shares." *New York Times,* 20 December 1993, B2.

Bowers, Norman, and Paul Swaim. *Probing (some of) the Issues of Employment Related Training: Evidence from the CPS.* Washington, D.C.: U.S. Department of Agriculture, Economic Research Service, 1992.

Bowman, Edward H., and Harbir Singh. "Corporate Restructuring: Reconfiguring the Firm." *Strategic Management Journal* 14 (1993): 5–14.

———, and Harbir Singh. "Overview of Corporate Restructuring: Trends and Consequences." In *Corporate Restructuring,* edited by Milton L. Rock and Robert H. Rock. New York: McGraw-Hill, 1990.

———, Michael Useem, and Raja Bhadury. "When Does Corporate Restructuring Influence Economic Performance?" *California Management Review,* forthcoming.

Bradbury, Susan L. "Dual Career Couples in R&D Labs." *Research and Technology Management* 31, no. 1, January–February (1994): 45–47.

Branch, Shelly. "MBAs Are Hot Again—And They Know It." *Fortune,* 14 April 1997, 155–157.

Brandeis, Louis D. *Other People's Money, and How Bankers Use It.* New York: Harper and Row, 1967.

Bridges, William. "The End of the Job." *Fortune,* 19 September 1994, 62–74.

Briner, Rob. "Feeling for the Facts: Relationship between Employee Stress and Performance." *People Management,* 9 January 1997, 73.

Brockner, Joel. "The Effects of Work Layoffs on Survivors: Research, Theory, and Practice." In *Research in Organizational Behavior,* 10 (1990): 212–255.

Brockner, Joel, Steven Grover, Michael N. O'Malley, Thomas F. Reed, and Mary Ann Glynn. "Threat of Future Layoffs: Self-Esteem, and Survivors' Reactions: Evidence from the Laboratory and the Field." *Strategic Management Journal* 14 (1993): 153–166.

Brockner, Joel, Steven Grover, Thomas F. Reed, and Rocki Lee DeWitt. "Layoffs, Job Insecurity, and Survivors' Work Effort: Evidence of an Inverted-U Relationship." *Academy of Management Journal* 35 (1992): 413–425.

Brown, Clair, ed. *The Competitive Semiconductor Manufacturing Human Resources Project.* Berkeley, Calif.: Competitive Semiconductor Manufacturing Program at U.C. Berkeley, July 1997.

Brown, James, and Richard Light. "Interpreting Panel Data on Job Tenure." *Journal of Labor Economics* 10 (1992): 219–257.

Brynjolfsson, Eric, Thomas Malone, Vijay Gurbaxani, and Ajet Kambil. "Does Information Technology Lead to Smaller Firms?" *Management Science* 40, no. 12 (December 1994).

Buch, Kimberly. "Quality Circles and Employee Withdrawal Behaviors: A Cross-Organizational Study." *Journal of Applied Behavioral Science* 28, no. 1 (March 1992): 62–73.

Bureau of National Affairs. "The Changing Workplace: New Directions in Staffing and Scheduling." Washington, D.C.: Bureau of National Affairs, 1986 (BNA Special Report).

Buttrick, John. "The Inside Contracting System." *The Journal of Economic History* 12, no. 3 (Summer 1952): 205.

Byrne, John A. "The Horizontal Corporation." *Business Week,* 20 December 1993, 76–81.

Callaghan, Polly, and Heidi Hartmann. *Contingent Work.* Washington, D.C.: Economic Policy Institute, 1991.

Cameron, Kim S., Sarah J. Freeman, and Aneil K. Mishra. "Downsizing and Redesigning Organizations." In *Organizational Change and Redesign,* edited by George P. Huber and William H. Glick. New York: Oxford University Press, 1993.

Cappelli, Peter. "Are Skill Requirements Rising? Evidence for Production and Clerical Workers." *Industrial and Labor Relations Review* 46, no. 3 (March 1993).

———. "Examining Managerial Displacement." *Academy of Management Journal* 35 (1992): 203–217.

———. "Technology, Work Organization, and the Structure of Wages." Working paper, Wharton School, Philadelphia, September 1997.

Cappelli, Peter, Laurie Bassi, Harry C. Katz, David Knoke, Paul Osterman, and Michael Useem. *Change at Work.* New York: Oxford University Press, 1997.

Cappelli, Peter, and Keith Chauvin. "An Inter-plant Test of the Efficiency Wage Hypothesis." *Quarterly Journal of Economics* 106, no.3 (August 1991): 769–787.

———. "A Test of an Efficiency Model on Grievance Activity." *Industrial and Labor Relations Review* 45, no. 1 (October 1991): 3–14.

Cappelli, Peter, and K. C. O'Shaughnessey. *Changes in Skill and Wage Structures in Corporate Headquarters, 1986–1992.* Philadelphia: National Center on the Educational Quality of the Workforce (EQW), 1995.

Cappelli, Peter, and Daniel Shapiro. *Employer Participation in School-to-Work Programs: Results from the National Employer Survey.* Philadelphia: National Center on Post-Secondary Improvement, 1997.

Cappelli, Peter, and Peter D. Sherer. "Assessing Employee Attitudes under Two-Tier Pay Plans." *Industrial and Labor Relations Review* 43, no. 2 (January 1990): 223–244.

———. "Satisfaction, Market Wages, and Labor Relations: An Airline Study." *Industrial Relations* 27, no. 1 (1988): 56–74.

Cappelli, Peter, and Stephanie Wilk. "The Determinants and Consequences of Selection Decisions." Working paper, Wharton School Department of Management, Philadelphia, 1997.

"Career Development and Employee Orientation Practices Aim to Increase Retention and Productivity." *Business Wire,* 29 May 1997, 7.

Carsten, Jeanne M., and Paul E. Spector. "Unemployment, Job Satisfaction, and Employee Turnover: A Meta-analytic Test of the Muchinsky Model." *Journal of Applied Psychology* 27 (1987): 372–381.

Cascio, Wayne, Clifford E. Young, and James R. Morris. "Financial Consequences of Employment-Change Decisions in Major U.S. Corporations." *Academy of Management Journal* 40, no. 5 (1997): 1175–1189.

Causer, G., and C. Jones. "Responding to 'Skill Shortages': Recruitment and Retention in a High–Technology Labor Market." *Human Resource Management Journal* 3, no. 3 (1993): 202–221.

Chait, Richard, and Cathy A. Trower. *Where Tenure Does Not Reign*. Washington, D.C.: American Association for Higher Education, 1997.

Chandler, Alfred D., Jr. *Strategy and Structure: Chapters in the History of the American Industrial Enterprise*. Cambridge, Mass.: MIT Press, 1962.

———. "The United States: Seedbed of Managerial Capitalism." In *Managerial Hierarchies: Comparative Perspectives on the Rise of the Modern Industrial Enterprise*, edited by Alfred D. Chandler, Jr., and Herman Daems. Cambridge, Mass.: Harvard University Press, 1980.

———. *The Visible Hand: The Managerial Revolution in American Business*. Cambridge, Mass.: Harvard University Press, 1977.

Chauvin, Keith. "Firm-Specific Wage Growth and Changes in the Labor Market for Managers." *Management and Decision Economics* 15 (1994): 21–37.

Clark, Robert, and Ann McDermed. *The Choice of Pension Plans in a Changing Economy*. Washington, D.C.: American Enterprise Institute, 1990.

Clawson, Dan. *Bureaucracy and the Labor Process: The Transformation of U.S. Industry, 1860–1920*. New York: Monthly Review Press, 1980.

Clinton, Angela. "Flexible Labor: Restructuring the American Work Force." *Monthly Labor Review*, August 1997, 3–17.

Cohany, Sharon. "Workers in Alternate Arrangements." *Monthly Labor Review* 119, no. 10 (October 1996), 31–45.

Cohen, Arthur. "Upward Communications in Experimentally Created Hierarchies." *Human Relations* 11 (1958): 41–53.

Cole, Robert E., Paul Bacdayan, and B. Joseph White. "Quality, Participation, and Competitiveness." *California Management Review*, Spring 1993, 68–81.

Commerce Clearing House (CCH). "Mean Absenteeism Rate Up by Nine Percent to 2.68 Percent." *Ideas and Trends* 326 (27 April 1994): 1.

Commission on the Skills of the American Workforce. *America's Choice: High Skills or Low Wages!* Rochester, N.Y.: National Center on Education and the Economy, 1989.

Confederation of British Industries (CBI). *Flexible Labor Markets: Who Pays for Training?* London: CBI, 1994.

Conference Board. *Availability of a Quality Workforce*. Conference Board Report No. 1010. New York, 1992.

———. *Does Quality Work? A Review of Relevant Studies*. Report No. 1034. New York, 1993.

Constantine, Jill M., and David Neumark. *Training and the Growth of Wage Inequality*. Philadelphia: National Center on the Educational Quality of the Workforce (EQW), 1994.

Conte, Michael A., and Jan Svejnar. "The Performance Effects of Employee Ownership Plans." In *Paying for Productivity: A Look at the Evidence,* edited by Alan S. Blinder. Washington, D.C.: Brookings Institution, 1990.

Corporate Leadership Council. *Perfecting Labor Markets: Redefining the Social Contract at the World's High Performance Corporations.* Washington, D.C.: Advisory Board, 1995.

Davis, Gerald F., Kristina A. Diekman, and Catherine H. Tinsley. *The Decline and Fall of the Conglomeration Firm in the 1980s: A Study in the De-institutionalization of an Organizational Form.* Evanston, Ill.: Kellogg Graduate School of Management, Northwestern University, 1993.

Davis, Gerald F., and Suzanne K. Stout. "Organization Theory and the Market for Corporate Control: A Dynamic Analysis of the Characteristics of Large Takeover Targets, 1980–90." *Administrative Science Quarterly* 37 (1992): 605–633.

Davis, Steven J., and John Haltiwanger. *Wage Dispersion between and within U.S. Manufacturing Plants, 1963–1986.* Chicago: University of Chicago Graduate School of Business, 1990.

Davis-Blake, Alison, and Brian Uzzi. "Determinants of Employment Externalization: A Study of Temporary Workers and Independent Contractors." *Administrative Science Quarterly* 38, no. 2 (June 1993): 195–223.

Dawkins, P., and K. Norris. "Casual Employment in Australia." *Australian Bulletin of Labor* 16 (1990): 156–173.

DeCotiis, Thomas A., and Timothy P. Summers. "A Path Analysis of a Model of the Antecedents and Consequences of Organizational Commitment." *Human Relations* 40, no. 7 (1987): 445–470.

DeFillipi, R. J., and M. B. Arthur. "The Boundaryless Career: A Competency-Based Perspective." *Journal of Organizational Behavior* 15 (1994): 307–324.

Dennard, H. Lane, Jr., and Herbert R. Northrup. "Leased Employment: Character, Numbers, and Labor Law Problems." *Georgia Law Review* 23 (1994): 683–728.

Deutsch, Claudia H. "High-Technology Job Fair Is Now an Industry in Itself." *New York Times,* 29 September 1997, 4.

Diebold, Francis X., David Neumark, and Daniel Polsky. *Changes in Job Stability in the United States.* Philadelphia: National Center on the Educational Quality of the Workforce [EQW], 1995.

Doeringer, Peter B., Kathleen Christensen, Patricia M. Flynn, Douglas T. Hall, Harry C. Katz, Jeffrey H. Keefe, Christopher J. Ruhm, Andrew M. Sum, and Michael Useem. *Turbulence in the American Workplace.* New York: Oxford University Press, 1991.

Doeringer, Peter B., and Michael J. Piore. *Internal Labor Markets and Manpower Analysis.* Lexington, Mass.: D.C. Heath, 1971.

Donaldson, Gordon. *Corporate Restructuring: Managing the Change Process from Within.* Boston: Harvard Business School Press, 1994.

Donkin, Richard. "Career On and Off the Rails." *Financial Times,* 20 December 1995, 11.

Dorfman, N. "Route 128: The Development of a Regional High Technology." *Research Policy* 12 (1983): 299–316.

"DuPont Turns Over Its Computer Work to Two Contractors." *Philadelphia Inquirer,* 3 June 1997, C1.

Dyer, Lee, Felician Foltman, and George Milkovich. "Contemporary Employment Stabilization Practices." In *Human Resource Management and Industrial Relations: Text, Readings, and Cases,* edited by Thomas A. Kochan and Thomas A. Barocci. Boston: Little, Brown, 1985.

Economic Report of the President. Washington, D.C.: GPO, 1995.

Ehrlichman, John. "Who Will Hire Me Now?" *Parade,* 29 August 1993, 4–6.

Eisenberger, Robert, Peter Faolo, and Valarie David-LaMastro. "Perceived Organizational Support and Employee Diligence, Commitment, and Innovation." *Journal of Applied Psychology* 71, no. 3 (1990): 500–507.

"Employee Loyalty Takes Hit: Workplace Stress Weakens Job Commitment, Salaries Easily Lure Workers." New York: Reuters, 6 July 1998.

Employment Gazette. "The Flexible Workforce and Patterns of Working Hours in the U.K." London: Department of Employment, July 1994.

Epple, Dennis, Linda Argote, and Kenneth Murphy. "An Empirical Investigation of the Micro Structure of Knowledge Acquisition and Transfer through Learning by Doing." *Operations Research* 44, no. 1 (January–February 1996): 77–86.

EQW. *The EQW National Employer Survey: First Findings.* Philadelphia: National Center on the Educational Quality of the Workforce (EQW), 1995.

———. *Employers Who Work with Schools.* Philadelphia: National Center on the Educational Quality of the Workforce (EQW), 1995.

Ettore, Barbara. "The Contingency Workforce Moves Mainstream." *Management Review* 83 (February 1994): 10–16.

———. "How Are Companies Keeping the Employees They Want?" *Management Review* 86, no. 5 (May 1997): 49.

Farber, Henry S. "Are Lifetime Jobs Disappearing? Job Duration in the United States: 1973–1993." Working Paper #341, Industrial Relations Section, Princeton University, 1995.

———. "The Changing Face of Job Loss in the United States, 1981–1995." Working paper 360, Industrial Relations Section, Princeton University, 1996.

———. "The Incidence and Costs of Job Loss: 1982–91." *Brookings Papers on Economic Activity: Microeconomics,* no. 1 (1993): 73–119.

Faulkner, Robert R., and Andy B. Anderson. "Short-Term Projects and Emergent Careers: Evidence from Hollywood." *American Journal of Sociology* 92, no. 1 (1987): 879–909.

Feder, Barnaby J. "Recasting a Model Incentive Strategy." *New York Times,* 5 September 1994, 33.

Fierman, Jaclyn. "The Contingency Workforce." *Fortune,* 24 January 1994, 33.

"Finding the Time—A Survey of Managers' Attitudes to Using and Managing Time." *Management Services* 39, no. 6 (June 1995): 3–6.

Flynn, Gillian. "Contingent Staffing Requires Serious Strategy." *Personnel Journal,* April 1995, 50.

Flynn, Laurie J. "For Some, Steady Job Isn't the End of the Road." *New York Times,* 20 May 1996, D8

Forbes, F. S. and I. M. Jones. "A Comparative, Attitudinal, and Analytic Study of the Dismissal of At-Will Employees without Cause." *Labor Law Journal* 37 (1986): 157–166.

Fortune. "The End of the Job." 19 September 1994, 62–78.

———. "The New Deal: What Companies and Employees Owe One Another." 13 June 1994, 44.

———. "The Real Key to Creating Wealth." 20 September 1993, 1.

Foulkes, Fred. *Personnel Practices of Large, Non-Union Companies.* Englewood Cliffs, N.J.: Prentice-Hall, 1980.

Furchgott, Roy. "Earning It: Job Uncertainty Makes Offers Easier to Refuse." *New York Times,* 20 October 1996, 9.

Galinsky, Ellen, James T. Bond, and Dana E. Friedman. *The Changing Workforce.* New York: Families and Work Institute, 1993.

Gardner, Jennifer M. "Recession Swells Count of Displaced Workers." *Monthly Labor Review,* June 1993, 14–23.

Garone, Stephen J. *Building a High-Performance Organization.* New York: Conference Board, 1993.

Gerlin, Andrea. "Presbyterian Raids Cooper Cardiologists." *Philadelphia Inquirer,* 27 September 1997, 1.

Ghemawat, Pahkaj. "Sustainable Advantage." *Harvard Business Review,* May–June 1986, 69–74.

Gittleman, Maury B., and David R. Howell. "Changes in the Structure and Quality of Jobs in the United States: Effects by Race and Gender." *Industrial and Labor Relations Review* 48 (1995): 420–440.

Gokhale, Jagadeesh, Erica L. Groshen, and David Neumark. "Do Hostile Takeovers Reduce Extramarginal Wage Payments?" *Review of Economic Statistics* 77 (1995): 470–485.

Goldin, L., and E. Applebaum. "What Was Driving the 1982–1988 Boom in Temporary Employment? Preferences of Workers or Decisions and Power of Employers?" *Journal of Economy and Society* 51 (1992): 473–493.

Goozner, Merril. "A Musical of Japan's 'Salarymen.'" *Philadelphia Inquirer,* 28 December 1994.

Gorlin, Harriet. *Issues in Human Resource Management.* New York: Conference Board, 1985.

Gottschalk, Peter, and Robert Moffitt. "The Growth of Earnings Instability in the U.S. Labor Market." *Brookings Papers on Economic Activity,* no. 2 (1994): 217–272.

Gouldner, Alvin W. "The Norm of Reciprocity: A Preliminary Statement." *American Sociological Review* 25 (1960): 161–178.

Green, R., and D. MacDonald. "The Australian Flexibility Paradox." *Journal of Industrial Relations* 35 (1991): 142–156.

Greenberg, Jerald. "Equity and Workplace Status: A Field Experiment." *Journal of Applied Psychology* 23 (1998): 606–613.

Griffin, Abbie. "Metrics for Measuring Product Development Cycle Time." *Journal of Production Innovation Management* 10 (1993): 112–125.

Groshen, Erica L. "HRM Policy and Increasing Inequality in a Salary Survey." *Proceedings of the 44th Annual Meeting of the IRRA.* Industrial Relations Research Association, Madison, Wisconsin, 1993.

Grossman, Ron, and Charles Leroux. "Part-Timers Are the Cheap Labor of U.S. Colleges." *Chicago Tribune,* 20 August 1993, 1.

Gurbaxani, Vijay, and Seugjin Whang. "The Impact of Information Systems on Organizations and Markets." *Communications of the ACM* 34, no. 1 (January 1991): 59–73.

Gustman, Alan, Olivia Mitchell, and Thomas Steinmeier. "Retirement Research Using the Health and Retirement Survey." *Journal of Human Resources* 30 *(Health & Retirement Study Supplement)* (1995): 557–583.

Haas, Al. "Carmakers Look to Niche Markets to Bolster Sales." *Philadelphia Inquirer,* 25 May 1997.

Hakim, Catharine. "Core and Periphery in Employers' Workforce Strategies: Evidence from the 1987 E.L.U.S. Survey." *Work, Employment, and Society* 4 (1990): 157–188.

Hakim, Cliff. *We Are All Self-Employed.* San Francisco: Berrett-Koehler, 1994.

Hall, Gene, Jim Rosenthal, and Judy Wade. "How to Make Reengineering *Really* Work." *Harvard Business Review,* November–December 1993, 119–131.

Hammer, Michael, and James Champy. *Reengineering the Corporation: A Manifesto for Business Revolution.* New York: Harper Business, 1993.

Hammonds, Keith H. "Writing a New Social Contract." *Business Week,* 11 March 1996, 60.

Hampton, B. *History of the American Film Industry: From Its Beginnings to 1931.* New York: Dover Press, 1970.

Harley, William G. "The Politics of Flexibility: An Empirical and Theoretical Investigation of the Implications of 'Labor Flexibility' for Workers and Trade Unions in Australia." Unpublished Ph.D. thesis, Department of Government, University of Queensland, 1994.

Harris, Louis, and Associates. *Laborforce 2000 Survey.* New York: Louis Harris, 1991.

Haskel, Jonathan, and Christopher Martin. "Do Skill Shortages Reduce Productivity? Theory and Evidence from the United Kingdom." *Economic Journal* 105 (March 1993): 386–394.

Hays, Laurie. "IBM's Finance Chief, Ax in Hand, Scours Empire for Costs to Cut." *Wall Street Journal,* 26 January 1994, A1, A6.

———, and Gautam Naik. "Xerox to Cut 10,000 Jobs, Shut Facilities." *Wall Street Journal,* 9 December 1993, A2, A4.

Heckscher, Charles. *White-Collar Blues.* New York: Basic Books, 1995.

Hewitt Associates. Personal communication, 1994.

Hiam, Alexander. *Does Quality Work? A Review of Relevant Studies.* New York: Conference Board, 1993.

Hoerr, John. "Big Blues for Laid-Off IBM Workforce." *Business and Society Review,* 22 March 1994.

Holusha, John. "A Profitable Xerox Plans to Cut Staff by 10,000." *New York Times,* 9 December 1993, D1.

Hoppock, Robert. *Job Satisfaction.* New York: Harper and Row, 1935.

Hori, Shintaro. "Fixing Japan's White Collar Economy: A Personal View." *Harvard Business Review,* November-December 1993, 157–172.

Horwitz, Tony. "Jobless Male Managers Proliferate in Suburbs, Causing Subtle Malaise." *Wall Street Journal*, 20 September 1993, A1, A6.

Hoskisson, Robert E., Richard A. Johnson, and Douglas D. Moesel. *Corporate Restructuring Intensity: Effects of Governance, Strategy and Performance*. College Station, Tex.: College of Business Administration, Texas A&M University, 1993.

Houseman, Susan. *Temporary, Part-Time, and Contract Employment in the United States: New Evidence from an Employer Survey*. Kalamazoo, Mich.: W. E. Upjohn Institute for Employment Research, 1997.

———, and Machiko Osawa. "Part-Time and Temporary Employment in Japan." *Monthly Labor Review*, October 1995, 10–41.

Howard, Robert. "The CEO as Organizational Architect." *Harvard Business Review*, September–October 1992, 107–119.

"How Jobs Die—And Are Born." *Fortune*, 26 July 1993, 26.

HR Executive Review: Implementing the New Employment Contract. New York: Conference Board, 1997.

Hulin, Charles, and M. R. Blood. "Job Enlargement, Individual Differences, and Worker Responses." *Psychological Bulletin* 69 (1968): 41–55.

Hunter, Laurie, Alan McGregor, John MacInnes, and Alan Sproull. "The 'Flexible Firm': Strategy and Segmentation." *British Journal of Industrial Relations* 31 (1993): 383–407.

Ikeya, Akira. "Companies Relying on More Part-Time Workers." *Nikkei Weekly*, 2 October 1995, 3.

Institute of Management and Manpower, Plc. *Survey of Long-Term Employment Strategies*. London, 1994.

"Interim Managers: Tempers and Temporaries." *Director* 47, no. 2 (September 1993): 69–70.

Ippolito, Richard A. "Toward Explaining the Growth of Defined Contribution Plans." *Industrial Relations* 34 (1995): 1–20.

Jackson, Paul R., Elizabeth M. Stafford, Michael H. Banks, and Peter Warr. "Unemployment and Psychological Stress in Young People: The Moderating Role of Employment Commitment." *Journal of Applied Psychology* 68 (1983): 525–535.

Jacoby, Sanford M. *Employing Bureaucracy: Managers, Unions, and the Transformation of Work in American Industry, 1900–1945*. New York: Columbia University Press, 1985.

Jaeger, David A., and Ann Huff Stevens. "Is Job Stability in the United States Falling? Reconciling Trends in the Current Population Survey and Panel Study of Income Dynamics." Paper presented at the Russell Sage Foundation Conference on Job Stability and Security, February 1998.

Janger, Allen. *Measuring Managerial Layers and Spans*. New York: Conference Board, 1989.

Japan Association of Corporate Executives (Keizai Doyukai). "Management Focused on the Efficient Use of Capital." Tokyo, 1998.

Jensen, Michael C. "Eclipse of the Public Corporation." *Harvard Business Review*, September–October 1989, 61–74.

———, and Kevin J. Murphy. "CEO Incentives—It's Not How Much You Pay, but How." *Harvard Business Review*, May–June 1990, 138–153.

Johnson, Arlene S., and Fabian Linden. *Availability of a Quality Workforce.* New York: Conference Board, 1992.

Johnston, H. Russell, and Michael R. Vitale. "Creating Competitive Advantage with Interorganizational Information Systems." *MIS Quarterly,* June 1988, 153–165.

Jones, S. H. R. "The Origin of Work: A Historical Dimension." *Journal of Economic Behavior and Organization* 3 (1982): 117–137.

Kahneman, D., J. L. Knetch, and R. H. Thaler. "Fairness as a Constraint of Profit Seeking Entitlements in the Market." *American Economic Review* 76 (1986): 727–782.

Kalish, David E. "The Competition that Spawns Bidding War for High-Tech Talent." *Philadelphia Inquirer,* 22 May 1997, F4.

Kalleberg, Arne, and Torger Reve. "Contracts and Commitment: Economic and Sociological Perspectives on Employment Relations." *Human Relations* 45, no. 9 (1992): 1103–1132.

Kane, Mary. "Accounting Firm Leading Evolution of Corporate Office." *Newark Star Ledger,* 19 June 1994, 5.

———. "Downsizing: Profit vs. Pain." *The Atlanta Journal and Constitution,* 14 January 1996.

Kanter, Rosabeth Moss. *Men and Women of the Corporation.* New York: Basic Books, 1977.

———. "Transcending Business Boundaries: 12,000 World Managers View Change." *Harvard Business Review,* May–June, 1991, 151–163.

Kaplan, Steven N. "The Effects of Management Buyouts on Operating Performance and Value." *Journal of Financial Economics* 11 (1989): 5–50.

———, and Jeremy C. Stein. "The Evolution of Buyout Pricing and Financial Structure." Paper presented at conference on "Efficiency and Ownership: The Future of the Corporation." Sponsored by University of California, Davis, May 1992.

Katz, Harry C. *Shifting Gears: Changing Labor Relations in the U.S. Automobile Industry.* Cambridge, Mass.: MIT Press, 1985.

———, and Jeffrey H. Keefe. "Final Report on a Survey of Training and the Restructuring of Work in Large Unionized Firms." New York State School of Industrial and Labor Relations, Cornell University, Ithaca, N.Y., 1993.

Katz, Lawrence F., and Alan B. Krueger. "Changes in the Structure of Wages in the Public and Private Sectors." In *Research in Labor Economics,* vol. 12, edited by Ronald G. Ehrenberg. Greenwich, Conn.: JAI Press, 1991.

Kekre, Sunder, and Kannan Srinivasan. "Broader Product Line: A Necessity to Achieve Success?" *Management Science* 36, no. 10 (1990): 1216.

Kepner-Tregoe. *House Divided: Views on Change from Top Management—and Their Employees.* Princeton: Kepner-Tregoe, 1995.

Kilborn, Peter T. "The Workplace, after the Deluge." *New York Times,* 5 September 1993, Business section, 3–4.

Kilpatrick, David. "Lou Gerstner's First 30 Days." *Fortune,* 31 May 1993, 57.

King, Carole. "'Mentoring' May Be Remedy for Retention's Blues." *National Underwriter,* 28 June 1993, 11.

Kissler, Gary D. "The New Employment Contract." *Human Resource Management* 33, no. 3 (Fall 1994): 335–352.

Klebnikov, Paul. "Focus, Focus." *Fortune,* 11 September 1995, 42–44.

Kneale, Dennis, Gautam Naik, and Bart Ziegler. "Dialing for Dollars: AT&T's Heir Apparent Jumps to a Tiny Firm that Offers Huge Pay." *Wall Street Journal,* 20 August 1996.

Kochan, Thomas A., and Peter Cappelli. "The Transformation of the Industrial Relations and Human Resources Functions." In *Internal Labor Markets,* edited by Paul Osterman. New York: Oxford University Press, 1984.

Kochan, Thomas A., and Paul Osterman. *Mutual Gains Bargaining.* Boston: Harvard Business School Press, 1994.

Kochan, Thomas A., Harry C. Katz, and Robert B. McKersie. *The Transformation of Industrial Relations in the U.S.* New York: Basic Books, 1984.

Kramer, Michael. "Job Training Has to Be Reworked." *Time,* 20 January 1997, 20.

Krueger, Alan. "How Computers Have Changed the Wage Structure: Evidence from Micro Data, 1984–1989." *Quarterly Journal of Economics,* February 1993, 33–60.

Kuttner, Robert. "Talking Marriage and Thinking One-Night Stand." *Business Week,* 18 October 1993, 16.

Lambert, Richard A., David F. Larcker, and Robert E. Verrecchia. "Portfolio Considerations in Valuing Executive Compensation." *Journal of Accounting Research* 29 (1991): 129–149.

Lancaster, Hal. "Managing Your Career: If Your Career Needs More Attention, Maybe You Should Get an Agent." *Wall Street Journal,* 20 October 1998, B1.

Landes, David. *The Unbound Prometheus.* Cambridge: Cambridge University Press, 1969.

Lane, Randall. "Pampering the Customers, Pampering the Employees." *Forbes,* 14 October 1996, 74–80.

Lawler, Edward E., III, Susan Mohrman, and Gerald Ledford. *Employee Involvement and Total Quality Management: Practices and Results in Fortune 500 Companies.* San Francisco: Jossey-Bass Publishers, 1992.

"Lawmakers Vote to Require Early-Departing LAPD Recruits to Pay for Training." *Metropolitan News Company,* 17 January 1996, 14.

Lee, Chris. "Trust Me." *Training.* January 1997, 28–37.

Leete, Laura, and Juliet B. Schor. "Assessing the Time Squeeze Hypothesis: Hours Worked in the United States, 1969–1989." *Industrial Relations* 33, no. 1 (January 1994): 25–43.

Leigh, J. Paul. "The Effects of Unemployment and the Business Cycle on Absenteeism." *Journal of Economics and Business* 37 (May 1985): 159–170.

Levring, Robert, and Milton Moskowitz. *The 100 Best Companies to Work for in America.* New York: Doubleday, 1993.

Lichtenberg, Frank R., and Donald Siegel. "Productivity and Changes of Ownership of Manufacturing Plants." *Brookings Papers on Economic Activity,* no. 3 (1987).

Lohr, Steve. "I.B.M. May Quit Hilltop Headquarters." *New York Times,* 13 January 1994, A1, D3.

Lopez, Julie Amparano. "Many New Executives Are Being Discharged with Stunning Speed." *Wall Street Journal,* 4 March 1994, 1.

Louis Harris and Associates. *Laborforce 2000 Survey.* New York, 1991.

"Low Wage Lessons." *Business Week.* 11 November 1996, 108–116.

Lubin, Joann. "Japanese Are Doing More Job Hopping." *Wall Street Journal,* 18 November 1991, 1.

———. "Now Butchers, Engineers Get Signing Bonuses." *Wall Street Journal,* 2 June 1997, B1.

———. "Survivors of Layoffs Battle Angst, Anger, Hurting Productivity." *Wall Street Journal,* 6 December 1993, A1, A16.

———, and Joseph B. White. "Dilbert's Revenge: Throwing Off Angst, Workers Are Feeling in Control of Careers." *Wall Street Journal,* 11 September 1997, A1.

———. "More Companies Relocate CEO's in Style." *Wall Street Journal,* 7 April 1997, 1.

MacDuffie, John Paul, and John Krafcik. "Integrating Technology and Human Resources for High-Performance Manufacturing: Evidence from the International Auto Industry." In *Transforming Organizations,* edited by Thomas Kochan and Michael Useem. New York: Oxford University Press, 1992.

MacDuffie, John Paul, Kannan Sethuraman, and Marshall L. Fisher. "Product Variety and Manufacturing Performance: Evidence from the International Automotive Assembly Plant Study." *Management Science* 40, no. 3 (March 1996): 350–369.

Macy, Barry A., and Hiroaki Izumi. "Organizational Change, Design, and Work Innovation: A Meta-analysis of 131 North American Field Studies—1961–1991." In *Research in Organizational Change and Development,* edited by Richard W. Woodman and William A. Pasmore. Greenwich, Conn.: JAI Press, 1993.

Magnum, G., D. Mayhall, and K. Nelson. "The Temporary Help Industry: A Response to the Dual Internal Labor Market." *Industrial and Labor Relations Review* 38 (1985): 599–611.

Manufacturing Networks: A Report from the Partnership for a Smarter Workforce. Washington, D.C.: Partnership for a Smarter Workforce, 1996.

Marcotte, Dave. "Evidence of a Decline in the Stability of Employment in the U.S." Center for Governmental Studies, Northern Illinois University, 1994.

———. "Evidence of a Fall in the Wage Premium for Job Security." Center for Governmental Studies, Northern Illinois University, 1994.

Markels, Alex. "Signing Bonuses Rise to Counter Rich Pay Plans." *Wall Street Journal,* 21 August 1996, 1.

Markides, Constantine C. "Diversification, Restructuring, and Economic Performance." Working paper, London Business School, 1993.

Martin, Justin. "Job Surfing: Move On to Move Up." *Fortune,* 13 January 1997.

Mathieu, J. E., and D. M. Zajak. "A Review and Meta-analysis of the Antecedents, Correlates, and Consequences of Organizational Commitment." *Psychological Bulletin* 108 (1990): 171–194.

May, Troy. "Going to School on the Company Tab." *Business First—Columbus,* 28 February 1997, 17.

McGovern, Patrick. "To Retain or Not to Retain?" *Human Resource Management Journal* (United Kingdom) 5, no. 4 (Summer 1995).

McKinsey and Company. *Manufacturing Productivity.* Washington, D.C.: McKinsey Global Institute, 1993.

Medoff, James. *Middle-Aged and Out of Work: Growing Unemployment Due to Job Loss among Middle-Aged Americans.* Washington, D.C.: National Study Center, 1993.

——, and Katharine G. Abraham. "Experience, Performance, and Earnings." *Quarterly Journal of Economics* 90 (1980): 703–736.

Mercer, David. *IBM: How the World's Most Successful Company Is Managed.* London: K. Page, 1987.

Metcalf, Crysta J., and Elizabeth K. Briody. "Reconciling Perceptions of Career Advancement with Organizational Change: A Case from General Motors." *Human Organization* 54, no. 4 (Winter 1995): 417–428.

Meyer, John P., Natalie J. Allen, and Ian R. Gellatly. "Affective and Continuance Commitment to the Organization: Evaluation of Measures and Analysis of Current and Time-Lagged Relations." *Journal of Applied Psychology* 75, no. 6 (December 1990): 710–720.

Meyer, Stephen. *The Five Dollar Day: Labor Management and Social Control in the Ford Motor Company.* Albany: State University of New York Press, 1981.

Michaels, Ronald E., William L. Cron, Alan J. Dubinsky, and E. A. Joachimsthaler. "The Influence of Formalization on the Organizational Commitment and Work Alienation of Salespeople and Industrial Buyers." *Journal of Marketing Research* 25 (1990): 171–194.

Milligan, Patricia A. "Regaining Commitment." In *The New Deal in Employment Relationships: A Council Report.* Report No. 1162–96-CR. New York: Conference Board, 1996.

Mills, C. Wright. *The American Middle Class.* New York: Oxford University Press, 1953.

Mills, D. Quinn. *The IBM Lesson: The Profitable Art of Full Employment.* New York: Times Books, 1988.

——. "Seniority versus Ability in Promotion Decisions." *Industrial and Labor Relations Review* 38 (1985): 421–427.

Minderman, Dean. "Big Blues." *Credit Union Management,* February 1995.

Mirvis, Philip H., ed. *Building a Competitive Workforce: Investing in Human Capital for Corporate Success.* New York: John Wiley, 1993.

Mishel, Lawrence, and Jared Bernstein. *The State of Working America, 1994–1995.* Washington, D.C.: Economic Policy Institute, 1995.

Montgomery, David. "Workers' Control of Machine Production in the Nineteenth Century." *Labor History* (Fall 1976): 488.

"More than a Dying Fad?" *Fortune,* 18 October 1993: 66.

Mori, Kiyoshi. "Industrial Sea Change: How Changes in Keiretsu Are Opening the Japanese Market." *Brookings Review* 12 no. 4 (1994): 20.

Morris, Charles E. "Why New Products?" *Chilton's Food Engineering* 6, no. 6 (1993): 130.

Moskal, Brian. "Company Loyalty Dies, a Victim of Neglect." *Industry Week* 242, no. 5, 1 March 1993, 11–12.

——. "Hide This Report Card!" *Industry Week* 243, no. 17, 19 September 1994, 27–29.

Mowatt, Raoul V., Dean Takahashi, and Brandon Bailey. "The Big High-Tech Thieves: Employees." *Philadelphia Inquirer,* 30 May 1996, F3.

Mowday, R. T., L. W. Porter, and R. M. Steers. *Employee-Organization Linkages.* New York: Academic Press, 1982.

Nadler, David A., Marc S. Gerstein, Robert B. Shaw, and Associates. *Organizational Architecture: Designs for Changing Organizations.* San Francisco: Jossey-Bass, 1992.

Nadler, David A., and Michael Tushman. *Strategic Organization Design.* Glenview, Ill.: Scott, Foresman, 1988.

Nardone, Thomas, Diane Herz, Earl Mellor, and Steven Hipple. "1992: Job Market Doldrums." *Monthly Labor Review,* February 1993.

National Association of Temporary and Staffing Services (NATSS). "Profile of the Temporary Workforce." Alexandria, Va., 1994.

————. "Temporary Help/Staffing Services Industry Continues to Create Employment Opportunities." Alexandria, Va., 1994.

National Employer Survey conducted for the National Center on the Educational Quality of the Workforce by the Bureau of the Census. Unpublished figures, August 1997.

Nelson, David. *Managers and Workers: Origins of the New Factory System in the United States, 1880–1920.* Madison: University of Wisconsin Press, 1975.

Neumark, David, Daniel Polsky, and Daniel Hansen. "Has Job Stability Declined Yet? New Evidence for the 1990s." Presented at the "Conference on Labor Market Inequality," University of Wisconsin, revised October 1998.

Newman, Katherine S. *Falling from Grace: The Experience of Downward Mobility in the American Middle Class.* New York: Random House, 1989.

New Social Contract: Redefining GTE's Employment Relationship. Stamford, Conn.: GTE Corporation, August 1996.

Nocerra, Joseph. "Living with Layoffs." *Fortune,* 1 April 1996, 69.

Northrup, Herbert R., and Margot E. Malin. *Personnel Policies for Engineers and Scientists: An Analysis of Major Corporate Practice.* Philadelphia: Industrial Research Unit of the Wharton School, 1985.

"Office Workers Rub Elbows as More Workplaces Shrink." *Wall Street Journal,* 7 May 1977, B1.

Oi, Walter Y. "The Fixed Employment Costs of Specialized Labor." In *The Measurement of Labor Cost,* edited by Jack Triplett. Chicago: University of Chicago Press, 1983.

Olson, Judith S. et al. "Computer-Supported Cooperative Work: Research Issues for the 1990s." *Behavior and Information Technology* 12, no. 2 (1993): 115–129.

"On the Air, But Not the Payroll." *Philadelphia Inquirer,* 3 August 1995, E6.

O'Reilly, Brian. "The New Deal: What Companies and Employees Owe One Another." *Fortune,* 13 June 1994, 44.

O'Reilly, Charles, III, and Jennifer Chatman. "Organizational Commitment and Psychological Attachment: The Effects of Compliance Identification and Internalization on Prosocial Behavior." *Journal of Applied Psychology* 71, no. 3 (1986): 492–499.

Organization for Economic Cooperation and Development (OECD). *Employment Outlook, 1993.* Paris, 1993.

————. *Labor Market Flexibility: Report by a High-Level Group of Experts to the Secretary General.* Paris, 1986.

Osterman, Paul. "How Common Is Workplace Transformation and How Can We Explain Who Does It?" *Industrial and Labor Relations Review* 47 (January 1994): 173–188.

————. "The Impact of Computers on the Employment of Clerks and Managers." *Industrial and Labor Relations Review* 39 (1986): 175–186.

————. "Skills, Training, and Work Organization in American Establishments." *Industrial Relations,* April 1995, 125–146.

————. "Work Organization." In *Change at Work,* edited by Peter Cappelli. New York: Oxford University Press, 1997.

Ouchi, William G. *Theory Z.* Reading, Mass.: Addison-Wesley, 1984.

Pearce, Jone L. "Toward an Organizational Behavior of Contract Laborers: Psychological Involvement and Effects on Employee Co-Workers." *Academy of Management Journal* 43, no. 2 (January 1990): 225–244.

Peck, J. A. "Outworking and Restructuring Processes in the Australian Clothing Industry." *Labor and Industry* (Australia) 3 (1990): 302–39.

Pennar, Karen. "Economic Anxiety." *Business Week,* 11 March 1996, 50.

Petzinger, Thomas, Jr. "A Creative Staff Finds New Strength in Its Differences." *Wall Street Journal,* 11 April 1997, B1.

Pfeffer, Jeffrey, and James N. Baron. "Taking the Workers Back Out: Recent Trends in the Structuring of Employment." In *Research in Organizational Behavior,* vol. 10, 257–303, edited by Barry Staw and L. L. Cummings. Greenwich, Conn.: JAI Press, 1988.

Pfeffer, Jeffrey, and John Lawler. "Effects of Job Alternatives, Extrinsic Rewards, and Behavioral Commitment on Attitudes toward the Organization: A Field Test of the Insufficient Justification Paradigm." *Administrative Science Quarterly* 25 (1980): 38–56.

"Pinnacle Alliance Delivers Benefits to J. P. Morgan during First Year of Operation." *M2 Presswire,* 16 July 1997.

Piore, Michael J., and Charles F. Sabel. *The Second Industrial Divide.* New York: Basic Books, 1984.

Plunkett, Marguerite M. "County Grants $280,000 in Jobs Incentives." *Palm Beach Post,* 4 October 1995, 4B.

Podgursky, Michael. "The Industrial Structure of Job Displacement, 1979–89," *Monthly Labor Review,* September 1992, 17–25.

Pollert, A. "The 'Flexible Firm': Fixation or Fact?" *Work, Employment, and Society* 2 (1988): 281–316.

————, ed. *Farewell to Flexibility?* Oxford: Basil Blackwell, 1991.

Polsky, Daniel. "Changes in the Consequences of Job Separations in the U.S. Economy." Working paper, University of Pennsylvania, October 1996.

Potter, Edward, and Judith Youngman. *Keeping America Competitive: Employment Policy for the 21st Century.* Lakeland, Colo.: Glenbridge Publishers, 1994.

Prahalad, C. K. and G. Hamel. "The Core Competence of the Corporation." *Harvard Business Review,* May–June 1990, 79–91.

Price, James L. *The Study of Turnover.* Ames: Iowa State University Press, 1977.

"Productivity Point International Announces Enterprise-Wide Training Solutions via the World Wide Web." *Business Wire, Inc.,* 11 November 1996.

Raff, Daniel M. G., and Lawrence H. Summers. "Did Henry Ford Pay Efficiency Wages?," *Journal of Labor Research* 5, no. 2 (1987): S57–S86.

Regan, Donald T. "Effects of a Favor and Liking on Compliance." *Journal of Experimental Social Psychology* 7 (1971): 627–639.

Reich, Robert B. "Companies Are Cutting Their Hearts Out." *New York Times Magazine,* 19 December 1993, 54–55.

Reichheld, Frederick F. *The Loyalty Effect: The Hidden Force behind Growth, Profits, and Lasting Value.* Boston: Harvard Business School Press, 1996.

Reilly, Anne H., Jeane M. Brett, and Linda K. Stroh. "The Impact of Corporate Turbulence on Managers' Attitudes." *Strategic Management Journal* 14 (1993): 167–179.

Reinemer, Michael. "Work Happy." *American Demographics* 17, no. 7 (July 1995): 26–30.

"Report on Employer Provided Training," U.S. Bureau of Labor Statistics, press release, 19 July 1996.

"Rethinking Work." *Business Week,* 19 October 1994.

Richman, Louis S. "How Jobs Die—And Are Born." *Fortune,* 26 July 1993, 26.

Rifkin, Jeremy. *The End of Work: The Decline of the Global Labor Force and the Dawn of the Post-Modern Era.* New York: Putnam, 1996.

Riverside Economic Research. *Brancato Report: Equity Turnover and Investment Strategies.* Fairfax, Va.: Victoria Group, 1994.

Robinson, Peter. "The British Labor Market in Historical Perspective: Changes in the Structure of Employment and Unemployment." London: Center for Economic Performance Discussion Paper No. 202, 1994.

Robinson, Sandra L. "Trust and the Breach of the Psychological Contract." *Administrative Science Quarterly* 41 (1996): 574–599.

———, Matthew S. Kraatz, and Denise M. Rousseau. "Changing Obligations and the Psychological Contract." *Academy of Management Journal* 37 (1994): 137–152.

Roethlisberger, F. S., and William J. Dickson. *Management and the Worker.* Cambridge, Mass.: Harvard University Press, 1927.

Rogers, Everett M., and Judith K. Larsen. *Silicon Valley Fever.* New York: Basic Books, 1984.

Rogers, Rolf E. "Managing for Quality: Current Differences between Japanese and American Approaches." *National Productivity Review* 12, no. 4 (1993): 503.

Rose, Stephen. *The Decline of Employment Stability in the 1980s.* Washington, D.C.: National Commission on Employment Policy, 1995.

Rosenau, Milton D., Jr. "From Experience: Faster New Product Development." *Journal of Production Innovation and Management* 5 (1988): 150–153.

Rosenbaum, James. "Tournament Mobility: Career Patterns in a Corporation." *Administrative Science Quarterly* 24, no. 2 (1979): 220.

Rotondi, Thomas. "Organizational Identification and Group Involvement." *Academy of Management Journal* 18 (1975): 892–897.

Rousseau, Denise. "Organizational Behavior in the New Organizational Era." *Annual Review of Psychology* 48 (1997): 515–546.

———. "Psychological and Implied Contracts in Organizations." *Employee Responsibilities and Rights Journal* 2, no. 2 (1989): 121–139.

———. *Psychological Contracts in Organizations.* Thousand Oaks, Calif.: Sage Publications, 1995.

———, and R. J. Anton. "Fairness and Obligations in Termination Decisions: The Role of Contributions, Promises, and Performance." *Journal of Organizational Behavior* 12 (1991): 287–299.

Rucci, Anthony V., Steven P. Kirn, and Richard T. Quinn. "The Employee-Customer Profit Chain at Sears." *Harvard Business Review* 76, no. 1 (January–February 1998): 83–97.

Ruhm, Christopher J. "Secular Changes in the Work and Retirement Patterns of Older Men." *Journal of Human Resources* 30, no. 2 (Spring 1995): 62–385.

Ryan, R. "Flexibility in New Zealand Workplaces: A Study of Northern Employers." *New Zealand Journal of Industrial Relations* 17 (1992): 129–147.

Rynes, Sara L., Marc O. Orlitzky, and Robert D. Bretz, Jr. "Experienced Hiring versus College Recruiting: Practices and Emerging Trends." *Personnel Psychology* 50, no. 2 (1997): 309–339.

Sager, Ira. "The Few, the True, and the Blue." *Business Week,* 30 May 1994.

Saxenian, AnnaLee. *Regional Advantage: Culture and Competition in Silicon Valley and Route 128.* Cambridge, Mass.: Harvard University Press, 1994.

Schellhardt, Timothy D. "Talent Pool Is Shallow as Corporations Seek Executives for Top Jobs." *Wall Street Journal,* 26 June 1997, 1.

Schleifer, Andrei, and Lawrence H. Summers. "Breach of Trust in Hostile Takeovers." Working paper 2342, National Bureau of Economic Research, Cambridge, Mass., 1987.

Scott, Elizabeth D., K. C. O'Shaughnessy, and Peter Cappelli. "The Changing Structure of Management Jobs in the Insurance Industry." In *Broken Ladders: Managerial Employment Systems in the New Economy,* edited by Paul Osterman. New York: Oxford University Press, 1997.

Scott Morton, Michael S., ed. *The Corporation of the 1990s: Information Technology and Organizational Transformation.* New York: Oxford University Press, 1991.

Seavey, Dorie, and Richard Kazis. *Skills Assessment, Job Placement, and Training: What Can Be Learned from the Temporary Help/Staffing Industry? An Overview of the Industry and a Case Study of Manpower, Inc.,* report. Boston: Jobs for the Future, 1994.

———. *1997 Update to Jobs for the Future Report on Manpower.* Boston: Jobs for the Future, 1997.

Sedgwick, David. "Proving Ground: Brazil Offers Makers and Suppliers a Place for Beta Testing Manufacturing Ideas." *Automotive News,* 4 August 1997.

Segal, Louis M., and Daniel G. Sullivan. "The Growth of Temporary Services Work." *Journal of Economic Perspectives* 11, no. 2 (Spring 1997): 117–136.

Shank, Matthew, Gail Paulson, and Thomas Werner. "Perceptual Gaps in the American Workforce." *Journal for Quality and Participation* 19, no. 6 (October–November 1966): 60–64.

Shankar, Ganesan, and Barton A. Weitz. "The Impact of Staffing Policies on Retail Buyer Job Attitudes and Behaviors." *Journal of Retailing* 72, no. 1 (Spring 1996): 31–56.

Shellenbarger, Sue. "Employers Are Finding It Doesn't Cost Too Much to Make a Staff Happy." *Wall Street Journal*, 19 November 1997, B1.

Sheridan, John E. "Organizational Culture and Employee Retention." *Academy of Management Journal* 35, no. 5 (1992): 1036–1056.

Silicon Valley Joint Venture. *Joint Venture's Index of Silicon Valley: Measuring Progress toward a 21st Century Community*. San Jose, Calif.: Silicon Valley Joint Venture, 1997.

Slater, Stanley F. 1993. "Competing in High-Velocity Markets." *Industrial Marketing Management* 22 (1993): 255–263.

Slichter, Sumner H. *The Challenge of Industrial Relations*. Ithaca, N.Y.: Cornell University Press, 1947.

————, James J. Healy, and E. Robert Livernash. *The Impact of Collective Bargaining on Management*. Washington, D.C.: Brookings Institution, 1960.

Smith, Robert S. "Comparable Worth: Limited Coverage and the Exacerbation of Inequality." *Industrial and Labor Relations Review* 41 (1988): 227–239.

Stalk, George, Jr. "Time—The Next Source of Competitive Advantage." *Harvard Business Review*, July–August 1988, 41–51.

Steers, Richard M. "Antecedents and Outcomes of Organizational Commitment." *Administrative Science Quarterly* 22 (1977): 76–84.

Stone, Katharine. "The Origins of Job Structures in the Steel Industry." *Review of Radical Political Economics* 6, no. 2 (Summer 1974): 113–173.

Storper, Michael. "The Transition to Flexible Specialization in the U.S. Film Industry: External Economies, the Division of Labor, and the Crossing of Industrial Divides." *Cambridge Journal of Economics* 13 (1989): 273–305.

Sugaliski, Thomas D., Louis S. Manzo, and Jim L. Meadows. "Resource Link: Reestablishing the Employment Relationship in an Era of Downsizing." *Human Resource Management* 34, no. 3 (Fall 1995): 389–403.

Sullivan, Kevin, Linda Chan, Don Shapiro, and Chris Pomery. "Wage Spiral Makes Bosses' Heads Spin." *Asian Business* 48, no. 8 (August 1988): 59–60.

Swinnerton, Kenneth A., and Howard Wial. "Is Job Stability Declining in the U.S. Economy?" *Industrial and Labor Relations Review* 48, no. 2 (January 1995): 293–304.

Szymankiewicz, Jan. "Contracting Out or Selling Out? Survey into the Current Issues Concerning the Outsourcing of Distribution." *Logistics Information Management* 7, no. 1 (1994): 28–35.

Takahashi, Dean. "Trade School Grads Wooed by Flurry of Job Offers." *Philadelphia Inquirer*, 27 June 1995, G1.

Tannenbaum, Jeffrey A. "Making Risky Hires into Valued Workers." *Wall Street Journal*, 19 June 1997, B1.

Taylor, Judith Combes. *Learning at Work in a Work-Based Welfare System: Opportunities and Obstacles—Lessons from the School-to-Work Experience*. Boston: Jobs for the Future, April 1997.

Taylor, Robert. "Europe's Unhappy World of Work." *Financial Times*, 14 May 1997, 18.

"Temporary R&D Employees in Unique Roles at DuPont and Henkel." *Chemical and Engineering News* 72, no. 9 (28 February 1994): 26–27.

Thompson, J. D. *Organizations in Action*. New York: McGraw-Hill, 1977.

Towers Perrin. *1997 Towers Perrin Workplace Index.* New York, 1997.

"Towers Perrin 1997 Workplace Index Reveals Growing Concerns in Employee Delivery on 'the New Deal' Contract." Towers Perrin press release, 15 September 1997.

Training. "Give 'Em that Old-Time Ambition." February 1992, 74.

Trist, E. L., and K. W. Bamforth. "Some Social and Psychological Consequences of the Long Wall Method of Coal-Getting." *Human Relations* 4, no. 1 (1951): 6.

Uchitelle, Louis. "More Are Forced into Ranks of Self-Employed at Low Pay." *New York Times,* 15 November 1993, A1, B8.

———. "More Downsized Workers Are Returning as Rentals." *New York Times,* 8 December 1996, 1.

———. "Strong Companies Are Joining Trend to Eliminate Jobs." *New York Times,* 26 July 1993, A1, D3.

United Nations. *World Investment Report: Transnational Corporations and Integrated International Production.* New York, 1993.

United Shareholders Association. *Executive Compensation 1,000.* Washington, D.C., 1993.

"Upsizing of America." *Wall Street Journal,* 20 September 1996.

U.S. Department of Labor. *Guide to Responsible Restructuring.* Washington, D.C.: GPO, 1995.

———. *High-Performance Work Practices and Firm Performance.* Washington, D.C., 1993.

Useem, Elizabeth. *Low-Tech Education in a High-Tech World: Corporations and Classrooms in the New Information Society.* New York: Free Press, 1986.

Useem, Michael. "Corporate Restructuring and the Restructured World of Senior Management." In *Broken Ladders: Changes in Managerial Career Paths,* edited by Paul Osterman. New York: Oxford University Press, 1997.

———. "Management Commitment and Company Policies on Education and Training." *Human Resource Management* 32 (1993): 411–434.

———. *The New Investor Capitalism.* New York: Basic Books, forthcoming.

Valetta, Robert G. "Has Job Security in the U.S. Declined?" *Federal Reserve Bank of San Francisco Weekly Letter,* No. 96-07, 16 February 1996.

Walk, Mary Anne. "Building a New Deal Around a Concept." In *The New Deal in Employment Relationships.* Report No. 1162–96-CR, 27. New York: Conference Board, 1996.

Walkup, Carolyn. "Companies Vie for Workers as Labor Pool Evaporates." *Nation's Restaurant News,* 20 February 1995, 1.

Weber, Joseph. "Scott Rolls Out a Risky Strategy." *Business Week,* 22 May 1995, 48.

Weick, Karl E. "Enactment and the Boundaryless Career: Organizing as We Work." In *The Boundaryless Career: A New Employment Principle for a New Organizational Era,* edited by Michael Arthur and Denise Rousseau. New York: Oxford University Press, 1996.

Weinstein, Jeff. "Personnel Success." *Restaurants and Institutions* 102, no. 2 (9 December 1992): 113.

Welbourne, Theresa M., David B. Balkin, Luis R. Gomez-Mejia. "Gainsharing and

Mutual Monitoring: A Combined Agency-Organizational Justice Interpretation." *Academy of Management Journal* 38 (1995): 881–899.

Wellington, Alison J. "Changes in the Male/Female Wage Gap." *Journal of Human Resources* 28, no. 2 (1993): 383–411.

Wessel, David. "Up the Ladder: Low Unemployment Brings Lasting Gains to Town in Michigan." *Wall Street Journal*, 24 June 1997, A1.

Whyte, William H. *The Organization Man.* New York: Simon and Schuster, 1956.

Wiatrowski, William. "Small Businesses and Their Employees." *Monthly Labor Review,* October 1994, 29–35.

Wilk, Steffanie L., and Elizabeth A. Craig. "Should I Stay or Should I Go? Occupational Matching and Internal and External Mobility." Working paper, Department of Management, Wharton School, 1998.

Williamson, Oliver E. *Markets and Hierarchies.* New York: Free Press, 1975.

———. "The Organization of Work: A Comparative Institutional Assessment." *Journal of Economic Behavior and Organization* 1 (1980): 5–38.

Winstanley, D. "Recruitment Strategies and Managerial Control of Technical Staff." In *White Collar Work: The Non-Manual Labor Process.* London: MacMillan, 1991.

Womack, James, Daniel Jones, and Daniel Roos. *The Machine that Changed the World.* New York: Rawson-Macmillan, 1990.

Worrell, Dan L., Wallace N. Davidson III, and Varinder M. Sharma. "Layoff Announcements and Stockholder Wealth." *Academy of Management Journal* 34 (1991): 662–678.

Wyatt Company. *Best Practices in Corporate Restructuring.* New York, 1993.

———. *Measuring Change in the Attitudes of the American Workforce.* New York: Wyatt WorkUSA, 1995.

———. *Wyatt's 1993 Survey of Corporate Restructuring—Best Practices in Corporate Restructuring.* New York, 1993.

Yago, Glenn. *Junk Bonds: How High-Yield Securities Restructured Corporate America.* New York: Oxford University Press, 1991.

Yankelovich, Daniel. "How Changes in the Economy Are Reshaping American Values." In *Values and Public Policy,* edited by Henry J. Aaron, Thomas E. Mann, and Timothy Taylor. Washington, D.C.: Brookings Institution, 1993.

———. "The Meaning of Work." In *The Worker and the Job,* edited by Jerome M. Rosow. Englewood Cliffs, N.J.: Prentice-Hall, 1974.

Index

About the Author

Peter Cappelli is a Professor of Management and the Director of the Center for Human Resources at The Wharton School of the University of Pennsylvania. He recently served as Co-Director of the U.S. Department of Education's National Center on the Educational Quality of the Workforce. Before coming to Wharton, he held positions at MIT, the University of California at Berkeley, and the University of Illinois. He received his B.S. in Industrial Relations from Cornell University and his Ph.D from Oxford where he was a Fulbright Scholar. He has written widely on employment issues. His other books include *Change at Work*, an account of the effects of corporate restructuring on employees.